A Forgotten Front

Portrait of Confederate soldier Washington Mackey Ives
from the 4th Florida Infantry taken in Chattanooga, Tennessee,
courtesy of State Archives of Florida, Florida Memory

A FORGOTTEN FRONT
FLORIDA
DURING THE
Civil War Era

EDITED BY

SETH A. WEITZ & JONATHAN C. SHEPPARD

THE UNIVERSITY OF ALABAMA PRESS TUSCALOOSA

The University of Alabama Press
Tuscaloosa, Alabama 35487-0380
uapress.ua.edu

Hardcover edition published 2018.
Paperback edition published 2019.
eBook edition published 2018.

Typeface: Adobe Caslon

Cover images: Above, *Fort Taylor, Key West, Florida*, 1861; below, *Re-enforcement of Fort Pickens by Company A, First Artillery, on Saturday Morning, April 13, 1861*; images courtesy of the State Archives of Florida, Florida Memory
Cover design: Michele Myatt Quinn

Paperback ISBN: 978-0-8173-5982-9

A previous edition of this book has been catalogued by the Library of Congress.
ISBN: 978-0-8173-1982-3 (cloth)
E-ISBN: 978-0-8173-9182-9

Contents

List of Illustrations vii

Acknowledgments ix

Introduction: From Territory to Twenty-Seventh State
Seth A. Weitz 1

1
Extreme Measures: Florida and the Crisis of 1850
Seth A. Weitz 18

2
"The Rights, Causes, and Necessity for Secession":
The Interplay of Race, Class, and Politics in Antebellum Florida
Lauren K. Thompson 42

3
"So Exposed as Recently to Encounter Serious Disasters":
The Defense and Capture of Amelia Island, 1861–1862
Jonathan C. Sheppard 59

4
"Our Necessary Resort": Confederate Guerrillas in East
and Middle Florida, 1861–1865
Zack C. Waters 72

5
Embattled Executive: Governor John Milton's Civil War
R. Boyd Murphree 89

6
"The Church Did Not Die": Religion in Florida during the Civil War
David B. Parker 115

7
Civil War and Florida's New Legal Paradigm
Chris Day 135

8
Grander in Her Daughters: Florida's Women during the Civil War
Tracy J. Revels 163

9
Florida Hispanics in the Civil War
Robert A. Taylor 183

10
Battles of Olustee: Civil War Memory in Florida
David Nelson 196

Bibliography 227
Contributors 251
Index 253

Illustrations

Frontispiece.
Portrait of Confederate soldier Washington Mackey Ives ii

Figure 1.
Map of the state of Florida, 1860 19

Figure 2.
Florida Ordinance of Secession 43

Figure 3.
Portrait of John Milton, Florida's Civil War governor 90

Figure 4.
Ellen Thompson, former slave of Martha Margaret Murry May 164

Acknowledgments

In the process of researching, writing, and editing this collection of essays, I have benefited greatly from family, friends, colleagues, and mentors who have encouraged me in numerous ways. Firstly I would like to thank my wife Jill who not only put up with me during this long process, but also aided me with some of the more technical aspects of the project. Also, I obviously could not have completed this venture without my coeditor Jonathan, who is much more than a coeditor. Jonathan has been a colleague, but much more importantly a friend since 2002 when we both began graduate school at Florida State. We have shared a love of history and sports (especially college football) over the past fifteen years. I am honored to call him a friend, and look forward to future collaborations with him. I am also forever indebted to Jim Jones who was my mentor at Florida State. He helped me grow as a historian, expanded my knowledge and love for Civil War and Florida history, and whom I am proud and honored to call a friend.

I would like to thank the staff at the Florida State archives as well as Strozier Library at FSU where the bulk of my research was conducted, as well as my colleagues at Dalton State College, specifically Matt Hipps, Sarah Mergel, and my department chair, Judy Cornett, who all stood by me, and helped me in various ways. I cannot forget The University of Alabama Press, who agreed to take on this work, and helped both Jonathan and myself through the process. I want to specifically thank Donna Cox Baker and Dan Waterman for their time, effort, and especially patience. This would never have come to fruition without the numerous authors who contributed time, effort, and ultimately chapters to the work. Lauren, Zack, Boyd, David, Chris, Tracy, Robert, and David, thank you.

I would also like to thank my parents, who provided me with moral support over the past couple of years, as well my in-laws. Lastly I would like to thank the two brightest lights in my life, my children, Max and Ellis, who thankfully did not erase any of the chapters of the book. I guess I should also acknowledge and thank the nonhumans who have played an important role in my life, our two dogs, the late General Montgomery, and the new addition to my family, Bernie.

SETH A. WEITZ

Without mentors, family, and friends, this book could not have been attempted, much less accomplished. I would like to extend my gratitude and appreciation to those who accompanied me on this journey.

This book began as an idea developed years ago by Seth Weitz and myself. Seth and I met in Historical Methods (or the further adventures of James Cook) in the fall of 2002 and discovered we shared a passion for football and Florida History. Though life has taken us to different locales our determination to see this project through has endured. Seth is an excellent historian, fantastic teacher, and more than that, a great friend. I am proud to be a coeditor on this work with him.

My wife Courtenay has provided love and encouragement for the duration of this project and I cannot thank her enough for being the wonderful woman she is.

Seth and I both studied under professor Jim Jones, whose disdain for Florida History is known and legendary. It is natural then, that we dedicate this work to him. His examples and inspirations are found throughout this work, and Seth and I are honored to call him our major professor and friend. Our other dedication goes to the late-professor Joe M. Richardson. Joe M. provided his students with a passionate and solid foundation of the history of Reconstruction, and any student at Florida State that passed through one of his courses should consider themselves fortunate.

All of our contributors deserve a special mention as they each put aside their own projects to provide a chapter for this compilation. Also, a special thank you is due to Dan Waterman and all the staff at The University of Alabama Press.

Lastly, I need to thank my grandparents and other family members for their support, and for my mother and late-father, whose love and guidance I shall never forget.

Jonathan Sheppard

A Forgotten Front

Introduction

From Territory to Twenty-Seventh State

Seth A. Weitz

Florida is often the forgotten front of the Civil War, both for scholars and in memory, as many often overlook the subject and tend to focus on what they deem to be the more significant theaters and participants in the conflict. In spite of this, the war did touch Florida, and it left a lasting impact on the state. More than fifteen thousand Floridians took up arms for the Confederacy, of which close to five thousand died from either combat or disease. Another twelve hundred white Floridians served in Union forces during the war, as did more than one thousand freed slaves and free black Floridians.[1] Union troops occupied most of the coastal areas for the entirety of the war, while Confederate forces held the interior, keeping Tallahassee out of the reach of Union forces and thereby making it the only Confederate capital east of the Mississippi River to never fall into Union hands. While there was only one major campaign and battle in the state, the Battle of Olustee, or Ocean Pond, in 1864, the state did see its share of action from guerrilla fighting and blockade-running along the coast. Florida also was vital to the Confederate war effort, as the state was a valuable supplier of cattle and other items such as salt and cotton, which were shipped to the rest of the South.

This edited collection of essays sheds light on this lesser known theater of the war and illuminates the lives and struggles of Floridians during the trying times of the 1850s and 1860s. The first chapter in this work, "Extreme Measures: Florida and the Crisis of 1850," was written by Seth A. Weitz of Dalton State College and looks at the changing political landscape in Florida during the antebellum period, focusing on the "Crisis" of 1850. Weitz also analyzes the demise of the two-party political system in Florida, which mirrored events in the Deep South a decade before secession and the Civil War. Through his work, Weitz shows how the Old South was reconstructed within Florida's borders, mostly due to the efforts of transplanted

Virginians, Georgians, and South Carolinians, the latter of which tending to be more radical and filling the ranks of the fire-eating secessionists.

Following Weitz is Lauren K. Thompson of McKendree University, whose chapter, "'The Rights, Causes, and Necessity for Secession': The Interplay of Race, Class, and Politics in Antebellum Florida," deals with Florida and secession. Thompson picks up where Weitz's chapter ends and takes the story through the Secession Winter of 1860–1861. She examines the motives that drove Florida to become the third state to break the bonds of Union, following South Carolina and Mississippi out of the Union in January 1861. As Thompson illustrates, the decision to secede was not unanimous, but Florida's fire-eaters ultimately prevailed and the state mirrored its Deep South brethren, especially South Carolina. In her work, Thompson also looks at the demographics in the state and how that played a role in the decision to secede.

Jonathan C. Sheppard, executive director of Mission San Luis: Florida's Apalachee-Spanish Living History Museum, looks in his chapter, "'So Exposed as Recently to Encounter Serious Disasters': The Defense and Capture of Amelia Island, 1861–1862," at various wartime policies along Florida's coastline. Jefferson Davis believed that the Confederacy's viability, and status in the world, rested in its ability to defend its vast territory. In Florida, with Governor John Milton's acquiescing, Davis's policy meant defending the numerous inlets and bays necessary for maritime operations. The chapter, thus, examines the reasons Fernandina was chosen as a focal point for defense and the manpower and resources expended on the town's defenses. It also analyzes the Union's operation in March 1862 to occupy the town and the operation's place in the overall collapse of Davis's coastal defense scheme. Zack C. Waters, in his chapter, "'Our Necessary Resort': Confederate Guerrillas in East and Middle Florida, 1861–1865," looks at the guerrilla war in Florida, including how the East Gulf Blockading Squadron used escaped slaves in their effort and how Southern partisans sustained their presence near St. Augustine in 1865, toward the conclusion of the war.

In "'The Church Did Not Die': Religion in Florida during the Civil War," David B. Parker of Kennesaw State University shows the role religion played during not only the Civil War in Florida but also the secession debate. Drawing on sermons and political journals alike, Parker highlights the fact that the two, war and religion, were intertwined in Florida, as well as in the Deep South, and demonstrates how many used religion to justify secession. R. Boyd Murphree, project manager at the Florida Family and

Community History at the George A. Smathers' Library at the University of Florida, analyzes the administration of John Milton, Florida's wartime governor, in his chapter, "Embattled Executive: Governor John Milton's Civil War." Murphree illuminates Milton's pro–Jefferson Davis stance and its effect on Florida's citizens and wartime efforts, as well as this relationship, and that of Florida, to the rest of the Confederacy during the war. Chris Day of the Maclay School looks at the role race and slavery played in Florida during the Civil War and Reconstruction in his chapter, "Civil War and Florida's New Legal Paradigm." By studying specific court cases and other documents, Day presents the reader with evidence of how African Americans were marginalized in Florida before and during the Civil War and how their lives would be forever changed by the Emancipation Proclamation and their impending freedom.

Tracy J. Revels of Wofford College, in "Grander in Her Daughters: Florida's Women during the Civil War," highlights the often-forgotten roles played by Florida's women, whose lives were dramatically and drastically altered when their husbands, sons, and fathers enlisted and were sent hundreds if not thousands of miles away to fight for the Confederacy. She focuses not on the single plantation mistress or on the wife of one prominent politician or officer but rather provides the reader with a widespread analysis of the lives of the state's female population, from the planter "Cottonocracy" to the yeoman farmer, from the slave to the free black Floridian. She also looks at the wives and mothers of average soldiers, generals, politicians, and Unionists.

Robert A. Taylor of the Florida Institute of Technology examines the little-known role Hispanics played in Florida during the Civil War in his chapter, "Florida Hispanics in the Civil War." He examines this lesser known facet of the Civil War in Florida: the role played by soldiers of Hispanic descent in the conflict. Drawing from newspaper accounts, Confederate service rosters, rolls, official army records, and memoirs as well as secondary sources, Taylor paints a vivid account of who these men were, of their combat experience, and also of their background. This chapter is unique in Florida, Florida Civil War, and Civil War historiography in general, as it is a largely untold story of a segment of Florida's population.

Concluding the work is David Nelson of Bainbridge State College, with his chapter, "Battles of Olustee: Civil War Memory in Florida." Using the Olustee Battlefield as a case study and lens for Florida Civil War memory, Nelson includes in his study the United Daughters of the Confederacy, the Sons of Confederate Veterans, the war's centennial and 150th anniversary in Florida, and the preservation of the Marianna and Natural Bridge battlefields. He also examines the controversy surrounding the proposal to erect a Union memorial on the Olustee Battlefield as part of the 150th anniversary of the 1864 battle.

When Florida seceded from the Union, on January 10, 1861, it became the third state to take this action, following South Carolina and Mississippi. Emory Thomas, in *The Confederate Nation: 1861–1865* (1979), noted that while economically Florida was essentially an extension of Alabama and Georgia, politically it was an extension of South Carolina. Florida governor Madison Starke Perry, a native South Carolinian, issued an impassioned plea to his Legislature on the heels of Abraham Lincoln's election in November 1860, calling for a statewide convention to discuss the possibility of secession, a path his native South Carolina was about to undertake. Perry had attended the South Carolina secession convention and shared his insight with his political allies in Florida. On December 22 voters were given the opportunity to choose delegates for the convention, and they responded by selecting more ardent fire-eaters, forty-two, than moderates, or cooperationists, twenty-seven.[2] Despite a relatively large number of cooperationists, when they convened in Tallahassee in early January 1861, the secessionist majority was able to stave off attempts at moderation, and on January 10 they adopted the official Ordinance of Secession by a 62–7 vote, with twenty of the cooperationists joining the fire-eaters. One of the cooperationists, a former moderate Whig, Jackson Morton, was chosen to represent Florida in Montgomery, Alabama, for the formation of the Confederate States of America.[3]

The turn to radicalism and the associated decision to secede can be seen in the fact that Florida, which had been admitted to the Union only in 1845 and had been a part of Spain less than half a century before, was closely linked to its Deep South brethren, especially fire-eating South Carolina. This was not always the case in Florida, as many of the earlier settlers, including the planter elite, who made up Florida's political nucleus, hailed from Virginia and were more moderate in their political outlook.

The use of the term "radical" needs clarification before we can undertake an accurate study of Florida during the Civil War era, since it is a contentious word whose usage has been debated. Eric Walther, in his 1992 work, *The Fire Eaters*, questions whether "radical" and "fire-eater" can be used interchangeably. Walther states that there was, in fact, a difference between the two. Radicals advocated Southern rights but not necessarily secession, while fire-eaters were keen to break the bonds of the Union. Walther rationalizes that "all fire eaters, therefore, were radicals, but not all Southern radicals were fire eaters."[4] He abandons this distinction twelve years later, however, when he uses the terms interchangeably in *The Shattering of the Union.*

The term "radical" in this work will be used to describe Southern rights advocates and secessionists in Florida such as David Levy Yulee who swore an allegiance to John C. Calhoun in 1850 and eventually became engulfed in disunionist sentiment as the state moved toward secession a decade later. In 1859 L. W. Spratt, editor of the *Charleston Mercury*, proclaimed, "We stand committed to the South, but we stand more vitally committed to the cause of Slavery."[5] Nowhere was this statement closer to the truth than in Florida on the eve of secession. Economics and politics were intertwined in antebellum Florida, and, since the planter aristocracy controlled the economy of the state, they drove the political machine as well. While this was the case, Florida was ready to follow South Carolina's lead only after the planters defected from the ranks of the conservative Whig Party and joined the radical Democrats, who, by 1861, overwhelmingly favored disunion.

It has been more than a century since William W. Davis published his monumental, if not racially charged, Lost Cause–themed *The Civil War and Reconstruction in Florida* and more than fifty years since John E. Johns followed with his *Florida during the Civil War.* Despite the increase in the number of books and essays published on Florida in the Civil War in the last two decades, this remains an area largely neglected by scholars. Those two works were broad studies, analyzing the entire war, as was William Nulty's *Confederate Florida: The Road to Olustee*, published in 1990. Later works, such as George Buker's *Blockaders, Refugees, and Contrabands: Civil War on Florida's Gulf Coast, 1861–1865*, or regional works, such as Canter Brown's *Tampa in the Civil War and Reconstruction*, expanded the scope of study, as does this work, which encompasses various topics related to Florida's experience during the Civil War.

Before the events of 1861 or even 1850 can be studied in depth, it is essential to look back upon the earlier decades that paved the way for Florida's later extremist actions. Florida was a very different territory and state preceding the Civil War than it was when it followed South Carolina out of the Union in 1861. From the outset, Florida would prove distinct largely due to its access to and dependence on the sea. Before the Old South was recreated in Middle Florida's fertile soil, Florida was dominated by Pensacola in West Florida and St. Augustine in East Florida. These cities alternately held sessions of the Territorial Legislature, which left delegates scurrying back and forth between the two, situated four hundred miles apart. When the first session met in July 1822 in Pensacola, "the members from St. Augustine had traveled fifty-nine days by water to attend," with one delegate, Thomas Lytle, losing his life in a storm.[6] When the second session of the Florida Legislative Council met, in St. Augustine in 1823, the delegates from Pensacola were shipwrecked and barely escaped death.[7] The solution to this dangerous situation benefited the new settlers of Middle Florida, as commissioners John Lee Williams and William H. Simmons selected "the present day site of Tallahassee as the location for the new capital of Florida."[8] Not only was Tallahassee the midpoint between St. Augustine and Pensacola, but "Middle Florida also contained hundreds of thousands of acres of rich land suitable for plantations."[9] Richard Keith Call had "looked with favor upon the location and believed that it might allay the extreme east-west sectionalism in Florida."[10] The selection, or rather creation, of inland Tallahassee as the capital was a vital step toward replicating the Old South in Florida.

As settlers flocked to Florida, many sought a new and better life, feeling Florida was a land of opportunity. Florida was the nation's, but more importantly the South's, newest frontier. Despite more than three hundred years of Spanish, British, and French rule, Florida was largely a virgin land to white settlers in the 1820s. It was considered part of the old Southwest, which included Alabama, Mississippi, Louisiana, Tennessee, Arkansas, and eastern Texas and can account for the reason many felt Florida was a land of opportunity where settlers could begin new lives, an attitude somewhat similar to the idea known as Manifest Destiny that would fuel the westward expansion movements of the 1840s and 1850s.[11]

Not everyone who moved to Florida in the period after it became an American possession was looking for a different lifestyle. Most of the "elite men who moved to Middle Florida . . . sought, as did planters throughout the Old Southwest, to prosper and rule through the acquisition of land, control of dependents, and staple crop production."[12] These members of the South's planter aristocracy often hailed from South Carolina, Georgia, or Virginia and wished to replicate their own state's mentalities and values within Florida's borders. The early political prejudices can be traced back to these initial settlers. The Georgians and South Carolinians tended to be more radical and would make up the fire-eating Democratic element of

Florida's politics, while the Virginians, largely, would flock to the Whig and Conservative parties. An early settler in Middle Florida noted, "In time [Florida will] become an important Southern slaveholding state—producing as its staples, Cotton, Sugar, Rice and Fruit."[13] In 1823 John Lee Williams, speaking of Middle Florida, proclaimed, "The cotton fields exceed by one half, any I have seen and the sugar cane better than Mississippi affords."[14] In 1821, when Florida became a US Territory, the land held fewer than eight thousand people, including slaves, but by the mid-1830s, immigration to Middle Florida had caused the population of this region alone to swell to more than thirty-five thousand.[15] By the time the first Territorial Convention met to discuss statehood at St. Joseph in 1838, the state was home to 48,223 people, of which 21,132 were slaves.[16]

The population of West Florida, conversely, was in a constant state of decline after 1830. In 1830 the region boasted a population of 9,478, but the 1840 Territorial Census found only 5,500 people, while the populations of Middle and East Florida had more than doubled over the decade.[17] The state's regions also bickered with each other over the question of statehood. East Florida, jealous of the power and influence Middle Florida would have in the political arena based on the region's rapid growth in population and wealth, voted 614–255 against statehood. Middle Florida voted 1,152–226 for statehood and West Florida 732–324 in favor of the resolution.[18] The Constitutional Convention was made possible only because the legislature had placated the West and the East by giving them greater proportional representation than Middle Florida.[19] By 1839 Floridians had voted in favor of statehood in one final referendum after the close of the Constitutional Convention by a narrow 2,065–1,961 margin.[20] Despite the vote, statehood would not come to Florida until 1845. By this time planters had succeeded in constructing their new Southern society in Florida.

Florida was a vast territory, and to govern this land effectively a strong centralized government was essential. It was under this assumption that President James Monroe appointed William P. Duval as Florida's first territorial governor. Duval was later reappointed by Presidents John Quincy Adams and Andrew Jackson, of whom Duval was a close follower, as were all the men who made up what became known as the "nucleus" of Florida politics.[21] Ironically it was out of the nucleus that Florida's anti-Jackson parties, the Conservatives and later the Whigs, would emerge. These parties would include most of those who would later oppose immediate secession or secession in general.

Richard Keith Call, Florida's most famous governor during the Territorial period, was also a member of the nucleus and became one of Florida's most prominent Whigs and Florida's most loyal Unionist in the following decades. The nucleus, which dominated the legislature as well, was backed by the powerful Pensacola *Gazette* and drew more than nominal resentment from East and Middle Florida alike.[22] The nucleus did not begin as a political entity but rather as "a group of men having similar property and political interests who cooperated informally on matters in which they thought alike."[23]

The Democrats did not wield any power within Florida until after the deliberations of the Constitutional Convention, which lasted from December 3, 1838, to January 11, 1839, where, incidentally, they were known as the Jeffersonian Republican Party of Florida.[24] The convention kicked off a long and arduous debate between pro- and anti-banking factions: the Whigs, or Conservatives, as they were called at the time, sided with the banking groups, while the Democrats sat on the opposite end of the spectrum. The true victor of the convention was David Levy (he would add the surname Yulee, his Father's Sephardic Jewish surname, in 1846). He led the Democrats out of the convention as a force that could match the nucleus step for step in Florida's politics. Many members of the old guard, including Governor Call, did not realize how much power the Democrats had amassed until they convinced President Martin Van Buren to relieve Call of his office in 1839 and replace him with East Florida Democrat and Levy ally Robert Raymond Reid.[25] The battle that raged between Whigs and Democrats over Call's dismissal was the first of many that characterized antebellum Florida's political landscape.

The early 1840s were exemplified by an antimonopolist movement, which rallied to combat corporations created by the Conservative Party in the Territorial Legislature that aimed to help a select few, most of whom would later make up the Whig Party.[26] The movement was spearheaded by the Democratic Party, which quickly began referring to itself as the party of the people. The Conservatives made a bungled attempt to transpose blame on their opponents by labeling them as unpatriotic. They even denounced class distinctions and "ridiculed the idea that measures calculated for their benefit did not also benefit all other men."[27] It is ironic to note that the moderate planter aristocracy of the 1840s initially would not make up the majority of the fire-eating secessionists, whose goal would be to protect the "property" of the conservatives.

Florida's Whigs clearly lagged behind the Democrats in the early 1840s, as they were not united but rather split between States' Rights Whigs and conservatives.[28] Out of the States' Rights Whigs rose the newspaper that would ultimately become the main Whig organ in Florida, the *Florida Sentinel.* Originally based in Quincy, they moved their headquarters to Tallahassee in 1841.[29] With a Whig in the White House, the party in Florida looked to replace Governor Reid, whom they claimed had usurped Call's power. Call was named to the post that "so appropriately belonged to him" on March 19 by President William Henry Harrison, less than a month before the elderly chief executive's death.[30]

The return of Call to the governorship did not immediately unite the Whig Party, as the congressional elections in 1840 demonstrated. East Florida put forth the incumbent, an antistatehood conservative Charles Downing, while Middle and West Florida, whom Downing had alienated, threw their weight behind George Ward.[31] The Democrats, however, were united behind David Levy, who was referred to as "that little Jew politician" by opponents.[32] Levy easily won the election over the divided Whigs. The Whigs soon emulated the Democrats and organized local county and district conventions for the next round of elections with the hope that they would not see another split such as the one that had cost them the 1840 election. The Whigs ultimately rebounded and united behind the states' rights faction of the party and regained control of the legislature, which they held from 1843 through 1844.[33] It was during the period between 1841 and 1844 that Call again occupied the governor's chair and the Conservative Party officially disintegrated, with its pieces picked up by both the Democrats and the Whigs.[34]

Call's second term as governor was highlighted by several new movements and a solution to the so-called Indian problem. First, there was a revival of religious activity in Middle Florida, which many felt was long overdue.[35] Florida was a lawless frontier in the eyes of its numerous visitors and critics. Even Governor Call, in an address to the Florida Territorial Legislature, commended the temperance and religious movements that sprang up across Middle Florida and urged the "encouragement and support of the friends of morality and virtue."[36] Call's second term also saw peace in Florida for the first time since 1835 as President John Tyler negotiated an end to the Second Seminole War.[37] The peace was secured largely because of the actions of Missouri Senator Thomas Hart Benton, who had proposed "an armed occupation act to plant settlers on the frontier as a barrier against

Indian raids."[38] This act opened the door for more federal aid to Florida and ultimately to Tyler's intervention and the end of the war. Two new counties were created in 1844 out of land previously occupied by the Indians. One was named for David Levy (Levy County) and the other for Benton. In a show of Southern nationalism, Benton County was renamed Hernando County in 1850, when the Missourian displayed anti-Southern sentiment during the crisis surrounding the Compromise of 1850.[39] Alcohol, frivolous lifestyles, and Indians proved less of a threat to Florida than did the depression and the yellow fever epidemic that followed, the latter of which wiped out the town of St. Joseph and claimed the life of former governor Robert Reid and two successive editors of the *Floridian*.[40]

Out of the depression and chaos arose a new battle, the battle for statehood. Duval County's Isaiah D. Hart, a Whig, "introduced resolutions which would have nullified the St. Joseph's convention of 1838 and would have required the delegate to Congress to oppose Florida's admission until a new convention should be held."[41] These actions were carried out mainly for financial reasons, as Hart and his followers did not feel Florida could carry the financial burdens of statehood. The resolution did fail, but it began the debate that carried through Florida's ultimate admission into the Union in 1845. The 1844 session of the Territorial Legislature saw the antistatehood forces secure the passage of a resolution that called for Florida to be split into two separate territories with two separate governments.[42] Although this request was denied by Congress, it clearly showed that the sectional animosities that had been prevalent since Florida's creation as a territory were still present and a driving force in political life.

The leading advocate for statehood was David Levy, who had defeated George T. Ward in 1843 to return to Congress.[43] Levy's overall objective was the well-being of the South, and he argued that Florida's admission was necessary to offset Iowa's proposed admission as a free state. This he claimed would preserve balance within the Union. Levy also touted states' rights when he proclaimed that "statehood would mean freedom from federal interference" and more importantly "a greater voice in national politics."[44] By championing statehood, Levy forever tied the party to the eventual secession movement. In the short term the party rode Levy's coattails into securing a Democratic Legislative Council in 1844 whose goal was to renew Florida's application for statehood. This conflict was a moot point as the House of Representatives' Committee on Territories had already furnished a bill by January 7, 1845, calling for the admission of both Florida and Iowa.[45] The bill passed the House on February 13, the Senate on March 1, and was signed into law by President John Tyler on March 3. It is also important to note that Democrat John Branch had replaced Governor Call in July 1844 largely due to Call's open support for Henry Clay, Tyler's staunchest enemy in the question over the annexation of Texas. This meant that Florida's transition to statehood was made completely under Democratic auspices, thus furthering Levy's claim of a great victory for his party. Two decades after becoming a US Territory, Florida entered the Union as the twenty-seventh state. The state had already experienced several fiery political battles, but nothing could prepare Florida for the turmoil of the decade to come.

In 1850 Florida's statehood was only five years old, but the economic and social makeup of the state was already deeply rooted. The decade of the 1850s, which will be studied in greater detail throughout this collection, further entrenched these values and solidified the landscape that helped dictate the events of 1860–1861. After statehood was granted, the populated regions of the state included the areas known as East Florida, West Florida, and Middle Florida. Middle Florida became known as the "black belt" as it housed the majority of Florida's slaves working on the state's largest plantations and the richest soil. Middle Florida consisted of Jackson, Leon, Gadsden, Madison, and Jefferson Counties, and in 1850 all except Jefferson were staunchly Whig. Their shift to the Democrats in the mid-1850s helped tip the balance of the state away from the moderates and into the more radical, fire-eating camp.

According to William H. Nulty in his 1990 work, *Confederate Florida: The Road to Olustee*, the state was "psychologically, economically, socially and politically attuned with the other Southern states."[46] While this was true and will be examined in detail by several authors in this work, Florida was ill prepared to fight in 1861. With a population of around 140,000, of which close to half were slaves, there were simply not enough men available to defend Florida's vast coastline as well as to supply troops to the various armies fighting in other theaters of the war. The slaves, who were concentrated in Florida's black belt around the capital of Tallahassee, were seen as vital for Florida's war effort.

Florida's economy—largely undeveloped and one-sided, highly dependent on the institution of slavery, and lacking any real commercial manufacturing sector—would struggle and suffer through four years of fighting. With the Union blockade of Florida's coast, the state was unable to export one of its greatest and most lucrative assets, cotton, which only further confounded the problem. Florida also contained a measly four hundred miles of railroads, with virtually no connections to nearby states. It soon became clear that despite the loyalty and devotion that many Floridians had shown to the Southern cause, the war would be won on far-off battlefields, and many of the fifteen thousand Floridians who had been eager to join the war effort would be sent hundreds, if not thousands, of miles away to see action.

While numerous Floridians had shown a great amount of zeal and an almost blind allegiance to South Carolina in 1860 and 1861, there was a large Unionist segment within the population that opposed secession and later supported the Union forces, who occupied key cities such as Key West and Jacksonville as well as coastal forts such as Fort Clinch on Amelia Island, Fort Marion at St. Augustine, Forts Taylor and Jefferson off of Key West, and Fort Pickens near Pensacola, throughout the majority of the war. This led to tensions within the state and a savage form of guerrilla warfare, which was not seen in every state involved in the conflict. It also led to a somewhat contentious secession debate, though the fight did not reach the fever pitch it would in other Southern states such as Georgia or Tennessee, which had larger, more powerful Unionist segments.

Despite its separation and isolation from main theaters of the war, and despite the fact that Florida had been largely abandoned militarily by the Confederate military hierarchy and was an afterthought of Jefferson Davis and his government, Confederate General Robert E. Lee noted the importance of the state and made two wartime visits to Florida, both to Fernandina. It was during these trips that he decided that the interior of the state was to be held at all costs. Middle Florida was the interior, and not only was it home to the capital of Tallahassee, but as previously noted, it housed Florida's most fertile land and the majority of the population, both white and black, slave and free. Thus, Lee felt it was imperative that this region remain out of the Union's grasp.

Lee saw Florida as a vital cog in the Confederate war effort, as it also contained farmland and cattle ranches, which at the height of productivity were sending more than six hundred cattle north per week to help feed the rest of the Confederacy. Cattle raised in the St. Johns River Valley and in Central Florida were crucial to the Confederacy, and in 1863 a commissary agent was sent on an urgent appeal from Confederate General Braxton Bragg, who maintained that his army was entirely dependent on Florida for their resources, since South Carolina's and Georgia's stores had reportedly run dry. By 1864 the Richmond government "hoped for 25,000 cattle, 10,000 hogs, 100,000 gallons of syrup, and 20,000,000 pounds of fish from Florida."[47] South Florida was also cattle country, but the cattlemen in this region, according to historian Michael Gannon, "played both sides, selling to the highest bidder whether it was the Confederacy, the Union garrisons at Fort Myers and Key West, or the Cubans at Havana."[48] The Confederates understood the importance of cattle, and the Union threat, and in 1864 occupied Fort Brooke on the shores of Tampa Bay to protect and help grow the cattle industry of Central and South Florida. Later that year Captain James McKay organized what became known as the "Cow Cavalry," composed mostly of Floridian cowboys and cattle ranchers who were otherwise exempt from Confederate military service, for use in action along the west coast of Florida.[49]

Florida was also home to saltworks near present day Panama City and in Taylor County, where more than five thousand men, exempt from military service, were employed. The salt was in high demand, as it was needed to preserve the precious beef supply as well as help in the manufacturing of leather. Salt was also sold at a dollar a pound, and due to its importance, Confederate General Joseph Finnegan ordered three companies of troops to be stationed around St. Andrew's Bay, which housed one of the largest saltworks, to make sure it did not fall into Union hands.[50] While the Union Navy attacked and destroyed the saltworks on several different occasions, they were rebuilt each time, and General Lee sought to protect these industries as best as he could.[51]

The Union too noticed the importance of this region, and the Federal Department of the South, which comprised the coastal states on the South's Atlantic coast, made a concerted effort to capture Middle Florida through their ill-fated campaign in the winter of 1864, which was repulsed outside of Lake City at the Battle of Olustee, in between Jacksonville and Tallahassee. The goal of this campaign was to sever Florida's ties to the main body of the Confederacy while opening more of the state's ports to trade and use by the North and, possibly, to return Florida to the Union.

This was to be the largest campaign and subsequent battle fought in Florida and one of the bloodiest fought in the Civil War, as Union casualty rates were some of the highest proportionally that they would suffer in four years of fighting. The battle was also noteworthy because of the participation of several colored regiments within the Union order of battle. More than 5,500 Union troops marched west from Jacksonville toward

Tallahassee before they were turned back by 5,200 Confederate troops under the command of General Joseph Finnegan. The Federals suffered 1,800 casualties, while the Southerners lost around 900.[52]

Despite the victory, Governor John Milton still feared future attacks and raids, and in July 1864 he called on Florida's civilian population that was capable of bearing arms to rise to meet the challenge. In response, by November of the same year, three thousand men had been organized into forty-one companies with a promise of arms to be supplied to them by the Confederate government in Richmond. Unfortunately for the companies, Richmond could supply only about one-third of the men. While every able-bodied man between the ages of fifteen to fifty-five not in Confederate service was made a member of the militia, very few saw any action until the closing days of the war. The long-awaited attack on Tallahassee came in March 1865 by way of St. Marks, which resulted in the relatively small battle of Natural Bridge on March 6, 1865. During the battle, militia and teenagers from the nearby Florida Military and Collegiate Institute, which would later become Florida State University, were able to hold off an attack by the Second and Ninety-Ninth US Colored Infantry and protect Tallahassee.[53]

Florida's slaves, some sixty-three thousand at the outbreak of the war, did not openly rebel as many had feared, and many continued their work while their masters were away fighting in Virginia, Tennessee, or Georgia. Those who did not stay on the plantations and farms were pressed into service for the Confederate Armed Forces. In December 1862 the Florida General Assembly authorized the use of slave labor for defensive purposes. In 1863 slaves were put to work building defenses on the Apalachicola River, and in 1864 more than seven hundred slaves were used to build defenses around Jacksonville.[54]

As expected, with most able-bodied white men serving the war effort in some capacity, women felt the effects and bore the full brunt of the war. Frontier women, who had always worked, now took on more responsibilities, even much of the hard labor, usually set aside for men, with their husbands away. The women on Florida's largest plantations also had their lives altered, many living in fear of the inevitable slave uprising that never came. From firsthand accounts written by Ellen Call Long in *Florida Breezes* and Susan Bradford Eppes in *Through Some Eventual Years*, we gain a valuable insight into how two members of Florida's aristocracy viewed not only the war but also their slaves. They both commented on how loyal the slaves remained during the conflict, given it would have been easy for them to either rebel or escape.[55]

While Tallahassee did not fall into Union hands during the war, Federal troops entered the capital on May 10, 1865, without any opposition. They had feared the possibility of guerrilla-style warfare from factions of Confederate holdouts, but none came in Middle Florida. The massive slave revolt also never materialized, and many slaves remained with their masters after the war ended, mainly to help the women manage the farms and plantations with the men away or dead. Many of these slaves were not made privy to information about their freedom until the Emancipation Proclamation was read on the steps of the capitol building on May 20, 1865, by Union General Edward McCook, well after the war had come to an end. Florida's wartime governor, John Milton, was not present to welcome the Union troops to his capital as he had committed suicide the previous month, exclaiming, "Death would preferable to re-union."[56]

From slaves to slave owners, from soldiers to bishops, Floridians experienced the Civil War era in a multitude of ways. While the state was in its infancy when it left the Union, by January 1861, planters had helped recreate the Old South, especially in Middle Florida, while fire-eaters had allied themselves with South Carolina, whom they followed out of the United States. More than fifteen thousand white Floridians would take up arms for the Confederacy, while more than two thousand whites and African Americans donned bluecoats. Due to its long coastline and valuable natural resources, Florida would not emerge from the conflict unscathed.

Notes

1. Michael Gannon, *Florida: A Short History* (Gainesville: University Press of Florida, 1993), 46.

2. Emory Thomas, *The Confederate Nation: 1861–1865* (New York: Harper Torchbooks, 1979), 51.

3. Ibid., 52.

4. Eric Walther, *The Fire Eaters* (Baton Rouge: Louisiana State University Press, 1992), 2.

5. William L. Barney, *The Secessionist Impulse, Alabama and Mississippi in 1860* (Princeton: Princeton University Press, 1974), 1.

6. Thomas, *The Confederate Nation*, 122.

7. Gannon, *Florida*, 28–29.

8. Edward E. Baptist, *Creating an Old South: Middle Florida's Plantation Frontier*

Before the Civil War (Chapel Hill: University of North Carolina Press, 2002), 13.

9. Ibid., 14.

10. Hebert J. Doherty, *Richard Keith Call, Southern Unionist* (Gainesville: University of Florida Press, 1961), 41.

11. Baptist, *Creating an Old South*, 2–3.

12. Ibid., 2.

13. Ibid., 8.

14. Doherty, *Richard Keith Call, Southern Unionist*, 45.

15. Gannon, *Florida*, 30.

16. Ibid., 37.

17. Territorial Census of Florida, 1840.

18. Charlton W. Tebeau, *A History of Florida* (Coral Gables: University of Miami Press, 1971), 126.

19. Dorothy Dodd, *Florida Becomes a State* (Tallahassee: Florida Centennial Commission, 1945), 38–39.

20. Tebeau, *A History of Florida*, 126.

21. Doherty, *The Whigs of Florida, 1845–1854* (Jacksonville: Miller, 1959), 2.

22. Ibid., 3.

23. Doherty, *Richard Keith Call, Southern Unionist*, 49.

24. Herbert J. Doherty, *The Whigs of Florida*, 1.

25. Ibid., 8.

26. Doherty, *Richard Keith Call, Southern Unionist*, 118.

27. Ibid.

28. Tallahassee *Floridian*, September 5, 1840.

29. Doherty, *Richard Keith Call, Southern Unionist*, 122.

30. Tallahassee *Floridian*, February 13, 1841, published from the Pensacola *Gazette.*

31. Doherty, *Richard Keith Call, Southern Unionist*, 124.

32. Ibid., 125.

33. Doherty, *The Whigs of Florida*, 13

34. Doherty, *Richard Keith Call, Southern Unionist*, 125.

35. Comte de Castelnau, "Essay on Middle Florida," translated by Arthur Seymour, foreword by Mark Boyd, *Florida Historical Quarterly* 26, no. 3 (1948): 236–37.

36. *Florida Senate Journal*, 1843, reported in the *Florida Sentinel*, January 20, 1843.

37. *Presidential Message* quoted from US House of Representatives, Executive Documents, #27, 27th Congress, 2nd Session, 223.

38. Tebeau, *A History of Florida*, 149.

39. Ibid.

40. Doherty, *Richard Keith Call, Southern Unionist*, 130.

41. Doherty, *The Whigs of Florida*, 13.

42. Ibid.

43. Ibid., 14.

44. Ibid.

45. Ibid.

46. William H. Nulty, *Confederate Florida* (Tuscaloosa: University of Alabama Press, 1990), vii.

47. Tebeau, *A History of Florida*, 232.

48. Gannon, *Florida*, 43.

49. Tebeau, *A History of Florida*, 233.

50. Ibid., 234.

51. Gannon, *Florida*, 43.

52. Ibid.

53. Tebeau, *A History of Florida*, 216–17.

54. Ibid., 237.

55. Ibid., 238.

56. Gannon, *Florida*, 46.

1

Extreme Measures

Florida and the Crisis of 1850

Seth A. Weitz

After the abolition of slavery in the Northern states during and immediately following the American Revolution, the growing tension between North and South intensified as both regions looked to protect their own interests. The South felt threatened because the North was growing at a larger rate, and as the nation expanded westward during the 1800s, Northerners proved more mobile. Whenever the United States gained territory, the question of whether slavery should be allowed on this land was brought to the forefront in the form of fiery rhetoric in newspapers and lively, and also often violent, debate on the floors of the House of Representatives and the Senate. Many Southerners viewed the institution of slavery as not only their livelihood but also a means to justify their existence and define their culture and values. This sectional tension and the debate over the expansion of slavery climaxed in 1850, after the United States defeated Mexico in the Mexican-American War and found itself in possession of what are today the states of California, New Mexico, Nevada, Arizona, and parts of Utah and Colorado. As the debate raged in the halls of Congress, many in the South felt that their way of life was being threatened by the possibility of numerous new free states. Not only did the Southern states have to deal with opposing beliefs in the North over slavery, but they also had to contend with more moderate elements within their own society who did not wish to antagonize the rest of the nation and thereby risk endangering the institution of slavery where it already existed.

Nowhere in the South was this political struggle more evident than in Florida, where moderates and radicals battled for the supremacy of the state's political apparatus during the 1850s. The decade preceding the Civil War was a crucial period in Florida's antebellum political history as the

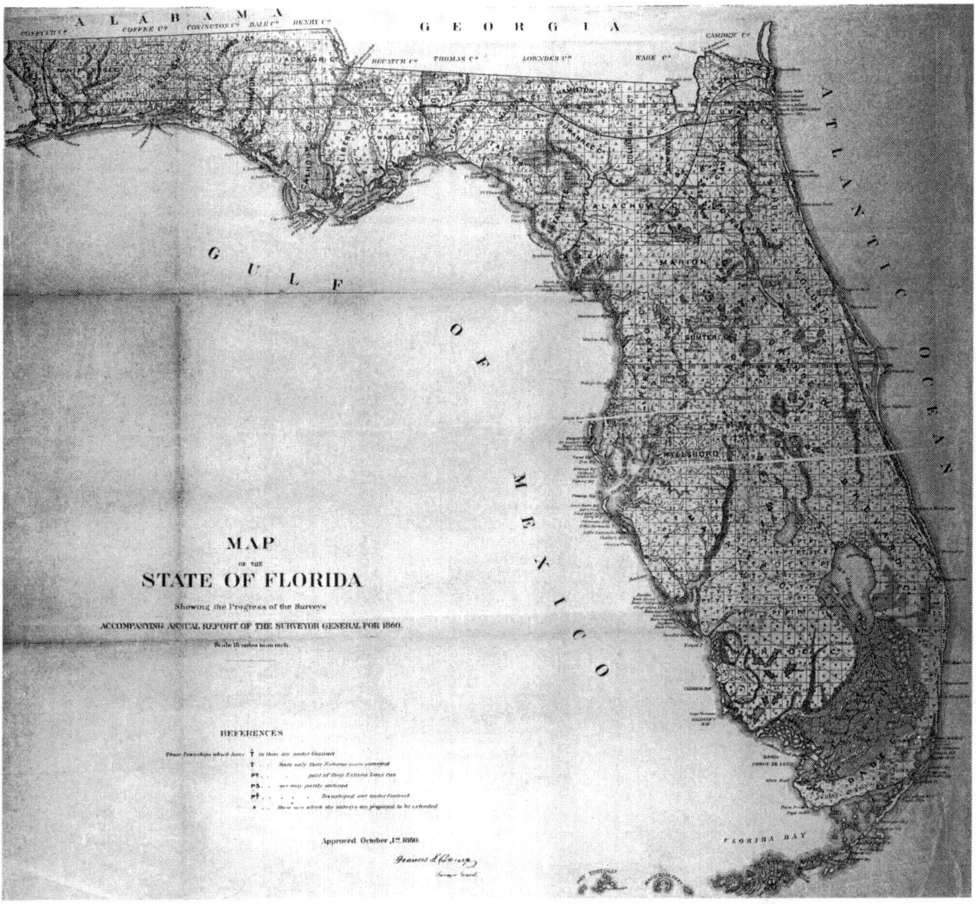

Figure 1.
State of Florida, 1860, courtesy of State Archives of Florida, Florida Memory

state underwent a metamorphosis beginning with the Crisis of 1850 and coming to an end with the collapse of the two-party political system in 1856. Antebellum Florida politics were dominated by the region of Middle Florida, known as the "black belt" both because of the unique color of the soil and because its economy was driven by the institution of slavery. This region, except for Jefferson County, staunchly supported the Whig Party in the early years of statehood. The radical element of society, mainly fire-eating Democrats led by David Levy Yulee, John C. McGehee, James E.

Broome, and Madison Starke Perry, wanted to ally the state with extremist South Carolina but could not do so as long as the planter aristocracy felt a strong allegiance to the more moderate Whigs. The Crisis, or Compromise, of 1850, which temporarily mollified the tensions between North and South on the national level, also proved to be a watershed moment in Florida's history. After the events of 1850, Florida, which had previously been dominated by the more moderate Whig Party, saw a shift toward extremism and the more radical Democratic Party that would eventually lead the state out of the Union during the so-called Secession Winter of 1860–1861.

Noted Civil War diarist and South Carolina fire-eater Mary Boykin Chesnut proclaimed on a visit to Florida in 1860 that "no-one could live in this state unless he *were* a fire-eater."[1] This feeling was not far from reality among the state's white citizens. Florida's population was 140,424; however, of this population, only 77,746 were white. Fourty-four percent of the inhabitants of the state were slaves.[2] The plantation system dominated Florida despite the fact that there were only 5,152 slave owners in the state in 1860. With these demographics, the Whig Party reached the height of their power in Florida between 1848 and 1850 in the years and months leading up to the Compromise of 1850. Henry Clay's compromise had saved the Union from bloodshed, albeit for a mere decade. The Whig Party had won back the governor's mansion, and the Democrats, at least initially, appeared to be divided and frazzled. While Florida succumbed to moderate forces, it was clear by the end of 1850 that the state's political culture was in fact transforming. Extremism and emotionalism slowly gained ground in the state as the perceived threat to the institution of slavery increased and the planter elite of Middle Florida began to question their political allegiance to the Whigs. Whichever party had the support of the so-called Cottonocracy would therefore dominate Florida. The demographic makeup of the state also slowly changed during the 1840s and 1850s, and this favored the Democrats and spelled doom for those with dreams of compromise and conciliation within Florida and the South.

In the late 1840s, the Democrats were seen as the party of emotion and irrationalism, and the speech of lame-duck governor William Dunn Moseley opening the 1848 session was filled with patriotic fervor that echoed these sentiments. Moseley had just witnessed his party endure an embarrassing defeat at the hands of the Whigs on the national level, and he was trying to stir up support for the Democrats by playing on Southern sentiments and interests. Moseley tried to paint the Democrats as the true "party of the South," but, as the voters proved in the 1848 elections, enflaming sectional animosity was not on the minds of most voters.[3]

The governor spoke correctly of ominous "clouds now lowering over our Southern horizon enveloping in darkness the future destiny of our glorious confederacy."[4] Moseley foresaw that a "systematic and incendiary assault upon the peculiar institutions of the South will soon be made, with a determination and strength which can no longer be regarded with contempt."[5] He clearly did not feel that compromise was the answer and was not in favor of following the policies that had won the Whigs the election. He continued by stating, "I have no fears that when the issue is distinctly presented, the South will be united in its resistance to this wanton aggression on its rights; and that all the differences of opinion . . . will be merged."[6] In his fiery speech Moseley tried to warn the state and the South against becoming complacent and thus further sacrificing Southern ideals for the sake of stability and compromise. Moseley's words echoed those of the radical fire-eaters who would draw Florida and the South out of the Union a decade later.

The Florida General Assembly, controlled by the Whigs, pushed aside Moseley's warnings and continued with the business of everyday government in the state, turning their attention toward electing a senator to serve the state's needs in Washington. This election was for the seat currently held by Democrat James Westcott, whom the Whigs did not wish to see reelected in March.[7] Since senators were not elected based on popular vote, there was no statewide campaigning, and in the months leading up to the elections several people were nominated by various members of the assembly. Samuel Burritt of Jacksonville, a lawyer, was nominated, along with Jackson Morton of Escambia County. Joining them were Jesse J. Finley, nominated by Nicholas Long of Jackson County, and George T. Ward of Tallahassee, who was nominated by William Maxwell and represented Leon County.[8] All these candidates were Whigs. Finley had support of the *Florida Whig* since he was from Jackson County where the paper was published, while the *Pensacola Gazette* backed Jackson Morton of Pensacola, largely because they felt West Florida was neglected by the rest of the state.[9]

The first vote in the assembly proved inconclusive, as no one candidate earned a majority; Burritt led the way with twenty-six votes, followed by Ward with sixteen, Finley with seven, and Morton with six.[10] A second vote was immediately called and the results again were indecisive. Burritt led the pack with eighteen, followed by Ward with sixteen, Finley with seven, and Morton with six. The third vote again saw Burritt in the lead with twenty-six votes again, followed by Ward with seventeen, Finley with seven, and Morton with five.[11] At this point a motion to adjourn until the following week was voted down 29–28, continuing the painfully prolonged process of selecting Florida's senatorial representative in Washington.[12] To complicate matters further, Walker Anderson, a Democrat from Pensacola, was nominated by John Ghent, an independent, in an attempt to draw away support from Burritt.[13] The subsequent vote saw Burritt and Ward leading the way; but without a majority, no election was valid, and when a second vote for adjournment was brought before the assembly, it was again defeated 33–25.[14] The fifth vote again did not produce a senator, and upon the third motion for adjournment, the assembly voted 29–28 in favor of postponing the election until the following day.[15] On December 12, the assembly voted 24–14 to indefinitely postpone the vote.

The seeming deadlock was due largely to sectional differences that remained within the state and even within the Whig Party itself. The Whigs had united to defeat the Democrats in the statewide elections of 1848, but the state as a whole could not shed the cloud of regional animosity and jealousy that had gripped Florida since the beginning of the territorial period in 1821. Both the *Pensacola Gazette* and the *Florida Republican* attacked the Whigs of Middle Florida for trying to horde the power in the state, and they also both in turn mocked the Middle Florida Whigs for "graciously" allowing them the right to even furnish the state with representatives.[16]

To fully understand the sectional tension and shifting political landscape, it is important to examine how Florida had changed between 1821 and 1850 and, more significantly, in the five years since it had become a state. In 1845 the state had a population of 66,500, but by 1850 it had grown to 87,445, an increase of almost 21,000, or 31.5 percent.[17] Florida remained the smallest state in the nation but had seen a population boom and an increase in size by close to 35,000 over the 1840s, with most of these immigrants coming from neighboring Southern states, mostly Georgia and South Carolina. Before the 1840s Florida had been settled by a great number of Virginians, who for the most part were more moderate than their Deep South brethren. Middle Florida still held the power in the state, as the region boasted 34,959 people, or 39.9 percent of the state's population.[18] The heartbeat of Middle Florida, Leon County, home of the capital city of Tallahassee, had a population of 11,442, of which 8,203, or 71.6 percent, were slaves. The slaves in Gadsden and Jefferson Counties, which bordered

Leon on the West and the East, respectively, also constituted more than 50 percent of their populations, 4,880 out of 8,784 in Gadsden and 4,938 out of 7,718 in Jefferson.[19] As a whole, Florida was home to 39,310 slaves in 1850, which accounted for 44.9 percent of the population, and Middle Florida alone was home to 46.8 percent of the state's slaves. Florida also had 4,143 plantations and farms in 1850, with the majority located in Middle Florida reinforcing the importance of slavery and the influence of the middle region of the state.[20]

Florida, with a slave population of 45 percent, was fourth behind South Carolina (57.6 percent), Mississippi (51.1 percent), and Louisiana (47.3 percent), and ahead of Alabama (44 percent) and Georgia (42 percent), in slave population, and of the three states ranked above Florida, two (Mississippi and South Carolina) preceded the state in seceding from the Union in 1860 and 1861.[21] The other state, Louisiana, was also one of the seven Deep South states to secede before the firing on Fort Sumter in April 1861. Florida's transformation into a Deep South state dependent on the institution of slavery was well underway by 1850, and the state was locked into the same trap that befell South Carolina and the other radical states in their dependence on slavery. Florida was commercially prosperous due to its long coastline, but this prosperity too was deeply tied to slavery, as Florida's cotton was exported from ports such as Apalachicola, Pensacola, and Jacksonville bound for England and other destinations in Europe. Pensacola also served as a port to export cotton from Eastern Alabama by way of the Escambia River to the Gulf of Mexico.

Largely due to the surprising growth rate of Middle Florida compared to that of East and West Florida, sectional differences dominated the state. The other two regions, which had dominated the state during the early territorial stage, were now growing at a much slower pace than Middle Florida and were jealous of its increasing size and power. Escambia County, Florida's westernmost county and home to Pensacola, had a population of only 4,351 in 1850, with its neighbor, Santa Rosa, at 2,883. In East Florida, Duval County and St. John's County had populations of 4,539 and 2,525, respectively, and the fact that the East and West could not unite to combat Middle Florida confirmed the latter's political and economic dominance.[22]

When the General Assembly reconvened on January 1, 1849, a vote was once again called for the election of a senator. This time only George Ward and Jackson Morton were nominated, but the elimination of the other candidates did not change the situation. Even though Morton defeated Ward

29–27, the Speaker of the House ordered a revote.[23] In the subsequent vote, Morton, who had trailed badly in the initial elections in November, was certified as Florida's United States senator.[24] In the end, Morton, who became Florida's first Whig senator, received thirty votes to twenty-seven for Ward, with ironically twenty-two of the thirty coming from Democrats. Only eight Whigs voted for the Escambia politician.[25] The Democrats saw Morton as the lesser of two evils, since he was a novice compared to Ward, who had long been involved in Whig politics.[26]

Despite internal conflict, the brewing sectional conflict between the North and the South over slavery and its expansion could not escape the halls of Florida's General Assembly, and on January 3 a motion was introduced and passed in which Florida once again reaffirmed its allegiance to its neighboring Southern states. Florida vowed that it would do all in its power to support the South in Washington as well as in Tallahassee.[27] The resolution declared in defiant terms that the people of Florida were ready to join other Southern states in defense of their institutions and rights should the time come.[28]

After the conclusion of the Mexican-American War, the United States was in possession of roughly two-thirds of what used to make up the northern states and territories of the Mexican Republic. In Washington, Congress prepared to debate how the nation should incorporate these new lands. Regarding the proposed admission of California as a free state, Floridians resurrected the old argument that was used to bring Florida into the Union in 1845: a balance of slave states and free states. The majority of Floridians were discouraged by the lack of support given to those congressmen who sought to organize the territories annexed from Mexico under the guidelines of the Treaty of Guadalupe-Hidalgo, which had ended the war. Florida, though, was not united, as their new governor, Thomas Brown, a veteran of the War of 1812, spoke for the minority in the South who placed Unionism above all else. Despite this, it is undeniable that Brown was a proponent of Southern rights and states' rights, since, as a native Virginian, Brown had always displayed sympathy for the South. He was, though, deeply concerned with further upsetting sectional tensions. Despite not being able to officially take office until October 1849, because of contradictory statements in the territorial and state constitutions concerning the exact date of the succession of governors, Brown delivered his inaugural speech on January 11, 1849. Brown's speech differed greatly from that of Moseley only three months earlier. While he did reveal that his support lay with the rights of the individual states and the South, Brown also spoke of compromise and referred to the Founding Fathers. He condemned partisan politics, which many saw as a personal attack on the Democrats, while also stating, "The Northern fanatics have done much to weaken the attachment and reverence of the people of the Union; and I fear as much has been done by Southern demagogues as Northern fanatics."[29] This was a direct denunciation of former vice president and current South Carolina Senator John C. Calhoun and his young protégé from Florida, David Levy Yulee.

Brown's words shocked many Democrats, who deemed his speech an unnecessary assault on Southern radicals, who, led by Yulee and Calhoun on the national level, expressed their beliefs in the South Carolinians' "Southern Address," which had clarified the South's position on numerous issues. Many Democrats in Florida took their frustration out on their congressman in Washington, Edward C. Cabell. He was verbally abused along with the rest of the Whigs because he refused to sign Calhoun's address for the same reasons stated by Brown in his speech, noting that Calhoun's words were as much a threat to the nation as the abolitionists and the Free Soil Party in the North were.[30] In the face of these attacks, many Whigs did not feel that the time had come to further agitate the situation and therefore remained silent on the issue. Newspapers like the *Florida Republican* did in fact claim that most Floridians, whether Whigs or Democrats, would support the South if slavery were in fact attacked. They differed from the Democrats only because they felt that slavery was not being attacked by the majority of Northerners.[31] They claimed that radicalism "will kill, not cure the patient."[32] On the national level Cabell was clearly shaken by the negative reactions to the actions of his fellow Floridians, and he backed a measure put forth by his Southern colleagues to create a party platform to oppose ending the slave trade in Washington, DC, and exclude expansion of slavery into the newly acquired territories. Cabell withdrew from the Whig caucus along with eight other Southern Whigs when their plan was not approved by the party.[33]

At the same time, radical Democrats in Congress led by Calhoun began to push for a conference of Southern states to discuss what they saw as attacks on their way of life. Calhoun and his cohorts were angered by the prospect of California's admission to the Union as a free state and by resolutions passed by state legislatures in every Northern state except Iowa, which favored Congress's right to exclude the expansion of slavery into the former Mexican territories. As 1849 drew to a close, Yulee recommended to his colleagues that a meeting of Southern governors take place, and he suggested to Calhoun that if this was not enough that they split from the Democratic Party to form a new "Southern Rights Party" to combat the Free Soil Party and other antislavery forces rising in the North.[34] Yulee was not alone in these sentiments, as Calhoun already had a plan in mind. Calhoun proposed a convention to meet in Nashville, Tennessee, and for each Southern state to send delegates in June 1850.[35] The *Florida Sentinel*, Tallahassee's Whig organ, was appalled at the call for a conference, since, as a more moderate force than most Whigs, they felt this action would antagonize the antislavery forces in the North. They echoed Brown's sentiments of the previous year that more harm would come to the South from these actions.[36]

Initially Governor Brown remained silent on the issue, and he was encouraged by the Whig press, which did not want to see the issue brought to the forefront of Florida politics. They agreed with Brown that "passion was generally replacing intellect."[37] While some newspapers took a cautious approach toward the proposed convention, not wanting to antagonize the Democrats or even some of their fellow Whigs, the *Florida Republican* stated that it would rather see it "strangled in its birth than lend it countenance."[38] Brown's inaction angered Democrats and Whigs alike, since it meant that Brown refused to either endorse the convention or name Florida's delegates to it.[39] The path Florida would take in the Compromise of 1850 and beyond is significant in understanding the changes that were taking place in the state's landscape. Florida was being groomed by South Carolina much in the way David Levy Yulee was being mentored by John C. Calhoun. Florida was to prove one of South Carolina's most loyal allies during the secession crisis, and even though the Whigs controlled the state at the beginning of the decade, it was easy to see that moderate politicians such as Brown were in the minority when it came to dealing with the question of Southern rights. While it was difficult to find many whites in Florida who opposed states' rights and the institution of slavery, Florida's transition into a radical fire-eating state was not complete. Also noticeably quiet during the Crisis of 1850 was former governor and "Founding Father" of Florida, Richard Keith Call. Call had faded from the limelight in the five years since he had left office, but his sentiments had not changed much in that time. Call was confident of the path chosen by Governor Brown, and he therefore gave Brown his support out of the public's view.[40]

The conflicts in Florida mirrored the ones erupting on the national level, and fortunately for the nation a major conflict was averted, or at least postponed, when calmer heads prevailed and Henry Clay proposed what became the Compromise of 1850. In spite of this, the compromise did not sit well with radicals on either side, as the bill was referred to as the "surrender bill" by Florida's Democratic papers.[41] The *Floridian and Journal*, when referring to Clay's bill, claimed, "It was well said that not one man in a hundred would consider this plan a compromise. . . . It is an almost unconditional surrender to the North."[42] In their view, the admission of California as a free state and the proposed organization of Utah and New Mexico as free territories would leave the slave states completely surrounded. Fire-eating Democrats could feel the Northern yoke being tightened. However, the Whigs and their newspapers favored the compromise, even more so in Florida and throughout the South since the bill had measures that did protect slavery. The Whig newspapers spent most of their efforts assailing radicals such as Yulee in Florida and Calhoun on the national level.[43]

Nevertheless, Florida's Whig representatives in Washington did not take the moderate stance that their newspapers did, as they followed Yulee in endorsing his letter to Governor Brown calling for Brown to finally recognize the Southern Convention in Nashville and appoint delegates.[44] Cabell and Morton, both devout Whigs, united with Yulee since they felt the federal government was encroaching on the rights of the South. Democrats saw Morton as being malleable, and they approached him first before focusing their attention on Cabell, who would be the tougher convert since he had originally opposed a convention. Ultimately Cabell joined Morton and Yulee but felt it necessary to send an additional note to Brown in which he carefully defended his position and his reasons for endorsing the letter. Cabell was afraid that the antislavery forces had gained too much influence and that while his party had favored Clay's compromise, this bill, if left unchecked, could bring about an end to the Southern way of life.[45]

Governor Brown's response further ignited Florida's radicals while also damaging the already strained relations between Brown and his citizens. In the letter, he followed the path he had established in his speech a year earlier opening the state's General Assembly. He labeled the convention "revolutionary . . . and directly against the spirit if not the letter of the Constitution of the United States" and went further by stating his discontent with Cabell, Morton, and Yulee for putting him in such a precarious position.[46] Brown again refused to endorse and send delegates, saying, "The time has not arrived for such measures, and I pray God such a time may never arrive."[47] Interestingly enough, Brown stated that the South had not yet been put in a position that warranted such radical action. This statement illustrated that while he was one of the most, if not the most, moderate politicians in Florida in 1850, he was still a Southerner and did not condemn *future* action against antislavery forces if he deemed it *necessary*. Brown was a Unionist but still a Southerner, and, as he had in his speech of January 11, 1849, he attacked Northern radicals along with Southern radicals and charged both groups with antagonizing the other into making rash and unwise decisions.[48]

The Democratic press vilified Brown, labeling him as a traitor, while the Whig press praised his courage in standing up to the extremists.[49] Other Whig papers, such as Jackson County's *Florida Whig*, also supported Brown's conservatism, while the *Gazette* in Pensacola blasted their native son, Morton, for endorsing the convention. The paper went as far as to compare Brown's actions with the successful campaign President Andrew Jackson waged on South Carolina during the "Nullification Crisis" close to twenty years earlier.[50] In addition, the paper stated, "May we not hope that Governor Brown's letter has killed the nullification of 1850?"[51]

Most Whigs in Florida's General Assembly, despite their Southern patriotism, fell in line with the governor and criticized Morton unmercifully, claiming he was nothing more than Yulee's lapdog, afraid to think for himself and deviate from the path set forth by the powerful Democrat. Morton took these attacks to heart and lashed out at Brown and his fellow Florida Whigs in a letter published by the *Florida Republican*. In it he accused Brown of not acting in the best interests of the state but rather trying to appease Northern Whigs and President Zachary Taylor behind a guise of unionism. Morton further stated that the Nashville Convention, as it was now being called, was in the best interests of Florida and the South and was not an extreme action but rather a precautionary measure meant to implement a contingency plan in case the situation took a turn for the worse.[52] He complained that Brown represented the interests of neither of Florida's two political parties by the stance he had taken.

Brown did not give up the fight despite being outnumbered, and he counterattacked valiantly, but it was becoming clear that his views were too moderate for most Floridians, even members of his own party. The governor mocked his opponents by proclaiming that he did not wish to see "another revolution": "And if I feel called upon to blush in this connection, it is for those who pronounce this government a Russian despotism . . . who would call a convention of modern politicians to remedy the inherent defects in our great charter of liberties . . . who think themselves able to improve it . . . who in respect to anticipated grievances would change or destroy it, and who delude the people with dazzling schemes of a Southern Confederacy."[53]

In the end, most of Florida's Whigs, despite Governor Brown's protests, realized that they could no longer oppose the convention and still save face. The Whigs soon changed their tactics and set out to ensure that a moderate-laden, handpicked delegation would represent Florida in Nashville. The delegates were selected at meetings held in Florida's three regions. Each region, meeting in Ocala (East Florida), Tallahassee (Middle Florida), and Marianna (West Florida), chose both a Democrat and a Whig to represent the state. At Tallahassee, Charles H. Dupont was the Democratic selection, while Arthur J. Forman represented the Whigs. Marianna chose Congressman Cabell and Democrat James F. McClellan, while Ocala nominated Joseph M. Hernandez, a Whig, and B. M. Pearson from the Democratic Party.[54]

Brown's opposition to the convention could have been a deathblow to the Whigs and Brown himself, if tensions at the national level were not alleviated by the actions of Massachusetts Whig and famous orator Daniel Webster. Webster drew scorn from several Northern and Southern radicals for his "Seventh of March" speech in which he denounced radicalism, praised conservatism and moderation, and called for Henry Clay's compromise to be upheld. The positive reaction to Webster's speech allowed Cabell and Hernandez to decline the nominations to the convention. Cabell praised Webster's speech for helping to save the Union and lauded Clay and his work on the compromise, referring to both men as true patriots working with the nation's best interests in mind.[55] The radicals suffered a further blow to their cause when John C. Calhoun died, on March 31.

While many Florida Democrats moderated their extremism, the St. Augustine *Ancient City* did not. It still charged Southern Whigs with forcing the region to submit to the abolitionists and Northern radicals. The paper also did not endorse Clay's compromise, labeling it the driving force behind the submission.[56] These attacks embarrassed several of the state's leading Democrats who tried, largely in vain, to promote a more temperate compromising atmosphere and platform for their party.

It was under these auspices that the Nashville Convention began in the summer of 1850. While it did not attract either the attention or the enthusiasm that Calhoun, Yulee, and other fire-eaters had hoped, it still stood for division, which clearly countered the prevailing attitude of conciliation that the compromise had, for the most part, fostered. The president of the convention was William L. Sharkey of Mississippi, who himself was a moderate, and the tenor of the meeting followed his lead. Representatives from Florida, Alabama, Georgia, Mississippi, South Carolina, Tennessee, Texas, and Virginia were present, with only South Carolina maintaining an extremist posture.[57] While a resolution that condemned the compromise was passed, pushed through by the South Carolinians, Sharkey was able to use his influence to counter the fiery mood this created and shelve the action until Congress had come to a final decision concerning Clay's proposed bill, which was now being championed by Democrat Stephen A. Douglas of Illinois, as Clay himself had become gravely ill.[58] At home, Whigs such as George W. Call, son of the former governor and rising Whig politician, scolded the Democrats at a party meeting. In Alligator, now Lake City, Call placed the blame for the sectional crisis squarely on the shoulders of the Democrats. Once they had achieved victory through their support for the compromise at the national level many Whigs turned their attention toward inflicting further damage on their political opponents.[59]

The Compromise of 1850 was seen as a triumph for the Whigs, especially in Florida and the South, but, in the final analysis, it was a Pyrrhic victory. In Washington, Cabell and Morton joined Yulee in voting against the abolition of the slave trade in the District of Columbia. They also tried to stop the admission of California to the Union as a free state. Morton followed the fire-eating Democrat Yulee in opposing Texas giving up its claims to territory that would become New Mexico, while Cabell favored the measure. After the bill passed Congress, Cabell was the only Floridian to support it.[60] Cabell proclaimed, "We have not obtained all which I think should have been granted us, but no right has been taken away by the action of congress."[61] The passage of the bill was met with thunderous denunciations from the Democratic press, including from the editor of the *Floridian and Journal*, Tallahassee's leading Democratic paper. He proclaimed that the passage of the bill was met "with joyful acclamations from abolitionists and submissionists."[62] He persisted in saying that the compromise left the South with one choice, and that was disunion.[63]

It must be again noted that despite their opposition to sectional turbulence and inciting controversy between the North and the South, most Southern Whigs, such as Richard Keith Call, had little sympathy for free black people and even less for slaves. They also had the same disdain and scorn for Northern abolitionists that their radical Democratic counterparts displayed. The Whigs loathed radicals, both Northern and Southern. Call defended slavery, as did most Whigs in Florida, and felt that African Americans and slaves were mentally inferior to whites. In a letter written to John S. Littell, Call asserted his beliefs that black people were "wild barbarians, to be tamed and civilized by the discipline of slavery . . . an animal in the form of a man." He went further, proclaiming that "nobly has this race done the great work required. . . . They have been elevated in the scale of human beings."[64] These words condemning the black race are as harsh as those from any fire-eater in the antebellum South. Call and other Whigs made up the majority of Middle Florida's "plantation aristocracy," which helps to explain these views. Call's plantation, located in Tallahassee on Lake Jackson, was home to 140 slaves and 4,000 acres of land with an overall value of more than $6,000 per acre.[65] Yet Call, along with the majority of Whigs, was not willing to secede from the Union as a means of preserving the lifestyle to which he had become accustomed and that he fervently defended in his words to Littell.

The Compromise of 1850 did not end the sectional turmoil, as it merely served as a fleeting truce that did little to placate the sullen and implacable hostility that Southerners felt toward the North. In the midst of this ongoing tumult, Florida faced the prospects of an impending congressional election. The Whigs ran on a platform that stood by the compromise, while the Democrats attacked it outright. The Whigs nominated Cabell, while the Democrats nominated John Beard, a native of North Carolina who had moved to St. Augustine in 1838 and later settled in Tallahassee. Beard's most notable public job had been as registrar of public lands, a job given to him by Whig president John Tyler.[66] It was also rumored that Beard was a member of the Whig Party in 1840, because he supported Whig candidate William Henry Harrison in the presidential election of that year. He answered these assaults by launching a vigorous campaign across the state in which he conveyed the anticompromise sentiments of Democrats. He supported Yulee in favoring an extension of the Missouri Compromise line to the Pacific Ocean, which also meant that he opposed the admission of California as a free state. Beard tried to present himself as a Jeffersonian by claiming that he did have faith in the Union, which he felt was "based upon the truth and force of those principles which the immortal Jefferson made the ground work of . . . and which were illustrated by the lamented Calhoun."[67] He also added that the South had lost all in the compromise without any personal gain and further declared, "I love the Union with a reasonable affection" but "not with a servile or superstitious reverence as some great deity."[68] He dared Whigs to label him as a traitor or a disunionist, but he continued to follow the same platform throughout his campaign. In Beard's opinion, the compromise was the work of abolitionists.

Cabell proved equal to the task when he stated, "Major Beard is for a dissolution of the Union because (he opposed) the passage" of the Omnibus Compromise Bill. He clearly affirmed that he was a staunch Unionist by pronouncing that "the issues are Union and disunion. . . . I am for Union: peace or war . . . I am for peace."[69] Cabell went further, asserting, "Never, either as a Representative or Candidate, will I assume the awful responsibility of recommending to you dissolution of the Union."[70] The Democrats, as they waged their slanderous campaign, shot back by criticizing Cabell for refusing to stand firmly with his other Southern colleagues in protecting Southern rights and pointing out that the Northern wing of Cabell's party was associated with such loathsome men as William H. Seward. They accused Cabell of being a puppet for Seward and Joshua Giddings of Ohio, who, along with Benjamin Wade, had become one of the leading figures in the antislavery movement in the Midwest.

The Democrats recommended that Cabell and his fellow Southern Whigs break their bond with the abolitionists while in turn allying themselves with the Democratic Party. The "party of Jackson," as they often mislabeled themselves, was in their own minds the "only party in the North which has stood up, or will stand up, for the rights of the South, as secured and guaranteed by the constitution."[71] Cabell's vacillating feelings regarding the Nashville Convention were also brought forth by his opponents. Initially, in the letter he coauthored and endorsed along with Yulee and Morton, addressed to Governor Brown, Cabell had supported Florida's participation in the convention. When the convention finally took place, Cabell did not attend, even though he was the Whig delegate from West Florida, nominated at Marianna.[72] He was labeled a buffoon who possessed a "quivering uncertain character" and was further ridiculed for being someone who "professed Whiggery . . . [but] had not brains enough to classify their principles" in the midst of his political stance.[73]

To offset the Democratic aggression, the Whigs countered with someone other than Cabell on the campaign trail. Former governor and staunch moderate Richard Keith Call broke his self-imposed silence to trek around the state promoting Cabell while trying to maintain support for Clay's compromise. Call and the Whigs began their campaign confident that the passage of the compromise had virtually killed the Nashville Convention and settled the sectional controversy for the time being. The response from the Democratic press and candidates proved they were gravely mistaken. As shown above, the Democrats spun the sectional crisis to make it appear to have been perpetrated by the Northern Whigs, and by 1850 "Northern" was a soiled word south of the Mason-Dixon Line.

Call confronted Beard at a Democratic barbecue, marking the beginning of a heated series of interchanges between the two statesmen. Call took to heart what he saw as blatant assaults on the Union, which he cherished deeply, and vowed to fight Beard to the end. At the barbecue, Call scolded Beard in an emotional speech wherein he maintained that disunion was an unthinkable horror. He further asked, "Where would enslaved humanity [white humanity] throughout the earth, turn for succor, hope or comfort, if the great God of nations should withdraw his protecting arm, and permit this sun of liberty to sink in a night of strife and fraternal blood."[74] Call proved to be a more eloquent speaker than Beard, greatly aiding the Whig cause. Cabell's bid for reelection was also bolstered by George T. Ward of Tallahassee and David S. Walker, who himself was running for registrar of public lands, Beard's old position, against Mariano D. Papy.[75]

Much to the chagrin of Beard and the Democrats, proponents of severing political ties with the North were a small minority in Florida in 1850. Florida was not yet as radical as it would be in 1861 and clearly not on the same level in 1850 as South Carolina. The Democrats overestimated the degree of anti-Northern sentiment in the state, as did their major newspapers. The *Floridian and Journal* praised Beard for his stance on the compromise, reporting that he preferred disunion to subservience to the North. The following words from one of Beard's speeches were quoted in the same issue: "Fellow citizens, we all cherish a habitual and hereditary love for the Union: But it is the Union that our sires bled for . . . an Union of *equal rights* . . . an Union to promote the *general welfare* . . . not that of a *particular section*; an Union to secure 'domestic tranquility'; and not one to expose us to the horrors of a servile Negro war, excited by those who ought to be our friends."[76]

The Whigs responded sardonically, asking if Beard was in fact their candidate and if he had not proposed a Southern Confederacy as a viable means of action. Beard and the Democrats had indeed run on that platform and the election results of November verified that Florida was not yet ready for such extremism. When the election finally transpired, the Whigs were able to stave off a furious rally by the Democrats. Cabell and Walker defeated Beard and Papy, respectively, but it was not the decisive victory the party had enjoyed in 1848 and that many had predicted. While the Whigs proclaimed a great victory for conservatism, compromise, and peace, the election results showed the importance of Southern nationalism and how the crisis of 1850 was in many ways a Democratic victory in disguise.[77] The Compromise of 1850 had merely acted to prolong the inevitable schism that was destined to shake the foundations that the United States had been founded upon seventy-five years before. The bill was simply another fruitless effort aimed at mending a fatal wound with a simple bandage. These results in no way meant that Floridians approved the compromise, especially since Cabell had initially voted against various measures in Henry Clay's bill. By choosing the incumbent over Beard, the population showed that Beard had lost this election with his virulent tone more than Cabell had won it.

The majority from Cabell's 1848 victory was reduced by 86 votes, and while this might not seem a monumental change, one must keep in mind that a mere 8,581 votes were cast in the election. Cabell garnered 4,531 votes to Major Beard's 4,050, giving the Whig 52.8 percent of the popular vote. With his campaign closely linked to Cabell's, and his platform based on that put forth by the Whigs, David Walker defeated Mariano Papy 4,414–3,785, surpassing Cabell's margin of victory percentage. Papy attained a meager 46 percent of the vote as Walker took over Major Beard's old post as registrar of public lands.[78]

A further investigation of the statewide results showed that Cabell carried the "black belt" of Middle Florida where the state's wealthier landowners resided. This area, long a strong bastion of Whig support, had more to lose with the continuance of the agitation over the slavery question. In their minds, if slavery was undermined, then it would be a result of extremist uncompromising policies of the radical Democrats. Middle Florida, which continued to maintain a tight grasp over Florida politics as well as economic production, was a vital battleground, and one that the Democrats knew they would have to make immense strides in if they were going to wrest power away from the Whigs in future confrontations. The only county in Middle Florida to throw its weight behind Beard was Jefferson, which came as no surprise to Floridians.[79] Despite being the "buckle of the black belt," the city of Monticello, and Jefferson County as a whole, had long proved a Democratic stronghold, forever defying logic in refusing to succumb to the conservatism of the Whigs. Aside from Jefferson County, the major mustered most of his support from the poorer small yeoman farmers in South and East Florida.

Genuine shock, though, came when the Whigs failed to retain control of the General Assembly. The Whigs had swept state elections in 1848, but two years later they found their rivals in control of the legislature. Radicalism did not carry the day to the extent that many Democrats hoped it would, but the party of Calhoun *did* hold a feeble majority, an advantage of a solitary seat in the Senate and two in the House. The importance of this Democratic victory lay in the reality that the assembly would be charged with the task of electing a senator to represent Florida in the nation's capital, for David Yulee's term was set to expire in 1851.

When the dust settled from the calamitous events of 1850, Florida remained in the Union, but it was clear that the state's populace was growing more radical by the day. More importantly, Southern rights were quickly becoming a cause that many within the state would fight for, even if that meant breaking the bonds of the Union. The Whigs, who had risen to the apex of their power in the years preceding the Compromise of 1850, were slowly being swept aside by their political rivals, the Democratic Party. Florida, once a bastion of conservatism, was now becoming a hotbed of extremism.

Highlighting this shift, in the winter of 1851 various fire-eaters took it upon themselves to call several independent Southern Rights Conventions to be held at a variety of locations throughout the state. They affirmed that the time for "mere abstract propositions on the subject of the rights of slaveholders, or vague threats of what the South will be disposed to do, on the contingency of any specified encroachment upon those rights" had passed.[80]

The Southern Rights Association of Madison County met at the Madison Courthouse on June 7, 1851. The keynote address was given by Madison County's John C. McGehee, whose importance to secession would be felt ten years later, when he presided over Florida's Secession Convention. His speech echoed many sentiments expressed previously by Democrats in Florida's legislature. He charged the federal government with intending to overthrow Southern rights through its actions, especially the Compromise of 1850. McGehee followed that accusation with an attack on moderates throughout the South, labeling them weak and submissive. McGehee had been disappointed that the Nashville Convention had amounted to little but at the same time hopeful that through actions such as the creation of the Southern Rights Associations throughout Florida and the Deep South, their voices would be heard, their warning heeded, and their goals finally accomplished.[81] McGehee offered a pledge, readily accepted by those in attendance, who vowed to no longer "remain silent . . . under indignity and insult."[82]

McGehee, however, was unprepared for the type of reaction he got from some elements of Florida's press. He felt the denunciations were a slap in the face of the South, and McGehee was appalled to learn that his "name was used as a watchword of clamor and tumult to carry the crowd in opposition to principles I was known to entertain and advocate."[83] McGehee could not fathom why people would oppose what he viewed as a noble and just campaign to maintain a Southern lifestyle to which most were devoted. Unlike the Whigs and other moderates who felt, rightfully so, that extremists antagonizing the situation would culminate in disaster for the South, McGehee felt that radical measures were needed to safeguard Southern rights.

McGehee deviated from others before him by highlighting slavery as the main issue at stake. While others alluded to it, McGehee articulated the need for the system and what might occur should it be attacked and dismantled. He further exclaimed, "Florida is a slave state. . . . By her constitution and laws the right of property in slaves is guaranteed and protected. . . . The state as our sovereign is bound to protect every citizen equally and alike in the enjoyment of his life, liberty, and property."[84] McGehee challenged Governor Brown to provide protection for this cause. The fire-eater also readily employed common propaganda tactics to strike fear into the hearts of Floridians, alluding to gruesome images of mass rebellion, anarchy, and slaughter should abolitionists be afforded too much power in governing the nation. He evoked scenes of horror of the consequences of the slave rebellion in Haiti. McGehee reiterated his belief that the South was built on a pillar of white supremacy that would be shaken if the "naturally lazy, indolent, improvident and unscrupulous" black race was allowed the basic freedoms that he and his allies harped on endlessly in their cries for justice.[85]

The radicalism of John C. McGehee's words was unmistakable in his attack on not only slaves, abolitionists, and Northerners but also fellow Southerners, who he depicted as cowards and traitors for not employing fanatical measures to protect the institutions of Southern society. McGehee echoed the sentiments of the disunionists when he concluded his address by claiming that he expected others to respond with a "determination to spend our lives or meet our deaths in her cause."[86] At a Fourth of July picnic in Madison held by the Southern Rights Association, the fire-eaters proudly flaunted their mottoes "equality in the Union or Independence out of it" and "a Southern Confederacy should be the motto of every Southern man."[87] By calling on the patriotism of every Southerner, the radicals challenged their opposition to rally to the cause. In Leon County an estimated 10 percent of the voting population belonged to the Southern Rights Association, while in McGehee's home county of Madison that number ran as high as 33 percent.[88]

This transformation also played itself out in the subsequent elections of 1852 and 1854. In 1852, the Democrats regained the governor's mansion as South Carolina native and fire-eater James E. Broome defeated George T. Ward 4,628–4,336.[89] While the margin of victory was not overwhelming at 51.6 percent to 48.4 percent, the writing was clearly on the wall, even if the Whig press did not want to admit it. In a more shocking blow, Cabell was not reelected to Congress. The shifting of support in Middle Florida was apparent in that both Cabell and Ward had lost Leon and Gadsden Counties and Cabell had also lost three counties in East Florida that had helped to send him to Washington in 1850. These counties of Marion, Alachua, and St. Johns were all important economically, as the former two were driven by a plantation economy similar to that of the black belt.[90]

The Whigs' precarious situation worsened the following month when the results of the presidential election were announced, as 1,996 fewer votes were cast in the national election than in the statewide vote. This seemed to help Democrat Franklin Pierce, who routed Whig General Winfield Scott in Florida, polling 4,318 votes to the general's 2,875.[91] The landslide, which saw Pierce garner 60 percent of Florida's vote, clearly demonstrated the fear that Southerners had of the Northern wing of the Whig Party. The only counties Scott carried in Florida were Nassau, Walton, and Holmes. The embarrassing thrashing at the polls left a permanent scar on Cabell's once bold psyche. The promising, energetic, unionist stalwart was left distraught and disillusioned. He abandoned politics shortly after the election to assume the presidency of the Pensacola and Georgia Railroad, a title he held until he moved away from Florida before the Civil War, never to return. Cabell spent the remainder of his days quietly in Missouri until his death in 1896 at the age of eighty.[92] Although the Whigs would meekly muster candidates for the 1854 mid-term elections, 1852 is often cited as the true end of the party's run in Florida as well as on the national level.

The 1856 election was the last race of the antebellum period in Florida that saw the Democrats run opposed. Fire-eater Madison Starke Perry easily won the governor's mansion while the Democrats maintained their seat in Congress and even increased its stranglehold over the state legislature. When the dust cleared, the Democrats had won forty-two of Florida's sixty-five seats, or roughly 65 percent.[93] The rise of the Republican Party on the national level in 1856 was the deathblow for the old conservative camp in Florida as well as in the Deep South. The Republican Party would not even gain recognition in Florida and was absent from the ballots in both 1856 and 1860.

The great metamorphosis in Florida's political culture from 1848 to 1856, centered around the Crisis of 1850, was the key factor in the state's eagerness to join South Carolina and Mississippi by becoming the third state to secede from the Union, on January 10, 1861. The planter class, which controlled the black belt of Middle Florida, which in turn dominated the state's political structure, abandoned the moderates in favor of the radical fire-eating Democrats. It was only under Democratic leadership that they felt reassured that the peculiar institution of slavery and the Southern way of life to which they had grown accustomed were safe and could survive and prosper.

Notes

1. C. Vann Woodward, *Mary Chestnut's Civil War* (New Haven, CT: Yale University Press, 1981), 3.
2. Eighth Census of the United States—1860—Florida (available online at: www.census.gov).
3. Journal of the Proceedings of the House of Representatives of the General Assembly of the State of Florida, November 28, 1848, 17.
4. Ibid.
5. Ibid.
6. Ibid.
7. Marianna, *Florida Whig*, November 25, 1848.
8. House Journal, December 11, 1848, 47.
9. Marianna, *Florida Whig*, November 25, 1848.
10. Ibid.
11. House Journal, December 11, 1848, 48.
12. Ibid.
13. Tallahassee, *Florida Sentinel*, December 12, 1848.

14. House Journal, December 11, 1848, 49.

15. Ibid., 50.

16. Tallahassee, *Floridian*, December 9, 1848, and January 18, 1849.

17. Dorothy Dodd, "Florida in 1845," *Florida Historical Quarterly* 24, no. 17; Census of the United States—1850—Florida (available online at: www.census.gov).

18. Ibid.

19. Ibid.

20. Ibid.

21. Ibid.

22. Ibid.

23. House Journal, January 1, 1849, 127.

24. Ibid., 128.

25. Ibid., 127.

26. Tallahassee, *Florida Sentinel*, January 9, 1848.

27. House Journal, January 3, 1849, 145.

28. Jacksonville, *Florida Republican*, February 1, 1849.

29. Tallahassee, *Florida Sentinel*, January 16, 1848.

30. Jacksonville, *Florida Republican*, March 15, 1849.

31. Ibid., June 14, 1849.

32. Ibid.

33. Ibid., December 13, 1849.

34. Mills M. Lord Jr., "David Levy Yulee, Statesmen and Railroad Builder" (MA thesis, University of Florida, 1940), 73.

35. Jacksonville, *Florida Republican*, January 10, 1850.

36. Tallahassee, *Florida Sentinel*, January 14, 1850.

37. Herbert J. Doherty, "Florida and the Crisis of 1850," *Journal of Southern History* 19, no. 1 (February 1953): 36.

38. Jacksonville, *Florida Republican*, January 24, 1850.

39. Tallahassee, *Florida Sentinel*, January 29, 1850.

40. Herbert J. Doherty, *Richard Keith Call, Southern Unionist* (Gainesville: University of Florida Press, 1961), 142.

41. St. Augustine, *Ancient City*, February 14, 1850.

42. Tallahassee *Floridian and Journal*, February 9, 1850.

43. Jacksonville, *Florida Republican*, April 11, 1850.

44. "Yulee, Morton, Cabell to Governor Brown," February 6, 1850, published in Jacksonville, *Florida Republican*, March 7, 1850.

45. "Cabell to Governor Brown," February 12, 1850, published in Jacksonville, *Florida Republican*, March 7, 1850.

46. "Governor Brown to Yulee, Morton, and Cabell," February 22, 1850, published in Jacksonville, *Florida Republican*, March 7, 1850.

47. Ibid.

48. Ibid.

49. Jacksonville, *Florida Republican*, March 7, 1850.

50. Pensacola, *Gazette*, April 11, 1850.

51. Ibid.

52. "Morton to Governor Brown," March 10, 1850, published in Jacksonville, *Florida Republican*, April 4, 1850.

53. Tallahassee, *Floridian and Journal*, April 16, 1850.

54. Jacksonville, *Florida Republican*, May 23, 1850.

55. Ibid., March 21, 1850.

56. St. Augustine, *Ancient City*, June 22, 1850.

57. Jacksonville, *Florida Republican*, June 13, 1850.

58. Allan Nevins, *Ordeal of the Union*, vol. 1 (New York: Scribner, 1947), 315–17.

59. Tallahassee, *Florida Sentinel*, July 9, 1850.

60. Ibid., September 24, 1850.

61. Ibid., October 1, 1850.

62. Tallahassee, *Floridian and Journal*, September 28, 1850.

63. Ibid.

64. Doherty, *Richard Keith Call, Southern Unionist*, 140.

65. 7th Census of the United States—1850—Leon County, Florida (available online at: www.census.gov).

66. Jacksonville, *Florida Republican*, July 25, 1850.

67. St. Augustine, *Ancient City*, August 31, 1850.

68. Ibid.

69. Jacksonville, *Florida Republican*, September 26, 1850.

70. Tallahassee, *Florida Sentinel*, September 24, 1850.

71. St. Augustine, *Ancient City*, March 23, 1850.

72. Ibid., October 5, 1850.

73. Ibid., July 27, 1850.

74. Tallahassee, *Florida Sentinel*, September 10, 1850.

75. Ibid.

76. Tallahassee, *Floridian and Journal*, September 21, 1850.

77. Jacksonville, *Florida Republican*, October 16, 1850.

78. Pensacola, *Gazette*, November 9, 1850.

79. Tallahassee, *Florida Sentinel*, February 25, 1851.

80. Florida House Journal, December 30, 1850, 166.

81. "Address of John C. McGehee Before the Southern Rights Association of Madison County, June 7, 1851," *Florida Historical Quarterly* 5, no. 2: 68.

82. Ibid., 69.

83. Ibid., 71.

84. Ibid., 81.

85. Ibid., 86.

86. Ibid., 88.

87. Tallahassee, *Floridian*, July 19, 1851.

88. Dorothy Dodd, "The Secession Movement in Florida, 1850–1861, Part I," *Florida Historical Quarterly* 12, no. 1 (1933): 12.

89. Ibid., October 19, 1852.

90. Ibid.

91. Tallahassee, *Florida Sentinel*, November 23, 1852.

92. Herbert J. Doherty, *The Whigs of Florida, 1845–1854* (Jacksonville: Miller, 1959), 57–58.

93. Tallahassee, *Florida Sentinel*, November 29, 1856.

2

"The Rights, Causes, and Necessity for Secession"

The Interplay of Race, Class, and Politics in Antebellum Florida

LAUREN K. THOMPSON

On January 10, 1861, Florida's Secession Convention delegates voted sixty-two to seven in favor of secession.[1] Florida became the third state to secede from the Union, in 1861, only sixteen years after it was admitted as a state. Why did the Secession Convention delegates feel secession was the only option and did the majority of Floridians share this view? By synthesizing evidence from newspapers, personal correspondence, and the secession convention papers with the existing literature on the sectional crisis and Antebellum Florida, I expose Florida's decision to secede. Like other Southern states in the cotton belt, Florida had a political economy that revolved around chattel slavery. The planter class, a small percentage of the population, controlled the majority of wealth in Florida. These planters financially benefited from the production and sale of staple crops, mainly cotton, while serving as the local, state, and federal lawmakers. Also like the rest of the South, the majority of yeoman farmers in Florida did not own slaves but were attached to the slave labor economy through their virtues of self-made manhood and independence.[2] The heightened sense of hysteria swept through the planter class when the events of the 1850s negated the chance of compromise, polarized the nation, and, most importantly, threatened their extent of control. Concurrently, however, the secession crisis served as an opportunity for the transplanted slaveholders and second-generation Floridians looking to be taken seriously by the older Southern states. When Abraham Lincoln was elected in November 1860, the planter class persuaded Floridians that a "Black Republican"

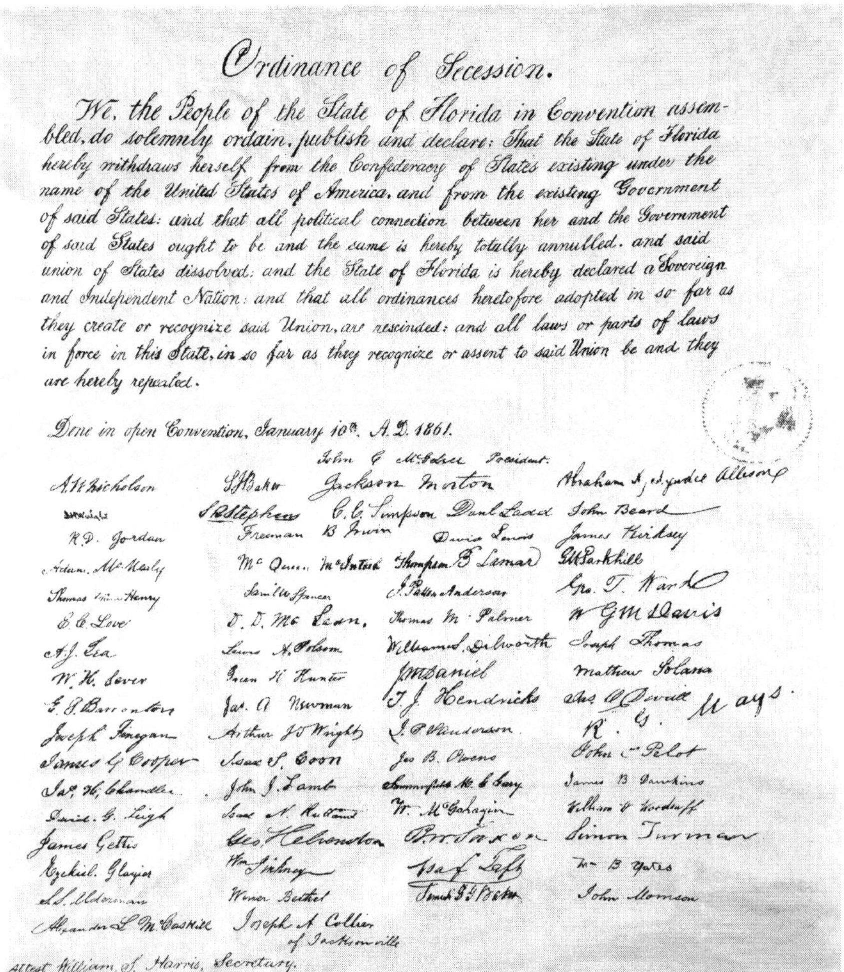

Ordinance of Secession.

We, the People of the State of Florida in Convention assembled, do solemnly ordain, publish and declare: That the State of Florida hereby withdraws herself from the Confederacy of States existing under the name of the United States of America, and from the existing Government of said States: and that all political connection between her and the Government of said States ought to be and the same is hereby totally annulled, and said union of States dissolved: and the State of Florida is hereby declared a Sovereign and Independent Nation: and that all ordinances heretofore adopted in so far as they create or recognize said Union, are rescinded: and all laws or parts of laws in force in this State, in so far as they recognize or assent to said Union be and they are hereby repealed.

Done in open Convention, January 10th. A.D. 1861.

John C. McGehee President.

Attest William S. Harris, Secretary.

Figure 2.
Florida Ordinance of Secession,
courtesy of State Archives of Florida, Florida Memory

would destroy the safety, traditions, and stability in Southern society. Middle Florida planters misconstrued Northern free-soil aims and constructed a threatening abolitionist message to persuade the masses from Pensacola to Key West that they were inherently tied to the preservation of slavery. By instilling the fear of racial equality and the death of white supremacy, Floridian slaveholders convinced the nonslaveholding majority that secession was their only option. In doing so, the slaveholding class simultaneously proved Florida's commitment to the confederate cause and legitimized its place among the Southern planter aristocracy.

The exceptional nature of Florida's settlement, particularly in terms of native peoples and slavery, explain why the fairly young state was so quick to join the Confederate States of America.[3] From the territorial acquisition in 1821 until secession in 1861, the major societal changes in Florida took place in the rich panhandle lands between the Suwannee and Apalachicola Rivers known as Middle Florida. As early as 1819, planters came to the Florida frontier hoping to stake their claim in the cotton market. Yet, these lands were already home to lower Creek native peoples known as Mikasuki. With the help of the federal government, planters coerced these people onto a reservation through the Treaty of Moultrie Creek in 1823. Thus, planters brought their slaves and ideologies to Middle Florida. Planters learned about the Florida frontier from private letters, oral reports, local newspapers, and travel narratives.[4] In the 1830s and 1840s, planters from the Upper South, mainly Virginia, the Carolinas, and Georgia, moved to the counties that made up Middle Florida: Madison, Jefferson, Jackson, Leon, and Gadsden.[5] For example, in 1830 planter Benjamin Whitner, a staunch Democrat from South Carolina, and Joseph Betton from Virginia came to Leon County to set up two of Florida's wealthiest antebellum plantations. Richard Croom came from Alabama with 139 slaves and Bryan Croom came from South Carolina with 197 slaves.[6] Planters moved to Middle Florida to maintain or acquire wealth, honor, and political positions for themselves and their family members.[7] By 1860, there were 5,152 slave owners in the state of Florida, which made up about 17 percent of the total population. Leon County had the largest number of slaves per capita, with 3,194 whites and 9,089 slaves on the eve of the Civil War.[8] The nature of this "planter paradise" seems as though it was settled with ease, but these planters, as well as others across the cotton belt, wanted full-scale removal of the native peoples.

This wave of planters that moved into Florida wanted complete control of the land and hence the removal of all native peoples from the Florida Territory. President Andrew Jackson signed the Indian Removal Act in 1830, and the subsequent Treaty of Payne's Landing in 1832 called for all lower Creeks, or Seminoles, to be forcibly relocated to the Oklahoma Territory. However, some Seminoles resisted by raiding United States Army outposts and in turn caused a prolonged set of guerilla attacks known as the Second Seminole War. Planters on the Florida frontier convinced the federal government that Seminole removal would contribute to broader notions of nationalism, expansion, and Manifest Destiny, when in actuality they wanted these lands for personal gain from slave labor cotton production.[9] The federal government continued to send money and resources until federal troops withdrew in 1842.[10] The estimated cost of the Second Seminole War alone was $40 million.[11] Leading scholar on the Seminole Wars John K. Mahon argues, "Obviously the Second Seminole War was connected intimately with the nation's number one problem of slavery. At the start the connection was not generally apparent, but as the war progressed, and the slavery issue grew year by year more deadly, the relationship became crystal clear."[12] The connection between clearing Seminole lands for the expansion of slavery grew apparent in the 1840s. An article in the *National Review* claimed, "Since the Missouri Compromise of 1820, the career of the Slave Power has been traced through every questionable transaction of foreign and domestic politics which the United States has taken part—through the Seminole War, Annexation of Texas, the Mexican War, and attempts at Cuba."[13] Thus, planter efforts to open Florida lands for cotton production not only led to long, expensive wars against native Floridians but also drew the entire state into a culture of solidarity against nonwhites.

Aside from Seminole resistance, enslaved black people heightened planter anxieties when they too pushed back by fleeing plantations and joining the Seminoles. These so-called black Seminoles or marooned societies created a fear among the planter class that racial hierarchies in Florida were on the verge of collapse.[14] Along with the growth in the populations of Seminoles and free blacks was the growth of the enslaved population. When the planters moved into the Florida Territory, in 1830, there were roughly 15,500 slaves. By 1860 there were more than 61,000 slaves in the state: two-thirds worked on plantations in Middle Florida, 17 percent in the Eastern region, and 8 percent in the Western panhandle.[15] The population of slaves grew through both natural reproduction and the importation of slaves from the Upper South, in what became known as the domestic slave trade. More than two-thirds of the slaves in Florida came from the Upper South.[16] The slave population grew faster than the white population did, especially on isolated plantations.

As the slave population grew, so did their acts of resistance. In East Florida, slaves violently expressed their objections to servitude by poisoning their master Mr. Randall at his plantation called Belmont. In Madison County, the slaves on Watt's Plantation killed their overseer in a violent act of resistance.[17] Although rare, these incidents confirmed planters' greatest fear. If so much brutality could occur on a lone plantation, planters wondered, what would the outcome be if a full-scale slave revolt took place in Florida? The hysteria spread like wildfire throughout the Florida plantation communities. Planters only exacerbated these anxieties when the critical events of the 1850s threatened the expansion of slavery westward into the new territories. Therefore, planters counterattacked with harsher slave codes and stricter punishments for their slaves. To maintain their supremacy, Florida planters pursued their quest for social control with the nonwhite population.

Planters, who reigned atop the racial hierarchy, attempted to gain dominance as a class through political control of the white masses. Parts of eastern Florida, inhabited by descendants of the Spanish, remained a diverse society based on trade. The peninsula contained pockets of yeoman farmers, while lands south of Tampa were virtually undeveloped. The western side of the state was mainly the port town of Pensacola, where a merchant class with economic ties to the North lived. In the 1840s and 1850s, the planter class and most whites held opposite views on issues such as a National Bank. Angry yeoman challenged the plantation system because they were against playing the subordinate role by the newly arrived planters. The Whig Party served as an option for yeoman farmers who supported the National Bank, which directly opposed the antibank sentiment of the wealthy Southern Democrats.[18] Floridian Whigs, mostly white middle-class inhabitants of the cities of Pensacola, St. Augustine, Tampa, Jacksonville, and Key West, along with the yeoman farmers scattered throughout the state, kept the planter class from gaining complete control of the state.

Slaveholding Floridians already loathed the Whig "compromisers" for allowing restraints on the expansion of slavery. After the Whig-orchestrated Compromise of 1850, Florida Representative Edward Cabell addressed Congress, "If Northern Whigs cannot meet us here; if they are resolved to go on with the slavery agitation, and to repeal the fugitive slave law, then the party ought not to be preserved."[19] Florida presses documented and embellished the threat of Northern aggression. In the wake of the Compromise of 1850, the *Floridian and Journal* published reflections on the US congressional debates. One article featured a debate between young Congressman R. R. Rhett and Henry Clay. Clay called Rhett a traitor for speaking on the favorable dissolution of the Union. Clay argued, "Is not Mr. Rhett entitled to his own opinion? Is the South to be trodden upon, cursed and desolated, and dare not a true son talk of revolution without being denounced a traitor?"[20] Rhett responded, "We admired and loved Mr. Clay. We stood by him through evil as well as good report, confiding in his justice, and believing that he would stand by the rights of the South. But Alas! He has turned his face to the North, and shall we follow him at the sacrifice of the South? That we can and will not do. We would yield our life before we would be such a traitor to our own section."[21] Another article, "Federalism and Something Worse, in Florida!," stated in regard to the Compromise of 1850, "The North having, by the admission of California, acquired complete control over the legislation of the country, having an Abolition President, a majority of the House of Representatives, *and* a majority in the United States Senate, it will only remain for her to carry out her cherished purpose of emancipating the Southern slaves *when she shall see fit*!"[22] This statement alludes to the socially constructed fear of a strong federal government with an abolitionist agenda. In 1850, Whig President Millard Fillmore supported peace between the sections and opposed abolitionism in any form. The article ends rhetorically, asking, "What Southern man does not tremble in contemplating the dangers which threaten his home? The scripture is fulfilled in our midst as the enemies of the South are they of her own household! Is it not enough that presses in New York, Philadelphia, Boston, Cincinnati, preach to us the doctrine of submission—nearly every Southern town has within it those from the strong holds of Abolition who are warning us of the consequences of resistance?"[23] The planter-driven campaign constructed fear and instability in the hearts and minds of Floridians through words like "tremble," "dangers," and "threaten." While the planter class chipped away at nonslaveholding moderates, national events drove a wedge between the sections.

The Kansas-Nebraska Act of 1854 passed when Southern Whigs allied with Southern Democrats, leading to the collapse of the Whig Party and ending any hope of a multisectional party. When Northern Whigs coalesced to form the Republican Party in 1854, only a very small minority in the party was abolitionist. Yet, to coerce former Floridian Whigs to their side, Democrats argued that the entire Republican Party was antislavery. The collapse of the Whig Party led to definitive sectional parties. Because Democrats claimed that the Republican Party stood for a Northern attack on Southern institutions, any Floridian who sided with the Republicans was deemed against the state, section, and very core of Southern pride and honor. Baptist argues, "The wounded honor of white men, the threat of slave insurrection, and the belief that the south must remain unchanged is what united whites in Florida. Common images and unified politics united most white Floridians."[24] In other words, class conflict over the banks and other issues that led the divisions during early statehood ended when the planter class wiped out any moderate stance on slavery. To support the Republican Party was tantamount to supporting equality between black people and white people, which was something even nonslaveholding whites vehemently opposed. With the help of planter mudslinging, Southern nonslaveholders could not align with the so-called Black Republican Party and in turn joined the Democrats. Floridian planters thus reigned supreme at the apex of their society. However, this planter-led campaign to scare the masses had only just begun.

As the election of 1860 approached, newspapers across the state promoted taking the hard line toward slavery. William Babcock of the *East Floridian* reported, "At the Democratic National Convention the Northern Democrats were blinded by sectional animosity and regardless of the rights of the south; principles hostile to our peculiar institutions. Therefore, we endorse fully the action of the delegates from Florida to the National Convention to withdraw."[25] In backing the delegates who walked out of the Democratic National Convention in Charleston, this paper suggests that Stephen Douglas and a popular sovereignty platform is simply too moderate and will not be tolerated. Floridians even attacked their own. In the *Key of the Gulf*, an article stated, "Governor R. K. Call is a Union Shirker because he was of a moderate pro-slavery position."[26] Yet, in a letter to his friend John Littell in Pennsylvania, Call wrote, "It [slavery] should be considered as it is, an institution interwoven and inseparably connected with our social and political system, as a domestic institution of the states, and a national institution created by the American people and protected by the Constitution of the U.S."[27] If their former governor, an advocate for slavery and a slaveholder himself, was attacked, it is understandable why in Florida Abraham Lincoln's name was not even on the ballot.[28] If the division between Northern and Southern Democrats was not already an issue for Democrat solidarity, the remnants of the Whig Party supported their own candidate, John Bell, under the new Constitutional Union Party. Thus, Florida had three candidates on the ballot during Election Day in November 1860. John Breckenridge won Florida with 8,543 votes, while

John Bell won 5,437 votes and Douglas a mere 376.[29] Breckenridge carried votes across the state, except for in the Western Florida counties, which supported John Bell. The former Whig presence was still intact, as seen by the votes that went to Bell. And although Bell carried the Upper South, in the cotton belt, the planter-class campaign was successful in making the majority of Southerners fearful of any moderate candidate. In Key West, the newspaper headline stated, "Breckenridge and Lane is the Ticket! Florida will support it with her whole strength and enthusiasm."[30] Because the South divided itself not once but twice, Abraham Lincoln won a decisive victory in the Electoral College, despite winning only 40 percent of the popular vote. For Floridian planters, the election of Abraham Lincoln, a former Whig who vowed not to touch slavery where it was already present, ended any final hope of compromise.

Almost immediately after the election of Lincoln, the Floridian planter class called for disunion. The *Fernandina East Floridian* predicted, "Seeing the dismemberment of the Union only as a matter of time, 'The South is as well prepared for that grave issue now.'"[31] Political leaders and the press preached that the only alternative to Northern oppression was secession.[32] Papers now amplified the threat of abolition and the destruction of the Southern racial hierarchy. The St. Augustine *Examiner* reported the week after Lincoln's election with a fervent caution. The article reads, "There is a danger from the aggressive and unconstitutional encroachment of the Northern States of the Union under the influence of Black Republicanism. There is an additional cause to believe the threats of the party will be against us by the election of ABRAM [*sic*] Lincoln. His policy is to attack the institution of slavery and equalize the black with the white race."[33] In this article, the journalist not only misspells Lincoln's name but also claims that Lincoln's policy was to free the slaves and encourage racial equality. President Lincoln argued that he would try to preserve the Union without touching the issue of slavery, yet the propaganda of Southern papers like the *Examiner* painted him as the Black Republican and abolitionist president. Ward's address, like others' across the South, continually equate Lincoln with abolition and, in turn, the destruction of all Southern values. The *Examiner* urges, "The Time has Arrived.—As the time has arrived which the people of the South must decide the important question, whether they will surrender their rights as freemen and remain in a union where denied the Equality secured to them by the compact under which the Northern states of the union have robbed, insulted, and degraded by it in every conceivable form in which a people can be subjected to such wrongs, indignities, and outrages."[34] This piece suggests that if Florida were to remain in the Union, white men would be treated as second-class citizens, kept from their entitled liberties, and oppressed.

Although slavery was the major issue at hand, the North became embittered at talks of secession, particularly in Florida, where the federal government incurred substantial debt from the Seminole Wars. Because Florida persuaded the federal government to protect its interests on the frontier by forcibly removing the Seminoles, Northern politicians became estranged when they heard rumors of Florida's secession. In the *Lowell Daily News*, an article titled "Personal and Political" claimed, "As Florida talks of secession, someone says that she had better have seceded before this government foolishly spent fifty millions for her benefit, under the pretext of expelling a small band of Seminoles."[35] At the height of the secession fear, Northerners were quick to recall the Seminole War and angrily preach against secession. The *New York Freedmen's Journal* states, "We purchased Florida from Spain, not for the sake of the people of Florida, but for the sake of the people of the Union. Can we permit the handful of white people now in Florida to march off with our purchase money, and our Seminole War money in their pockets?"[36] In response to these allegations, Southerners used this argument to their own advantage. One Southern paper, *What The South Has to Submit To*, claims, "Florida was an acquisition of territory they wanted and the intolerant North furnished the money to wage war to take it! They [The North] said The Seminoles must be removed and the arrogant North demanded to pay for their removal!"[37] Therefore, while Northerners attributed their sectional animosity to the expansion of the slave power, Southerners argued that Northerners were the voice behind Seminole removal and the wars.

Not only did Northerners and Southerners alike reference the Seminole Wars with hostile language, but both sides manipulated the cost of the war for their own defense. For instance, one Northern paper claimed, "We found that we have a rival element for the honors of the Seminole War. The paper referred to says the Federal Troops provided good food and powder, but the Georgia and Alabama volunteers did the work, and that but for them Florida would never have been freed from the Seminoles. It is only to be regretted that Georgia, Alabama, and Florida did not pay the twenty millions or so in expenses for this great achievement."[38] This example from the Southern perspective claims the cost is "twenty million or so." In terms of monetary value, the South downplayed the cost, while the North inflated it. For example, a Northern journal states, "Even Florida, pigmy State that she is, now not possessed of enough population for a representative in Congress, all forgetful of the blood and treasure expended to protect her in the sisterhood of the states—The Florida War with the Seminoles cost not far from a hundred millions of dollars—thinks she can stand alone and wants to try it. If she succeeds, the expatriated Seminoles have no right to remain on the reservations, but should be sent back to the Everglades of that state."[39] Similarly, another journal argues, "In 1840 the War with the Seminoles which cost about $100,000,000. Will anyone give into the claims that the secessionists who demand that Florida has professed to withdraw from the Union, she be 'let alone' and the United States lose the immense sums which have been expended."[40] In both pieces, the journalist's embellishment of the actual sum revealed the hostility and anger at the South for leaving after such a long, expensive war. Floridians, in turn, seethed with anger for being singled out. Secession was inevitable. The planter class did not need convincing but crafted a campaign to further alienate the masses from the federal government, because if a war was to come, they would need soldiers to fight it.

In November and December 1860, cries for secession echoed across the state. The *East Floridian* stated, "Secession of the State of Florida-Dissolution of the Union. Formation of a Southern Confederacy. THE TIME HAS COME!"[41] In Tampa, the *Florida Peninsular* stated, "Black Republican rule at Washington will not commence until the 4th of March. Before that all the Southern States do what should be done. What shall the South do? Grand Secession demonstrations in Apalachicola, Monticello, and St. Augustine."[42] On November 26, the Florida State Legislature called a meeting to discuss the formation of a Secession Convention. Governor Madison S. Perry addressed the Senate and House:

> A series of aggressions and insults, commencing forty years ago, by the Northern States against the Southern, and increasing in audacity as time rolled on and the South forbore, has been pushed to a point at which further forbearance of the South would justify the allegation that we are "afraid to resist."
>
> The election of Lincoln and Hamlin to the two highest offices in the confederacy, viewed in connection with the circumstances that led to the result, and the determination of Northern fanatics to urge their mad schemes, regardless of the welfare and the security of the

> Southern people, ought to extinguish any desire of the latter to prolong their connection with those who show such an utter disregard of covenanted rights and of plighted faith.
>
> I will not insult your intelligence or trespass on your patience by recounting the aggressions already perpetrated, or by referring to those that must follow our submission. For myself, in full view of the responsibility of my position, I most decidedly declare that in my opinion the only hope the Southern States have for domestic peace and safety, or for future respectability and prosperity, is dependent on their action now; and that the proper action is—Secession from our faithless, perjured confederates.
>
> But some Southern men, it is said, object to secession until some overt act of unconstitutional power shall have been committed by the General Government; that we ought not to secede until the President and Congress unite in passing an act unequivocally hostile to our institutions and fraught with immediate danger to our rights of property and to our domestic safety. My countrymen! If we wait for such an overt act, our fate will be that of the white inhabitants of St. Domingo.[43]

Perry's speech harkened to the Haitian Revolution, insisting that abolitionists were coming to free their slaves and lead a full rebellion against the Southern institution of slavery. This speech, along with the comments of other political leaders, led to the formation of a secession committee to draft a resolution for a Secession Convention. These members drafted a resolution that called for an election of delegates to take place on December 22, 1860, and the first Secession Convention meeting to be held on January 3, 1861.[44] This resolution was approved on November 30, 1860. Two days before the Secession Convention met, South Carolina became the first state to secede from the United States, on December 20, 1860.[45]

On December 22, sixty-nine delegates were elected to the Florida Secession Convention. Only seven of these delegates were born in Florida, while forty-seven were from Georgia, the Carolinas, and Virginia. Also, fifty-one, or 74 percent, of the delegates held slaves and the average age of the delegate was forty-three.[46] Therefore, the planters and elites who carried the state through the volatile decade of the 1850s and the Election of 1860 again would speak for the masses as they led their state into the decision to secede. The Secession Convention representatives, the majority of whom were slaveholders, successfully convinced the masses that disunion was their only option and that the protection of slavery was no secret.

On the morning of January 3, 1861, the sixty-nine delegates convened at the statehouse in Tallahassee, Florida. The floor opened with an address from the chair, John C. Pelot. The president of the convention, John C. McGehee, then stated, "The rapid spread of Northern fanaticism has endangered our liberties, our institutions and the election of Abram Lincoln, a wily abolitionist, to the Presidency of the United States, destroys all hope for the future."[47] McGehee went on to explain that all the Southern states that border Florida were holding similar conventions to propose a plan for secession. McGehee fully attributed the institution of slavery as the cause for secession: "At the South, slavery is the element of all value and a destruction of that destroys all that is property."[48] Slavery as a political economic institution concurrently assured the continuation of racial hierarchy wherein white men would always be dominant. The protection and expansion of chattel slavery was unanimously the reason Floridians wanted to secede. The question was not whether to secede but rather when it should be done.

Because of its vast border, both land and sea, a handful of secession delegates were hesitant to secede before the rest of the lower South. Some convention delegates proposed that Florida wait for Georgia, Alabama, and even Virginia to secede first. On January 6, representatives from these states visited Tallahassee to share their plans. Edmund Ruffin came from Virginia and Edward C. Bullock from Alabama. Bullock said to McGehee, "I fervently hope that Florida and Alabama will soon be united in that new Union of brotherly love—taking destiny into their own hands."[49] While these speeches were taking place, a small group of radical secessionists made up a committee to draft the "Ordinance of Secession." Most delegates were persuaded by the other state delegates that the time was right for Florida to secede. However, since only South Carolina and Mississippi had officially left the Union, a group of conservatives, known as the "Cooperationists," voiced the dangers of seceding too early.[50] This group, led by George T. Ward, felt that secession was indeed necessary but could be costly if done too hastily. Ward sat in the Secession Convention in Montgomery, Alabama, on January 6, 1861, and after listening to their plans, he opposed the immediate secession of Florida. Ward, in his address to the convention, stated, "As to separate and immediate secession, it must be obvious that Florida, from her geographical position, her resources, and her immense extent of sea coast frontier, is more than any other state bound to regard and to some extent await the movement of the other cotton states, particularly the adjacent states of Georgia and Alabama!"[51] Ward knew that Georgia and Alabama had stronger infrastructures, while Florida was still young in comparison to the larger South. Not only did Ward and his followers fear the repercussions of seceding too early, but they knew secession was a decision they could not repeal peacefully. Not to mention, the Confederate States of America would not be created until February 4, and without an organized coalition of other Southern states to form, Florida would stand alone. George T. Ward wrote, "I will only add that Florida is the outpost State, more exposed to predatory war than any other, and as it is through us that any foe, hostile to our institutions, will strike at the states north of us, Florida should be represented in an Convention of the Southern States that may be held. If these are the sentiments of my country, I stand ready, if elected, to serve you with alacrity."[52] While Ward and the other cooperationists wanted to wait, the fire-eaters saw this as the opportunity they had been waiting for—an avenue to propel themselves to the rank of slave power state.

Despite the opponents of immediate secession, an Ordinance of Secession was drafted. On January 10, 1861, the draft read, "The state of Florida is hereby declared a sovereign and independent nation; all laws or parts of laws in force in this state, in so far as they recognize or assent to said Union be and they are hear by repealed."[53] George T. Ward moved that the Ordinance of Secession be tabled until the results of the Georgia and Alabama secession conventions. A. K. Allison amended Ward's motion to table the Ordinance until Alabama and Georgia seceded. The immediate secessionists still held the majority, voting against Allison's motion forty-two to twenty-seven and against Ward's motion thirty-nine to thirty. When the delegates voted on the Ordinance of Secession, the motion passed by sixty -two to seven. The headline of the *Peninsular*, in Tampa, read, "May we hail the establishment of the great southern confederacy!"[54] Florida became the third of eleven states to secede from the Union in the spring of 1861. The planter class thus succeeded in falsifying Northern aggression in order to radicalize the majority of Floridians. The campaign against racial equality and white supremacy not only served as a call to arms but also propagated a message to the other Southern states that Florida was legitimate.

While the sixty-five delegates signed the Ordinance of Secession in

Tallahassee, a few hundred supporters cheerfully welcomed the official separation from the tyrannical federal government.[55] Silently, the nine thousand slaves in the surrounding fields of Leon County did not know the extent of the outcome. The perceived threat that their empire could dissolve without the ability to expand compelled planters in Florida to convince nonslaveholders that the North and the Lincoln administration threatened the very foundation of Southern sociocultural institutions and traditions and the South's constructed racial hierarchy. Most of these white men—the merchants, yeoman farmers, and nonslaveholders, cloaked in ideology and a commitment to slavery—were sent to battlefields in Tennessee, Mississippi, and Virginia. George T. Ward, who had so strongly opposed immediate secession, served as a colonel and was mortally wounded during battle at the Peninsula Campaign in 1862. Secession was the peak for the ruling class of the Middle Florida cotton empire. After four years of war, Floridians would see the demise of the slave society they built. Despite emancipation, these exconfederates never lost their place at the apex of society, and after the war, they would launch a new campaign built upon fear in order to protect and uphold their white supremacy.

Notes

1. William Rogers Warren and Erica R. Clark, *The Croom Family and Goodwood Plantation: Land, Litigation, and Southern Lives* (Athens: University of Georgia Press, 1999), 204.

2. Recent studies on yeoman farmers and nonslaveholders in the Antebellum South argue that while most Southerners did not own slaves, because a slave labor society allowed them to replicate mastery and autonomy in their own households, these white farmers benefited from being of the superior race. Some of these major works are Lacy Ford, *Origins of Southern Radicalism: The South Carolina Upcountry, 1800–1860s* (Oxford: Oxford University Press, 1988), Stephanie McCurry, *Masters of Small Worlds: Yeoman Households, Gender Relations, and the Political Culture of the Antebellum South* (Oxford: Oxford University Press, 1995), and Bertram Wyatt Brown, *The Shaping of Southern Culture: Honor, Grace, and War, 1760s–1880s* (Chapel Hill: University of North Carolina Press, 2001).

3. The other historiographical debate is rooted within the unique nature of antebellum Florida. Since Florida became a US Territory in 1821, most of the history of the Antebellum Florida focuses on the Seminole Wars. However, the planter class perpetuated these wars in an attempt to expand King Cotton and chattel slavery

across the Deep South. Therefore, planters from Virginia, South Carolina, and Georgia came to Florida in search of these virgin lands to claim their stake in the cash crop. The first historian to analyze the plantation settlements in Antebellum Florida is Julia Floyd Smith, in *Slavery and Plantation Growth in Antebellum Florida: 1821–1860* (1973). Smith argues that Southern planters adopted modern capitalist principles to develop and sustain plantations in Antebellum Florida. Recently, Edward Baptist revisits Smith's work in his book *Creating an Old South: Middle Florida's Plantation Frontier Before the War* (2002). While Smith looks at plantation slavery across the entire state of Florida, Baptist narrows his focus to Leon and Jackson Counties. Baptist expands on Smith's arguments to claim that honor and masculinity shaped public opinion and conflict in Middle Florida. Baptist offers insight into the public reactions to the events of the 1850s but only briefly summarizes the Secession Convention, with little analysis. This gap in the historiography calls for a bridge between the Middle Florida planters and the overwhelming vote in favor of secession on January 10, 1861. In *Slavery in Florida: Territorial Days to Emancipation* (2000), Larry Rivers examines the relationship between the planters, Seminoles, and blacks, which heightened racism and slave codes in Florida. Rivers concludes that alliances between Seminoles and free blacks created a sense of fear among planters. Also, Rivers explores the diversity of the Southern slave experience to argue that Eastern and Western Florida were very different from the Middle Florida slavery that Baptist focuses on. Overall, Smith, Baptist, and Rivers convincingly analyze the nature of Antebellum Florida to create a solid historiographical basis for the period, but when used in tandem gaps are revealed that require further investigation. Thus, current methodologies for investigating secession can be applied to the historiographical foundation of Antebellum Florida. In the planter class's attempt to establish a hegemonic paradise, Florida's diverse geopolitical makeup stood as an obstacle.

4. Edward Baptist, *Creating an Old South: Middle Florida's Plantation Frontier Before the War* (Chapel Hill: University of North Carolina Press, 2002), 156.

5. Warren, *Croom Family*, 1.

6. Warren, *Croom Family*, 125; 149–55.

7. Ibid., 19.

8. Warren, *Croom Family*, 195.

9. This argument is thoroughly analyzed by Adam Rothman in *Slave Country: American Expansion and the Origins of the Deep South* (Cambridge, MA: Harvard University Press, 2005).

10. Ibid., 156.

11. John K. Mahon, *History of the Second Seminole War, 1835–1842* (Gainesville: University Press of Florida, 1985), 326.

12. Ibid., 326.

13. "Slave Power and the Secession War," ed. Samuel Rhodes, *Friends' Review: A Religious, Literary and Miscellaneous Journal* 25 (1862): 15, 51.

14. Ibid., 158.

15. Larry Eugene Rivers, *Slavery in Florida: Territorial Days to Emancipation* (Gainesville: University of Florida Press, 2000), 253.

16. Baptist, *Creating an Old South*, 63.

17. Rivers, *Slavery in Florida*, 217–18.

18. Baptist, *Creating an Old South*, 177.

19. Edward Carrington Cabell, "Speech of Hon. E. C. Cabell of Florida on political parties, Whig Congressional Caucus, the Presidency: Delivered in the House of Representatives, June 12, 1852" (Washington, DC: Printed at the Congressional Globe Office, 1852), 3.

20. "Whig Mr. Rhett- a Traitor!" *Floridian and Journal* 2, no. 31: 1.

21. Ibid., 3.

22. "Federalism & Something Worse in Florida!" *Floridian and Journal* 2, no. 37: 1.

23. Ibid., 3.

24. Baptist, *Creating an Old South*, 264.

25. William Babcock, *East Floridian*, Fernandina, May 31, 1860, University of Florida P. K. Yonge Library of Florida History, Digital Collections of Florida Newspapers.

26. *Key to the Gulf*, Key West, September 1, 1860, University of Florida P. K. Yonge Library of Florida History, Digital Collections of Florida Newspapers.

27. Richard Keith Call, *Union, Slavery, and Secession: Letter from Governor R. K. Call of Florida to John S. Littell of Germantown, Pennsylvania* (Philadelphia: C. Sherman & Son Printers, 1861).

28. Baptist, *Creating an Old South*, 270.

29. Dorothy Dodd, "The Secession Movement in Florida, 1850–1861, Part I," *Florida Historical Quarterly* 12, no. 1 (July 1993): 8.

30. *Key of the Gulf*, Key West, Florida, July 14, 1860, University of Florida P. K. Yonge Library of Florida History, Collections of Florida Newspapers.

31. Dorothy Dodd, "The Secession Movement in Florida: 1860–1861, Part II," *Florida Historical Quarterly* 12, no. 2 (October 1933): 37.

32. John F. Reiger, "Secession of Florida from the Union: A Minority Decision?" *Florida Historical Quarterly* 46, no. 4 (April 1968): 360.

33. *Examiner*, St. Augustine, November 24, 1860, University of Florida P. K. Yonge Library of Florida History, Digital Collections of Florida Newspapers.

34. "The Time has Arrived!" *Examiner*, St. Augustine, December 22, 1860, University of Florida P. K. Yonge Library of Florida History, Digital Collections of Florida Newspapers.

35. "Personal and Political," *Lowell Daily Citizen and News*, November 24, 1860, vol. 10, no. 1405, 2.

36. "The Right of Secession," *Milwaukee Daily Sentinel*, November 23, 1860, vol. 2, no. 215, 2.

37. "What the South Has to Submit To," *Freedom's Champion, Weekly Champion and Press*, February 23, 1861, vol. 4, no. 3, 2.

38. "Florida," *Boston Daily Advertiser*, April 10, 1861, vol. 97, no. 14563, 2.

39. "Who is to Rule?" *Philadelphia Inquirer*, December 31, 1860, 4.

40. "Florida," *Easton Gazette*, August 31, 1861, vol. 44, no. 36, 2.

41. "The Time Has Come!" *East Floridian*, Fernandina, November 14, 1860, University of Florida P. K. Yonge Library of Florida History, Digital Collections of Florida Newspapers.

42. "Black Republican Rule," *Florida Peninsular*, Tampa Bay, Florida, November 24, 1860, University of Florida P. K. Yonge Library of Florida History, Digital Collections of Florida Newspapers.

43. M. S. Perry, *State Secession Debates, 1859–1862* (New Haven, CT: Research Publications, 1976), 8–9.

44. Reiger, "Secession of Florida from the Union: A Minority Decision?" 362.

45. Warren, *Croom Family*, 204.

46. Ralph Wooster, "The Florida Secession Convention," *Florida Historical Quarterly* 36, no. 4 (April 1958): 375–76.

47. *Journal of the Convention Proceedings. January 11, 1861* (Tallahassee, FL: Dyke and Carlisle), 1.

48. Ibid., 7.

49. Ibid., 36.

50. Warren, *Croom Family*, 204.

51. George T. Ward, *Secession Broadside*, 1860, Robert Manning Strozier Library Special Collections, Florida State University.

52. George T. Ward, "To the People of Leon County," *Floridian and Journal* 12, no. 51: 3.

53. *Ordinance of Secession-State of Florida*, Robert Manning Strozier Library Special Collections, Florida State University. The Special Collections has a copy of the Ordinance of Secession in their department, housed in oversize box #7.

54. *The Peninsular*, Tampa Bay Florida, January 15, 1861, University of Florida P. K. Yonge Library of Florida History, Digital Collections of Florida Newspapers.

55. *Ordinance of Secession-State of Florida*. Even though seven delegates voted against the Ordinance of Secession, five of those delegates still chose to sign the document.

3

"So Exposed as Recently to Encounter Serious Disasters"

The Defense and Capture of Amelia Island, 1861–1862

Jonathan C. Sheppard

Fernandina was, in 1860, a hamlet on the verge of a commercial boom. The completion of the Florida Railroad in that year signaled the beginnings of important times for the port, which clung to the western edge of Amelia Island. With one terminal at Fernandina and the other at Cedar Keys on the Gulf of Mexico, the Florida Railroad bisected the state from northeast to southwest. The railroad "penetrated a large district of the country in which cotton and sugar planting, as well as the naval store industry were increasing." The author of a US commerce report noted that "the export of these products from that region were then principally through Fernandina." Indeed, in that year more than $2 million in revenue was collected from Fernandina imports, and the port exported a portion of the more than sixty-five thousand cotton bales the state produced. The railroad's completion meant these figures would only increase.[1]

Located one hundred miles south of Savannah and twenty miles north of Jacksonville, Fernandina sat astride the best harbor that existed between these two points. Cumberland Sound, which separated Amelia Island from Cumberland Island to the north, offered plenty of water over the bar at high tide and a safe haven from the Atlantic rollers. The depth of the St. Marys River allowed vessels to reach the Fernandina docks with little fear of running aground. In addition to the port being friendly to mariners and the fact that it contained the eastern terminal of the Florida Railroad, Fernandina also benefited from being the southern entrance of the Inland Passage. This Intracoastal Waterway wound northward to Savannah behind the chain of barrier isles, known as the Georgia Sea Islands, providing an avenue of commerce that connected Georgia coastal communities with the world. This combination of location and transportation meant big things were in store for Fernandina as 1860 waned. Then, with the November election of Abraham Lincoln to the presidency and South Carolina's secession little more than a month later, the nation was plunged into turmoil.[2]

In April 1861, following both Florida's January 1861 secession and the Confederacy's establishment, US president Abraham Lincoln proclaimed a blockade of the southern coastline. The first blockader arrived off Cumberland Sound's entrance in mid-June and despite this threat a few "freighters darted into Fernandina and, after discharging a few supplies, maneuvered seventy miles up the inland passage to Savannah." One such vessel that ran into Fernandina during the war's first summer was the *Adaline*. A schooner hailing from Nassau, the *Adaline* deposited "a cargo of coffee, cigars and fruit, valued at $30,000." Yet the limited number of ships that dared challenge the Union blockade caused Amelia Island's citizens to become "discouraged as disruption of the coastal trade caused several shortages and emptied stores of merchandise." The majority of the trade in late 1861 was domestic, carried out by coastal lugs that regularly traveled between Savannah and Fernandina.[3]

Maintaining the blockade of not only Fernandina but also the entire Confederacy seemed to be a logistical nightmare for the Union Navy. As historian Craig Symonds notes, "Only steamships could perform the duties required of the blockading vessels. But steamers had to be refueled regularly" with coal. In the early summer of 1861, a Blockade Board, consisting of navy officers, the Superintendent of the Coast Survey, and an army engineer, convened in Washington with the purpose of refining the blockade. The board targeted Fernandina for seizure, not merely to deny its haven to blockade-runners but to utilize Cumberland Sound as a harbor for the refitting and resupplying of blockaders.[4]

The Blockade Board viewed Fernandina as the ideal location to establish a coal depot for the South Atlantic Blockade Squadron's vessels. With water enough on the bar to accommodate the navy's warships, the board's members agreed that "the anchorage in Amelia River possesses the quiet and safety of an enclosed dock. Repairs of all kinds may be carried on there without fear of accidents arising from motion of the water." In addition, another feature that attracted the Federal officers' attention was that the Florida Railroad's installations provided ready-made facilities for coal bunkers, and the island and its surrounding area could supply "wood and water in abundance." Further, the Blockade Board was drawn to the

Florida port because of its defensive nature; Amelia Island was surrounded on three sides by water, and impassable marsh separated the island from the mainland.[5]

Yet in the summer of 1861, the Blockade Board's ambitious plans for Fernandina went unfulfilled. In August, Flag Officer Samuel F. DuPont, a Blockade Board member and an experienced naval officer with forty years of sea duty behind him, was placed in command of the proposed expedition. Yet throughout the late summer months, "DuPont was frustrated that everytime he had a ship ready for service [Secretary of the Navy Gideon] Welles whisked it away on some duty." The army also had trouble obtaining troops for the assault on the Confederacy's coast. It took a meeting of Abraham Lincoln, his secretaries of war and the navy, and top military brass to make the proposed offensive a reality. But when DuPont's fleet finally sailed from New York in late October, its destination was no longer Fernandina but Port Royal, South Carolina. The Confederates on Amelia Island had taken advantage of this delay to strengthen their defenses.[6]

In May 1861, Florida politician George T. Ward expressed his concern to Confederate Secretary of War Leroy Pope Walker over Florida's coastal defenses, or, rather, its lack thereof. Ward predicted that as the Federals "press[ed] forward along the land toward Virginia they [would] make a strong diversion along the Atlantic and Gulf." In addition to suggesting that the Confederacy organize companies to man artillery batteries at important positions along the coast, he reminded the Confederate government that if the Federals occupied portions of the seashore and raided inland plantations, "the capacity of the country to contribute to the war is at an end."[7]

Pleas to the Confederate government for coastal defense measures were common in the spring and summer of 1861. Unfortunately for the infant Confederacy, it had no counterpart to the Blockade Board to identify strategic coastal locations and plan for their defense. Rather, in accordance with these many local requests, the Confederate government dispersed its forces to locales across the South, both strategic and nonstrategic. Historians have roundly criticized this decision. However, with the difficult subject of coastal defense, the Confederates faced a double-edged sword. True, the fledgling nation did not possess the military forces necessary to defend every inlet and coastal town. Yet, the Confederacy's "adequate defense along the coast played an important part . . . in sustaining civilian morale in these regions."[8]

Essentially, should the Confederacy surrender portions of its tidewater to the Union, defections among the populace were a possibility; state governors continually pointed this fact out to President Jefferson Davis, who obviously needed no prodding regarding the matter. Davis, in the words of a biographer, believed "there could be no abandonment of one portion of the nation in order to strengthen another. . . . Davis had to defend it all." Historian Donald Stoker recently noted that for Davis also, "a successful defense of the Confederacy's territorial holdings would prove that the Confederates had forged a nation, thereby helping the cause of recognition while also protecting the logistical support and recruiting base necessary for waging the war."[9]

Alas, Florida secession convention member George T. Ward was preaching to the choir when he wrote that from these coastal enclaves the Federals might launch raids to terrorize the inland regions, denying vital supplies to the Confederate war effort. Therefore, dispersal trumped necessity in early Confederate coastal defense strategy. Several months into the conflict, Richmond still had not found a balance between satisfying the local populations and governments and developing a coastal defense plan that defended only vital positions.[10]

Florida militia occupied Fort Clinch, the unfinished masonry fortification standing vigil over Cumberland Sound from the northern tip of Amelia Island, in January 1861. However, rather than incorporate the fort into the coastal defense of Amelia Island, the militia constructed a sand battery near the fort and equipped it with small-caliber artillery pieces. Following the arrival of the Third Florida Infantry Regiment on Amelia Island in July, the regiment's colonel, William Scott Dilworth, wrote of the previous defensive preparations: "On this island there is a sort of battery, but incomplete. The guns . . . are badly mounted, and would not stand continuous firing. I regard the battery and the guns as little protection, the range of the guns being too short to protect the channel." An anonymous Third Florida soldier seconded his commander's opinion in a letter to his hometown newspaper: "Our artificial defenses here are very deficient." Obviously, Colonel Dilworth and his regiment had their work cut out for them.[11]

In an attempt to better coordinate Florida's coastal defenses, on August 21, 1861, the Confederate War Department created the Department of Middle and Eastern Florida and placed Brigadier General John B. Grayson, an ailing career soldier, in command. The general, who was suffering through a losing battle with tuberculosis, arrived in Florida in early September and immediately undertook an inspection of Amelia Island's defenses. The general, needless to say, was dismayed by what he found.

With a sense of urgency, General Grayson informed the Confederate War Department: "As sure as the sun rises, unless cannon, powder, &c., can be sent to Florida in the next thirty days, she will fall into the hands of the enemy. Nothing human can prevent it." The general ordered the hastily built militia battery to be torn down and commanded Colonel Dilworth to construct new fortifications that could effectively defend Cumberland Sound against a Federal invasion.[12]

Following Grayson's departure, Dilworth redoubled his soldiers' efforts but soon realized that his regiment could not complete the task alone. He wrote of his Third Florida Infantry Regiment: "Men who never before have been accustomed to work, have been handling the spade, the shovel, and the wheelbarrow, with a hearty good will that would astonish their friends at home. After working night and day for a considerable time (Sundays not excepted,) they are becoming exhausted." One of Dilworth's soldiers informed his friends and family: "For a few weeks we were kept hard at work on the different fortifications; a party of ninety-six was kept continually employed." Teenage soldier Benjamin W. Partridge wrote, "We have been right hard at work and now I think the meanest place in the S.C. [Southern Confederacy] is now safe ie Fernandina."[13]

In a late-September plea issued to Florida planters, Dilworth revealed the depleted nature of his troops and asked that his fellow countrymen dispatch sixty slaves to assist in preparing the islands' defenses. The colonel ensured the patriots who responded to the request that "the Government will pay for the transportation and the feed of the negroes while engaged at work." By mid-October, more than twice the number of requested slaves toiled on Amelia Island's defenses. Samuel Pasco, a former school master among the Floridians' ranks, wrote of the slaves upon their arrival: "A finer set of hands I never saw, and they seemed proud of the honor of assisting in the defence of the country, and marched along with vigorous step making their own music as they advanced."[14]

Through the combined efforts of the Florida soldiers and the slave labor, by November's second week batteries of pine timber, palmetto logs, and sand took shape upon Amelia Island's northern shore and Cumberland Island's southernmost point. The gun emplacements, set en barbette, were soon ready, and carpenters and blacksmiths constructed carriages of pine to hold the cannon that were arriving frequently from Savannah. One such shipment arrived on October 27. Another delivery arrived on November 9, when the side-wheeler *Robert Habersham* slipped down the Inland Passage and landed five artillery pieces intended for the island's defenses.[15]

The new cannon could not have arrived soon enough, for during November's second week a renewed urgency gripped Amelia Island. On the seventh of that month, Flag Officer DuPont's fleet steamed into Port Royal Sound and, after a fierce bombardment, silenced the Confederate cannon. With the Confederate withdrawal, in but a few short hours, DuPont seized "a secure base and coaling station for the South Atlantic Blockading Squadron." Arriving in South Carolina also on November 7 was the newly appointed commander of the Confederate Department of South Carolina, Georgia, and Florida: Robert E. Lee. The former US Army colonel quickly dissected the Port Royal debacle, realizing the danger that the US fleet, and its ability to strike anywhere and at any time, posed.[16]

Flag Officer DuPont wanted to strike Amelia Island soon after securing Port Royal, but his warships had expended much of their ammunition reducing the Confederate defenses there and needed to replenish their magazine first. Yet while waiting for this resupply, the Federals took advantage of Confederate disorganization along the coast to reconnoiter numerous sounds and inlets and secure footholds for future operations. DuPont and General Thomas W. Sherman, commanding the expedition's soldiers, also turned their eyes to Savannah, one of the Confederacy's important Atlantic ports. DuPont and Sherman reasoned that should Savannah fall, because of its rail and sea communication with South Georgia and Florida, the Confederates would "abandon all forts south of St. Simons Sound and Brunswick."[17]

Following the fall of Port Royal Sound, portions of the Atlantic seaboard populations of Georgia and South Carolina panicked. Citizens of coastal areas fled, abandoning both their plantations and their slaves. Both Savannah and Charleston residents feared that the Yankees had marked their city as the next target. Working through the aftershock that Port Royal had upon Confederate morale, General Lee took immediate steps to bolster his department's defenses. One of the first actions Lee took was the dispatching of Confederate Navy Lieutenant William Webb to Amelia Island to supervise the training of artillery crews and to make suggestions regarding the mounting of weapons.[18]

On November 16, the general left South Carolina, where he kept his headquarters, and began a short inspection tour of his forces in Georgia and Florida. Author Douglas Southall Freeman claimed that following this journey, Lee made the "most important decision" of his "entire stay in the department." Lee, to the chagrin of many residents, forsook the destructive policy of stretching scant Confederate resources to defend every inlet and population center on the coast. In a letter to General Samuel Cooper, Lee explained that "the guns from less important points have been removed, and are employed in strengthening those considered of greater consequence. The entrance to Cumberland Sound & Brunswick and the water approaches to Savannah and Charleston are the only points which it is proposed to defend."[19]

Taking leave from the chaos in South Carolina, Lee might have hoped that he would find the southern end of his line ready to confront the enemy. If the general indeed harbored these anticipations, he was disappointed. He wrote in his official report, "At all of these places there is much yet to be done, but every effort is being made to render them as strong as the nature of the positions and the means at hand will permit. They ought, after their completion, to make a good defense against any batteries that are likely to be brought against them." Of the defenses, he informed his daughters: "They are poor indeed & I have laid off work to employ our people a month. I hope the enemy will be polite enough to wait for us."[20]

On Amelia Island, the first half of December passed by in relative quiet. The gun emplacements that the soldiers and slaves expended much efforts on were completed by the first of that month. The artillery, meant for the batteries and Fort Clinch, which was finally incorporated into the Confederate defenses, and dispatched from locations throughout the Confederacy, continued arriving throughout that month and required mounting. Ammunition and powder for the guns also reached Amelia Island but not in enough quantities if the garrison expected to successfully defend against a determined foe. Possibly expecting an amphibious assault on Amelia Island, Lee dispatched both the Twenty-Fourth Mississippi and Fourth Florida Infantry Regiments to Fernandina; both were encamped on the island by Christmas. Arriving with these regiments were the measles and mumps, which sent many soldiers to the general hospital.[21]

The Fernandina garrison had some excitement that month as well, for the week before Christmas a Spanish schooner, several days out of Havana, attempted to run the blockade into Fernandina. The ship's crew found the blockade too tight and instead ran aground on Cumberland Island and proceeded to begin unloading their cargo. As the Federal blockaders lowered boats for the purpose of boarding the stricken vessel, the Confederates assembled a relief expedition to salvage the valuable freight. Benjamin Partridge wrote that "ten men went from each company on a little steamer to see if they could save her." Before the Confederates reached the ship's location, the Federal boarding party secured the vessel, had their launches "loaded with coffee, cigars, shoes, and fruit and doomed schooner was soon wrapped in flames, the officers staying by her long enough to see that her destruction was inevitable." Yet a week later, a sloop successfully ran the blockade, bringing much needed salt into Fernandina, and in early February another vessel entered the harbor bearing foodstuffs.[22]

Off the coast of Savannah, Flag Officer Samuel Du Pont and Thomas Sherman focused their efforts on seizing the important Georgia port. Although formidable Fort Pulaski guarded the Savannah River's main channel, Du Pont explored the various cuts and passages that joined the river close to the city, thereby allowing a force to bypass the fortification. The War Department, however, having committed itself to Ambrose Burnside's operations on the North Carolina coast, balked at seizing Savannah. Furthermore, Du Pont felt that he would put his vessels at risk by maneuvering them through the shallow waterways above Fort Pulaski; General George McClellan ordered Sherman to reduce Fort Pulaski by siege and wrote, "Please concentrate your attention and forces upon Pulaski and Fernandina."[23]

By late February, Du Pont's invasion fleet, some twenty warships and eight transports, rode at anchor in Port Royal Sound. Poor weather caused delays in sailing, and Du Pont employed the extra time to devise an adequate plan for the reduction of the Amelia Island defenses. The Flag Officer was certain that all his vessels save two could navigate the Inland Passage and that he could use that waterway to attack the Confederate fortifications from their unprotected rear; the lack of reconnaissance of the sounds, however, gave him pause. Nevertheless, on February 27, the fleet weighed anchor and sailed into the Atlantic, bound for Wassaw Sound to embark the soldiers.

As Du Pont's fleet sailed south, the Confederates on Amelia Island worked frantically to dismantle the carefully built earthworks and dismount the many cannon on the island. For on February 10, General Lee had informed the Confederate Secretary of War Judah P. Benjamin that the Georgia troops defending St. Simons and Jekyll Islands had withdrawn to the mainland. In response to this retreat, evidently, Brigadier General

James Trapier, then commanding on Amelia Island, wrote to Lee expressing his view that Amelia Island was indefensible. On February 24, Lee concurred, writing, "The withdrawal of the troops from Saint Simons and Jekyl [*sic*] Islands can only affect the inland communication between Brunswick and Cumberland Sound, rendering it less secure and certain. The batteries commanding the principal entrance into Cumberland Sound can be easily turned." The general continued: "The withdrawal of the troops and guns will have to be done with extreme caution, and your arrangements for that purpose must be done quietly and executed so speedily as not to attract the attention of the enemy."[24]

While the Confederacy's abandonment of St. Simon's and Jekyll Island certainly rendered the majority of Fernandina's defenses useless, military setbacks in Tennessee and North Carolina also contributed to the decision to abandon Amelia Island. The latter disaster occurred at Roanoke Island, where a Confederate force was cut off from the mainland and forced to surrender. The geographic similarities between Roanoke and Amelia Islands were eerie, and the Confederates worried about the force in Florida suffering the same fate.

In the confusion that accompanied the evacuation, on March 1, no one on Amelia Island noticed a lone canoe pulling for the northern reaches of Cumberland Sound. The runaway slave in possession of the dugout happened upon Flag Officer Du Pont's fleet as it steamed through St. Andrew's Sound. Taken aboard a Union vessel, the slave described the scene at Fernandina, leaving Du Pont to write, "Well, everything is abandoned; all forts are being dismantled and the guns taken to St. John's Bluff at the St. Johns River on the main of Florida." Armed with this information, Du Pont ordered the captains of his shallow draft vessels to "proceed in haste, with the evening tide, through Cumberland Sound into Fernandina Harbor and, taking possession, you will exert yourself to preserve public and private property and to secure prisoners and munitions of war."[25]

On the morning of March 2, 1862, Commander Percival Drayton and his small squadron sailed through Cumberland Sound, passing west of Fort Clinch and the destroyed batteries, and took Fernandina under his guns. "Immediately on entering his harbor, Commander Drayton send Lieutenant White, of the *Ottawa*, to hoist the flag on Fort Clinch." Steaming into the Amelia River, the lookouts on the gunboats spotted the black smoke of a locomotive, pulling several cars onto the mainland. The *Ottawa* fired several rounds at the train, with one striking "the rear car—a platform car, loaded with furniture—and burst, scattering the furniture on all sides and killed two young men . . . who were riding on a sofa." Despite this well-placed shot, the gunboats failed to stop the train's progress.[26]

Ashore, the Yankees discovered Florida Railroad locomotives and cars, and Flag Officer Du Pont and his officers toured the remains of the rebel works. Thirteen cannon that the Rebels failed to evacuate remained in the various batteries on the northern shore. Du Pont marveled at the Confederate fortifications, writing: "It is impossible to look at these preparations for a vigorous defence without being surprised that they should have been voluntarily deserted." However, Du Pont and his fleet did not remain long in Cumberland Sound. Before March gave way to April, the combined force of naval vessels and army troops took advantage of the disorganized Confederates and successfully occupied both Jacksonville and St. Augustine.[27]

Amelia Island remained in Federal hands for the remainder of the war, and there, among the ruins of Confederate batteries, former slaves practiced their newfound freedom. A *Sacramento Daily Union* correspondent who visited the island in 1863 wrote of the island's houses: "Their homes are filled up with the contrabands, of whom over one thousand are now in the place, most of them being refugees from slavery." While the men enlisted in a United States Colored Troops regiment that formed on the island, others were "supplied with rations by the Government and . . . put to work upon plantations where practicable." In the same year that the Federals seized the island, the "Freedmen's Aid Society of Syracuse, New York, organized schools at Fernandina and St. Augustine" to educate ex-slaves.[28]

In the aftermath of Fernandina, the Confederate public, desperate to defend every inch of soil against the Yankees, leveled their criticisms against General James Trapier. Although General Lee had ordered the evacuation of Fernandina and other coastal enclaves, General Trapier was blamed for Fernandina's fall and for allowing possible access to Florida's interior. Yet newspapers contradicted their stance regarding Amelia Island's importance, with the *Savannah Republican* noting that even if Fernandina had been successfully defended, "it must have necessarily been accompanied with a sacrifice wholly unwarranted by the military importance of the place."[29]

While the Savannah newspaper spoke the truth when it declared that Amelia Island was of little military importance, the defense of the island and its subsequent evacuation provides an insight into the evolving nature of Confederate coastal defense policy. At the war's commencement, the Confederate strategy espoused by President Jefferson Davis involved blocking every possible avenue of Federal advance. When it became obvious that Federal naval power could penetrate this thin cordon at will, professional military men within the Confederacy developed a new stance, one in which only what they termed "valuable" locales, no matter the outcry from civilians, would be defended. Davis himself, in a rare admittance of error, noted in his inaugural of February 25, 1862: "In the effort to protect by our arms the whole of the territory of the Confederate States, Sea-board and inland, we have been so exposed as recently to encounter serious disasters." Although but one example of these "serious disasters" suffered during the first year-and-a half of the conflict, Amelia Island demonstrates the inability of the Confederacy to cultivate an effective coastal defense strategy and the advantage the Federals gained from the inadequacy.[30]

Notes

1. William F. Switler, "Report on the Internal Commerce of the United States," in House Executive Documents, 49th Cong., 2nd Sess., No. 7, Pt. 2 (Serial No. 2476), 400; James M. Merrill, *The Rebel Shore: The Story of Union Sea Power in the Civil War* (Boston: Little, Brown, 1957), 45; Robert A. Taylor, *Rebel Storehouse: Florida's Contribution to the Confederacy* (Tuscaloosa: University of Alabama Press, 2003), 18; Howell Cobb, "A statement showing the amount of revenue collected annually, in each collection district, from June 30, 1854, to June 30, 1859, together with the amount expended and number of persons employed in each district," in Senate Executive Documents, 36 Cong., 1 Sess., No. 33, 8.

2. Robert Browning notes that this Inland Passage was a series of sounds that connected Savannah with Fernandina and "allowed steamers not drawing more than five feet smooth water navigation for about 100 miles." Robert M. Browning Jr., *Success Is All That Was Expected: The South Atlantic Blockading Squadron during the Civil War* (Washington, DC: Brassey's, Inc., 2002), 9.

3. Stephen R. Wise, *Lifeline of the Confederacy: Blockade Running During the Civil War* (Columbia: University of South Carolina Press, 1988), 12; New Orleans *Times-Picayune*, June 25, 1861; Browning Jr., *Success Is All That Was Expected*, 13; Merrill, *The Rebel Shore*, 45–46; Macon *Daily Telegraph*, August 20, 1861; Taylor, *Rebel Storehouse*, 31; Marcus W. Price, "Ships That Tested the Blockade of the Georgia and East Florida Ports, 1861–1865," *American Neptune* XV (1955): 98.

4. Craig L. Symonds, *Lincoln and His Admirals: Abraham Lincoln, the U.S. Navy, and the Civil War* (Oxford: Oxford University Press, 2008), 62; Browning Jr., *Success Is All That Was Expected*, 14–15; *Official Records of the Union and Confederate Navies*

in the War of the Rebellion, 31 vols. (Washington, DC: Government Printing Office, 1894–1927), series 1, vol. 12, 195–96 (hereinafter cited as *ORN*).

5. ORN, vol. 12, 196–97; William M. Fowler, *Under Two Flags: The American Navy in the Civil War* (1990; Reprint, Annapolis: Naval Institute Press, 2001), 54–55; Browning Jr., *Success Is All That Was Expected*, 9; Symonds, *Lincoln and His Admirals*, 62.

6. Symonds, *Lincoln and His Admirals*, 65–66; Browning Jr., *Success Is All That Was Expected*, 24–26; Merrill, *The Rebel Shore*, 28.

7. *The War of the Rebellion: A Compilation of the Official Records of the Union and Confederate Armies*, 128 vols. (Washington, DC: Government Printing Office, 1880–1901), series 1, vol. 1, 466–67 (hereinafter cited as OR).

8. William H. Roberts, *Now for the Contest: Coastal and Oceanic Operations in the Civil War* (Lincoln: University of Nebraska Press, 2004), 35; Samuel H. Bright Jr., "Confederate Coast Defense" (PhD diss., Duke University, 1961), i; Richard E. Beringer et al., *The Elements of Confederate Defeat: Nationalism, War Aims, and Religion* (Athens: University of Georgia Press, 1988), 86; David M. Potter, "Jefferson Davis and the Political Factors in Confederate Defeat," in David Donald, ed., *Why the North Won the Civil War* (1960; Reprint, New York: Touchstone, 1996), 109; Robert G. Tanner, *Retreat to Victory? Confederate Strategy Reconsidered* (Wilmington, DE: A Scholarly Resource, Inc., 2001), 2.

9. William C. Davis, *Jefferson Davis: The Man and His Hour* (New York: Harper Collins, 1991), 372; Donald Stoker, *The Grand Design: Strategy and the U.S. Civil War* (New York: Oxford, 2010), 26.

10. OR 1, vol. 1, 466–67.

11. Don Hillhouse, *Heavy Artillery and Light Infantry: A History of the 1st Florida Special Battalion and 10th Florida Infantry* (Jacksonville: Privately published, 1992), 6; Monticello *The Family Friend*, August 5, 1861; *OR* 1, vol. 1, 471.

12. *OR* 1, Vol. 6, 276.

13. *Richmond Daily Dispatch*, October 12, 1861; Monticello, *The Family Friend*, October 19, 1861; B. W. Partridge to Dear Mother, October 13, 1861, Benjamin Waring Partridge Papers, 1824–1945, Manuscript Department, William R. Perkins Library, Duke University, Durham, NC. (hereinafter cited as Partridge Papers)

14. Monticello, *The Family Friend*, October 19, 1861, B. W. Partridge to Dear Brother, November 10, 1861, Partridge Papers.

15. B. W. Partridge to Dear Brother, November 10, 1861, Partridge Papers; *ORN* 1, vol. 12, 829; *OR* 1, vol. 6, 303.

16. Fowler Jr., *Under Two Flags*, 75–76; Symonds, *Lincoln and His Admirals*, 69–70; Douglas Southall Freeman, *R. E. Lee: A Biography*, vol. 1 (1964; Reprint, New York: Charles Scribner's Sons, 1932), 607–8. See Lee's statement to South Carolina governor Francis Pickens quoted in Merrill, *The Rebel Shore*, 41.

17. Browning Jr., *Success Is All That Was Expected*, 43, 58; *OR* 1, vol. 6, 203; Freeman, *R. E. Lee*, 610.

18. Merrill, *The Rebel Shore*, 38–39; Browning Jr., *Success Is All That Was Expected*, 43–44; *OR* I, vol. 53, 187.

19. Freeman, *R. E. Lee*, 613; *OR* 1, vol. 6, 327.

20. Ibid., R. E. Lee to Misses Annie and Agnes Lee, November 22, 1861, in *The Wartime Papers of R. E. Lee*, ed. Clifford Dowd and Louis H. Manarin (New York: Bramhall House, 1961), 89.

21. *OR* 1, vol. 6, 346, 351–52, 368; Augustus Henry Mathers to Dear Wife, December 22, 1861, in Franklin A. Doty, "The Civil War Letters of Augustus Henry Mathers, Assistant Surgeon, Fourth Florida Regiment, C.S.A.," *The Florida Historical Quarterly* 36, no. 2 (October 1957): 111, 113.

22. Franklin A. Doty, "The Civil War Letters of Augustus Henry Mathers, Assistant Surgeon, Fourth Florida Regiment, C.S.A.," 112, 119; *Harper's Weekly*, February 1, 1862.

23. *OR* 1, vol. 5, 39.

24. Ibid., vol. 6, 398–99.

25. *ORN* 1, vol. 12, 573–74.

26. Ibid., 576.

27. Ibid., 575; *Savannah Republican* quoted in the *Sacramento Daily Union*, May 1, 1862.

28. *Sacramento Daily Union*, July 21, 1863; Joe M. Richardson, *The Negro in the Reconstruction of Florida, 1865–1877* (Tallahassee: Florida State University, 1965), 98.

29. *Savannah Republican* quoted in the *New York Times*, March 28, 1862.

30. *OR* 4, vol. 1, 950–52.

4

"Our Necessary Resort"

Confederate Guerrillas in East and Middle Florida, 1861–1865

Zack C. Waters

Guerrilla warfare began in Florida even before the state voted to leave the United States. Five days before secession became official, a small band of armed men, in civilian attire, appeared out of the predawn darkness and forced the tiny caretaker crew at the Chattahoochee Arsenal at Apalachicola to surrender the federal facility, and its valuable supply of gunpowder, to the state. The following evening, twenty-five "volunteers" from Fernandina, likely reinforced by a local militia unit named the St. Augustine Blues, took possession of Fort Marion (Castillo de San Marcos) in the nation's oldest city. The fort's sixty-three artillery pieces would be employed by state, then Confederate, soldiers in early attempts to defend Florida's coastline. By the end of April 1861, citizen volunteers (described by the bluecoats as "gangs of pirates") had also disabled all the Federal lighthouses in the state, except for those at Jupiter Inlet and Dry Tortugas. Although seemingly inconsequential, a US naval officer described the guerrilla operation against the beacons as "disastrous" to shipping and blockading operations.[1]

After leaving the Union, some Floridians naively expected the new Confederate States government to protect their state, but many citizens realized that some form of irregular warfare would be the frontier region's primary defense. A Floridian, writing in the Macon, Georgia, *Telegraph*, expounded on this theme. "In the defence of the Florida coast," he wrote, "great assistance can be derived from guerrilla companies. If our enemies should effect a landing, the services of such companies would be invaluable. If our words [woods], which are very thick and heavy, become infected with guerrilla companies, the Yankees, if they attempt to march through the country, will conclude that Florida is a wilderness of destruction. We should lose no time; the Florida coast is in danger. . . . Florida will need the assistance of the other states; this assistance and her own exertions will enable Florida to bid defiance to the mymidours of Lincoln that certainly hover around her coast."[2]

Several factors combined to make irregular warfare seem an appealing option to Confederate sympathizers in the "Land of Flowers." An early study of Confederate partisans noted, "Long before the Civil War, guerrillas and guerrilla warfare had been popularized and romanticized in Southern Literature." Writers portrayed "the South [as a region] 'defending its unique way of life through the chivalric code like a medieval knight, a high-bred planter trained in arms and horsemanship [who] would use partisan tactics to repel invasion, inspire, and unify the Southern people.' Such writings helped create the myth of guerrilla warfare as 'patriotic, adventure, and above all, glorious.'" In addition to this literary propaganda, many people in the southernmost state knew from personal experience how a small band of Seminoles and their black allies used hit-and-run tactics to frustrate the United States Army for years during the Second Seminole War. Even the state's geography reflected the glorification of the guerrilla. Marion County, established in 1845, received its designation to honor Revolutionary partisan hero Francis Marion; and Sumter County, created in 1853, took its name from Thomas Sumter, the "Carolina Gamecock."[3]

Despite popular belief in the efficacy of guerrilla warfare, the administration of Jefferson Davis initially opposed the use of irregular combatants. In mid-1861, Judah P. Benjamin, the Confederacy's acting secretary of war, unequivocally declared: "Guerrilla companies are not recognized as part of the military organization of the Confederate States, and cannot be authorized by this department." This policy statement undoubtedly echoed the personal philosophy of the chief executive. Two concerns likely influenced Benjamin's proclamation. As a graduate of West Point, Davis confidently believed that regular troops, commanded by military academy graduates, provided the new nation's best chance of battlefield success. He may have also feared that guerrilla warfare might lead to the unrestrained butchery that enveloped Missouri and some sections of the Mountain South. That type of slaughter rarely occurred in Florida, except when the Rebels encountered black troops. Most of the irregular troops in the southernmost state fit into Daniel E. Sutherland's description of "partisans." These soldiers were "official, government-sanctioned guerrillas . . . [who] were expected to obey government regulations and coordinate their movements with local military commanders. . . . [T]hey operated on 'detached service' to provide reconnaissance, conduct raids, and attack small groups of enemy soldiers." (Union troops failed to appreciate such distinctions, invariably labeling their foes as "guerrillas.") As more and more territory fell to the enemy, Jefferson Davis reluctantly modified his stance on the use of "shadow warriors." In mid-1863 he wrote: "Irregular bodies of troops are not as efficient as disciplined and instructed soldiers, but when we have not enough of the latter, the former is our necessary resort."[4]

One of the first examples of guerrilla activity in Florida occurred months before the initial Federal invasion. At Union-occupied Key West, the military commanders awarded a contract to Lyman D. Stickney, a man with a reputation as a "professional opportunist" and "a person who mixed politics and private business indiscriminately for his pecuniary advantage." He contracted to bring trees from the mainland to the nation's southernmost city, where the wood would then be turned into coal to fuel the US steamers patrolling Florida's coastline. Stickney's work crew went to the area around Fort Myers, an abandoned Third Seminole War fort, to harvest the timber. Jacob Summerlin, an ardent Confederate and "the foremost cattleman in South Florida," protected that region, and a Georgia journal reported: "A posse of Capt. J[acob]. Summerlin's Cow Boys last week made a descent on a body of Lincolnites who were engaged in cutting timber . . . and succeeded in capturing four of them." As a result of Summerlin's quick, effective action, the woodcutters beat a hasty retreat, leaving behind their felled trees.[5]

Beginning in the first week of March 1862, Flag Officer Samuel F. DuPont led a combined naval and infantry force from Port Royal, South Carolina, to North Florida. Amelia Island fell on March 4. Southern defenders, in their haste to escape capture, relinquished a substantial part of the artillery taken from Fort Marion as spoils of war. The loss of Fernandina constituted a serious setback for Confederate interests, and Gov. John Milton quickly recognized the extent of the disaster. The fall of Amelia Island, he observed, gave the enemy "access to Jacksonville and the St. Johns [which] opened a pathway into the heart of East Florida." The Union flotilla quickly occupied Jacksonville on March 8, going upriver as far as Palatka. St. Augustine fell into Yankee hands on March 11, with two rebel militia units and a large number of pro-Confederate residents fleeing south to New Smyrna as the Union fleet began crossing the bar into Mantanzas Bay. Gen. Robert E. Lee, Confederate commander of coastal defenses in South Carolina, Georgia, and Florida, took a realistic approach to the Yankee incursion. Upon his advice, the Richmond government basically abandoned Florida. He ordered the removal of virtually all Florida troops to the rebel armies in Virginia and Tennessee, leaving only scattered companies and a small force along the Apalachicola River to prevent an invasion into South Georgia. Lee also directed state authorities to give "primary importance" to protecting the interior of the state. Although the Confederate general tactfully refrained from stating the obvious, the writing was on the wall. The state's defense now rested entirely upon the shoulders of small bands, which the Federals designated as "guerrillas," and militia groups.[6]

As the Federal gunboats ascended the St. Johns, Col. J. C. Hemming and his son Charles towed two vessels, the steamer *St. Mary's* and yacht *America*, a Confederate blockade-runner and celebrated winner of the 1851 challenge race against Great Britain, south to the mouth of Dunn's Creek. Col. Hemming, a native of England, had been a resident of Jacksonville for more than twenty years, where he held several public and private offices. His son had recently enlisted in the Third Florida Infantry, and the two rebel patriots scuttled the *America* and *St. Mary's* to keep them from falling into Union hands. Governor John Milton sent two units—a small cavalry unit called the "St. Johns Rangers," commanded by Lt. Winston Stephens, and an infantry company commanded by Capt. John W. Pearson—to protect the ships. Stephens's horsemen arrived too late to prevent the enemy from raising *America*, and they quickly retreated to safety.[7]

Captain Pearson, a Marion County planter who also owned a machine shop and a half-interest in the famed Orange Springs watering spa, with his "Oklawaha Rangers," explored the region south of Jacksonville, and what he learned disgusted the hard-bitten Confederate. "I regret very much to report to you," Pearson wrote to Milton, "that at least three-fourths of the people on the Saint Johns River and east of it are aiding and abetting the enemy; we could see them at all times through the day communicating with the vessel [Federal gunboat] in their small boats. It is not safe for a small force to be on the east side of the river; there is a great danger of being betrayed to the enemy." The threat of being double-crossed by area residents caused Pearson to adopt guerrilla tactics; hiding his camp, remaining close-lipped regarding his movements, and trusting no one with his plans. During his stay east of the river, Pearson arrested four Caucasians as suspected collaborators, and they hanged a black man for the same offense. As a result of what he discovered, Pearson recommended that the state's chief executive declare martial law in East Florida.[8]

Pro-Confederate citizens of East Florida had a few rays of hope during the early days of the invasion. The *Hard Times*, a small steamer laden with arms and ammunition for the Southern army, escaped from a pursuing Union blockading vessel by running up the St. Marys River and taking refuge in a creek too small for the Federal ship to enter. Lt. Frank J. Clark, a Nassau County resident, raised "a number of volunteer citizens" and took position to ambush the Yankee steamer as it returned toward the Atlantic. According to a news account, Clark's unit sprang the trap with "each [rebel] man taking [cover behind] a tree, and with their Maynard rifles and double barrel shotguns, as the enemy gunboat got within sixty yards, the first of the ambuscade line opened, and the fire told with deadly effect upon the thickly crowded decks of the gunboat. . . . One . . . volunteer, a noted hunter and excellent marksman, fired five times, and each time selected his man—the one with brass buttons on [officers]." A Home Guard unit from adjoining Camden County, Georgia, commanded by Capt. George Lang, joined the assault on the steamer from the northern bank. The Rebels estimated Union casualties (almost certainly inflated) at forty-seven dead and sixteen wounded. A New Orleans paper suggested "all our troops will profit by the example set by this guerrilla movement"; and it would be almost a year before the Federals, on Amelia Island, would again venture in force into the Nassau County hinterlands.[9]

Another thing quickly became apparent to the bluecoats occupying St. Augustine. They, and Pearson, had seriously overestimated the amount of loyalist sympathy in the region east of the St. Johns River. A historian reported: "In 1862 guerrilla warfare in East Florida reached its peak. Several Unionists were hung in St. Johns County where guerrillas even grew bold enough to slip into St. Augustine to snipe at Federal sentinels." Several months later the situation had not improved. A member of the occupation force encamped at the oldest city informed a Northern newspaper: "The inhabitants [St. Augustine] are not privileged to have ingress or egress . . . [from the] city owing to the hordes and bands of guerrillas who are organizing themselves. This has produced a terror in the neighborhood, as the guerrillas do not hesitate to kill those who differ with them when once they get into their power. The Halfway House, as it is called, between Jacksonville and St. Augustine, has become a rendezvous for the guerillas, who not long since attacked a party [of] reconnoitering [Union] cavalry and drove them back with success." The Federals eventually established a modicum of control over the region, but problems continued to flare up throughout the conflict. The provost marshal in East Florida received an offer from a civilian named G. W. Long, in January 1865, to raise "a company for the purpose of repelling and capturing rebel scouts [guerrillas] on the East side of the St. Johns River." At the time of his request, Long had enlisted only ten men for this dangerous undertaking.[10]

More good news came to the rebel populace from the Atlantic Coast. The Union blockading ships sought to close Mosquito Inlet, near New Smyrna, a haven for fleet ships carrying arms and supplies for the Southern armies. A small blockade-runner named *Kate* [or *Katie*] had brought a large cargo of English Enfield rifles to the Confederacy. On March 23, 1862, when a party of Federals came ashore, the Florida companies of Capts. Daniel E. Bird and Matthew H. Strain, of Companies E and H, of the Third Florida Infantry, respectively, and Capt. W. E. Chambers' Marion County cavalry company ambushed the enemy. A local bushwhacker named George Huston (or Houston) captured and hanged the black pilot who had guided the bluecoats ashore. "This skirmish left a bitterness with the Federal crews," which seems to have led to the later "shelling and burning of Smyrna." The Yankee seaman also determined to avenge the death of the pilot. Led by Lt. J. G. Sproston, a seventy-man naval squad approached Huston's residence, on the west bank of the St. Johns River, and demanded his surrender. Although outnumbered seventy to one, the Florida guerrilla proved game. "He appeared at his door, armed with a double-barreled gun, two pistols, and a bowie knife," opened fire, killing Sproston, and died in a hail of gunfire.[11]

By mid-1862 a new leader appeared on the scene who would become Florida's most famous, and effective, partisan leader. John J. Dickison, a forty-year-old transplant from South Carolina and a wealthy Marion County planter. After failing to be reelected as lieutenant of the Marion Light Artillery, he received permission from Gen. Joseph Finegan to raise the final company for the Second Florida Cavalry: "His company, along with various other units temporarily under his command, patrolled areas along the St. Johns and eastward to the coast, ambushed Union foraging expeditions, and captured pickets and isolated bodies of troops. Even when he was not actually attacking the enemy, fear of Dickison and his men kept the Union forces for the most part bottled up in St. Augustine and a few scattered posts. The Federals could occupy the towns, but they were never able effectively to control the countryside." Nicknamed "The Swamp Fox," "War Eagle," or simply "Dixie," a modern historian has concluded that "most of the credit for holding on to [the interior of] Florida belonged to one man—John Jackson Dickison."[12]

Few regularly enrolled Florida Confederates received uniforms until ordered to the Army of Northern Virginia or the Army of Tennessee. Wearing everyday apparel allowed the shadow warriors to blend in with the general populace and aided their surprise attacks, but it created a feeling of suspicion among Federals. A letter from a bluecoat summed up the feelings of many Northern soldiers in the occupied South. "They called themselves partisan rangers," he complained, "but claim to be part of the Rebel army, and expect all the immunities of civilized warfare. They wear citizens' clothes, seize all the property that falls their way, and shoot our pickets when they succeed in 'slipping up' on them. . . . [Before a battle] they go to swell the Rebel ranks, and after the battle detach themselves to prowl, rob, and murder as before. The only treatment for these cutthroats is to shoot them on sight, or hang them when taken prisoner."[13]

In late 1862, a few weeks after the signing of the Emancipation Proclamation, several Abolitionist officers in the Union armies began enrolling former slaves into United States Colored Troops (USCT) regiments. The First South Carolina Loyal Volunteers, composed of many former Florida slaves, received orders in March 1863 to garrison the city of Jacksonville. General Rufus Saxton bluntly stated: "The object of the expedition was to occupy Jacksonville and make it the base of operations for the arming of negroes and securing in this way possession of the entire state of Florida." The outpouring of hatred and outrage from many white Floridians was predictable. In a typical response, a Confederate soldier stated: "If those niggers are brought out into the State as they say they intend, you'll hear some of the 'damndest fights' you ever heard tell of, as every man of us is determined to do his best towards wiping them out completely." In the USCT's first expedition along the St. Marys River, in early 1863, the guerrillas who opposed the black troops acted with foolhardy desperation, exposing themselves as if their lives meant nothing as long as they could kill black men. With the notable exception of J. J. Dickison, the sable soldiers learned to expect little mercy from Confederate irregulars if captured.[14]

The military situation in Middle Florida differed considerably from the more populous, wealthier St. Johns River region. Until very late in the war, Federals along Florida's lower Gulf occupied no mainland towns but established outposts on a few small islands such as Cedar, Seahorse, and Egmont Keys. Rather than making the enlistment of black soldiers a priority, the

Yankees along the Gulf made allies of the region's Unionists and deserters. Supplied and aided by the United States East Gulf Blockading Squadron, enough of these dissidents enlisted to create the Second Florida (US) Cavalry. The abandonment of Florida by the government in Richmond and the strict enforcement of the hated Conscript Law, coupled with the disastrous rebel losses at Shiloh, Perryville, and Stones River, caused many men to desert or "lay out" in the swamps and woods. "This group of allies enabled the [Federal] blockaders to establish partisan combat actions on the mainland, which disrupted the Confederate government." Some of the groups of deserters numbered more than a hundred, and knowing that a hangman's noose or firing squad would be their fate if captured added desperation to their raids and operations.[15]

On rare occasions, the Federals used contrabands, as they characterized runaway slaves, as guerillas to harass the rebel irregulars along the Gulf. Capt. Sam Hope, who fashioned a record as a fine Confederate combat officer in both Florida and Virginia, reported the results of a skirmish with such a group of black guerrillas. Writing on September 8, 1863, from Hernando [modern Citrus] County, he reported: "I had succeeded in capturing the boat [used to transport the black partisans from Seahorse Key] and had the negroes cut off. . . . After chasing them about two miles through the saw Grass we came up [with]in gun shot of them. We began to fire at them, and [they] returned fire very cool and deliberately but we got in close range of them and killed them. One of these negroes was recognized by some of my men as belonging to Mr. Everett, who lives near hear [here], which ran away from him about nine months ago. He was styled Captain of the party, as I learned from the negroes recaptured of Mr. King." They could not find three of the seven-man squad, and with tongue firmly in cheek, Hope added: "I could not get any information [on the three missing men] from any of the four that was killed."[16]

Not only did the East Gulf Blockading Squadron supply arms and intelligence to the Union guerrillas and grant refuge to white and black refugees, but it also carried on an active campaign to destroy rebel shipping, saltworks, and communities near the coast. These forays were usually successful and damaged Confederate interests in the backcountry. "The Union blockade," Dr. Joe Knetsch asserts, "proved to be more effective as time wore on and the resources of the Confederacy dwindled. Florida, with its lack of manpower, extended coastlines and few exploitable resources necessary for military production, was always open to attack. The large and destructive raids upon the numerous salt works along the coast are legendary in Florida's colorful history. The [May 28, 1864,] burning of the [former Senator David Levy] Yulee [Homosassa] plantation symbolizes the extreme vulnerability of the coastal settlements throughout the state. The shelling of the city of Tampa [on numerous occasions, but particularly October 16–17, 1863] indicates the relative ease with which the Union forces could operate without too much fear of retaliation." Coming ashore, however, involved a great deal of danger to the Union sailors. Groups of Confederate irregulars invariably hid nearby hoping to kill unwary seamen, as happened on June 29, 1862, near Crystal River to a seven-man landing party from the schooner USS *Beauregard*.[17]

Tampa remained a hotly contested battleground from early 1862 until the state's remaining battalions received orders to Virginia in April 1864. Some of the state's finest officers, including W. L. L. Bowen, William I. Turner, John W. Pearson, and John Westcott, effectively defended the town at various times throughout that period. Pearson especially proved a thorn in the side of the Union blockaders. He brought in two rifled cannons, made at his machine shop at Orange Springs, to keep the blockading ships at a distance. On March 23, 1863, Pearson's men lured Yankee seamen into a trap at Gadsden Point on Tampa Bay. He lured one of the blockading vessels close to shore by having some of his men wear dresses and blackface—posing as escaping slaves—and signaling with a white flag for the US boat to rescue them. When the bluecoats neared shore, Pearson's men opened fire from the nearby sand dunes, though the number of killed and wounded remains a point of contention. In October, a Federal expedition, guided by local Unionists, came ashore. The invasion force burned a couple of blockade-runners but retreated to their ships under an intense fire from Westcott's "Swamp Marines." The Federals finally captured Tampa in May 1864, but Northern news accounts noted this occurred only after the previous defenders "left to reinforce Lee's army."[18]

The situation changed dramatically in the Land of Flowers in mid-1863. The surrender of Vicksburg on July 4, 1863, allowed the Mississippi River to flow "unvexed to the sea," and Union gunboats rapidly moved to shut off the movement of cattle and foodstuffs from the Trans-Mississippi region to the Confederate armies in the East. Florida suddenly assumed a very prominent position in the future of the Confederacy. Robert A. Taylor, author of a groundbreaking study on Florida's role in the Confederate supply system, explains: "As supply officers pondered their options, it was known that Florida had large herds of cattle, some of which it had already been providing the military. More Florida beef was needed to help ease the shortage. If meat were not obtained, it would be impossible to feed the Army of Tennessee. The disintegration of a major Confederate field army hung in the balance." The Federals almost immediately became aware of the importance of the Florida beef and tasked the US Second Florida Cavalry and a regiment of USCT troops with halting the stream of meat on the hoof to Chattanooga and Charleston.[19]

Confederate commissary officers recognized that they needed a military force whose main assignment was to collect the cattle, fight off Union efforts to halt the flow of beef, and drive the cattle to the railheads in South Georgia. Jefferson Davis selected Maj. Charles J. Munnerlyn, a former Georgia representative in the Confederate Congress, to direct the newly organized First Battalion, Florida Special Cavalry (called the "Cow Cavalry"). In all, Munnerlyn managed to enlist nine companies. Cattle soon began flowing into holding pens from extreme southwest Florida (near Union-occupied Fort Myers), the lower St. Johns River Valley, central Florida, and as far north as Tallahassee, awaiting the long drives to the railhead in South Georgia. Veteran Florida cowmen from Braxton Bragg's army and the Sixth Florida Battalion comprised the core of the unit, supplemented by local rebel sympathizers, youths too young to join the army, and even deserters from the army who agreed to aid the Confederacy rather than join the Second Union Florida Cavalry. In addition, "a number of veterans from units like J. J. Dickison's cavalry . . . [used] their hard-learned skills as soldiers to add to the battalion's efficiency. These troopers were rugged individuals who had banded together for a common purpose, so they may have lacked the military bearing of professionals." The work required a special skillset, for "collecting and driving semi-wild bovines was an assignment that only experienced wranglers could handle effectively." The Yankees considered Munnerlyn's men to be guerrillas, of course, and treated them accordingly.[20]

The new importance of Florida beef led to a marked increase in the number of skirmishes and smaller battles all across the southernmost state. A large part of this escalation of violence resulted from Union attempts to curtail the shipment of cattle and swine to the Southern armies. Robert Taylor asserts: "While it was not the only reason for the Olustee Campaign, the desire to interdict the flow of cattle into Georgia was an important factor in General Truman A. Seymour's ill-fated march toward Lake City."

Following the defeat and panicky retreat from Ocean Pond, Gen. Seymour received orders from his superiors to undertake "no offensive operations" until Jacksonville had been sufficiently fortified to withstand *any* rebel attack. The bluecoats seemed content to rely upon the wide St. Johns as a barricade to keep the Confederates at bay, but they stepped up their efforts, in the St. Johns River Valley and in South Florida, to cut off the food supply to the Army of Tennessee and the graycoats defending Charleston.[21]

The subordinates of Gen. P. G. T. Beauregard, who commanded the Department of South Carolina, Georgia, and Florida, believed attacking Jacksonville would devastate their forces, and as long as the Yankees controlled the river with their gunboats it would be impossible to occupy the town. In April, the horrendous losses suffered by Lee's army at the battles of the Wilderness and Spotsylvania Court House resulted in a call for any available Florida troops. Gov. Milton responded quickly, sending the Sixth Florida, the First Florida (Special), Second Florida, and Fourth Florida Battalions to Virginia. Companies of these troops had been stationed at sensitive points from Tampa to the Apalachicola River, and their removal put additional pressure on the irregular bands left behind.[22]

The Southern victory at Olustee did little to improve conditions in Middle Florida. The state's Confederate commander, in fact, reported "considerable alarm [is] felt by many citizens of Middle Florida on account of recent depredations committed or threatened by bands of deserters, disloyal persons, and bandits, who had been gathering and forming semi-organizations along the coast." Beauregard tried to help by offering amnesty to men absent from their units, Unionists, and conscript evaders in North Florida, but his "offer met with little success." Meanwhile, the Federals established a base at Palatka, sixty miles south of Jacksonville and on the west bank of the St. Johns, believing loyalists and runaway slaves would flock to the Putnam County town for sanctuary. It proved no more successful than Beauregard's decree.[23]

The Rebels stepped up their efforts to break Union control of the St. Johns and force the evacuation of the fort at Palatka. During April and May of 1864, Lt. Thomas E. Buckman, chief of ordinance for Florida, ably assisted by men like Jacob Mickler, constructed and positioned a series of torpedoes in the channel near Mandarin. Within weeks, the *Maple Leaf*, the *General Hunter*, and the *Harriett A. Weed* all sank after striking torpedoes. Adding insult to injury, J. J. Dickison, on May 22, captured the *Columbine*, with her crew and cargo, at Horse Landing. Shortly thereafter,

Florida's Swamp Fox forced the capitulation of the Federal garrisons at Welaka and Saunders, on the eastern side of the St. Johns. A major Yankee expedition to Gainesville in August, to gather up slaves, burn cotton, and collect supplies, also suffered a disastrous defeat. Following the fight, Union survivors scattered in the wildest disorder through Central Florida as they attempted to reach safety on the east side of the St. Johns. As a result of these setbacks, the danger involved in supplying the Palatka outpost by water, having small units snatched up by guerrillas, and the reduction of the number of Union troops in the southernmost state, the bluecoats decided to "reduce . . . major permanent garrisons to those at St. Augustine, Jacksonville, and Fernandina."[24]

The situation in the rest of Middle and South Florida appeared much less positive for rebel supporters. Confederate partisans and militia proved incapable of dealing with William Strickland's Independent Union Rangers and other deserter groups centered in the state's (modern) Big Bend region. After receiving numerous complaints from citizens of the area, Gen. Franklin Gardner, at Monticello, determined to "bring them to punishment, and to use every effort to prevent the recurrence of similar acts of lawlessness and plunder." In late March, Lt. Col. Henry D. Capers led a combined force of South Georgia infantry and cavalry into Strickland's stronghold, burning houses, meeting camps, and even taking the wives and children of the deserters as hostages. The war against women and youngsters proved too much for Confederate sympathizers at Tallahassee, and Gov. Milton sent the deserters' families to the coast, turning them over to the East Gulf Blockading Squadron. This took some of the wind out of Strickland's sails for a while, but other deserter companies continued to disrupt Southern operations along Florida's northern Gulf region.[25]

The cattle wars in South Florida had only one battle, but numerous small skirmishes resulted in a considerable amount of bloodshed and suffering. Collecting beef and moving the animals to railhead constituted the primary purpose of Munnerlyn's units. The rebel wranglers were generally spread over a large area of scrubland in squads of six to twelve men, which meant the bluecoats almost always had the advantage in numbers. For example, the Union force that marched toward Brooksville in the first week of July 1864 consisted of 120 members of the Second Florida (Union) Cavalry and 120 men of the Second USCT. They advanced almost forty miles inland, skirmishing with the Cow Cavalry, capturing one hundred head of cows, and "the plantations of Capt. [David] Hope, Capt. [L. G.] Leslie

[Lesley] and sons, and Capt. [William B.] Hooker, all commanding guerrilla parties of the enemy, were destroyed." By the time they approached the county seat of Hernando County, a number of townsmen and cowmen had assembled, and after a brief skirmish the Federals retreated toward Bayport. Such expeditions annoyed the Rebels but did not seriously disrupt the movement of cattle to the graycoated armies in Georgia and South Carolina. According to Robert Taylor: "Cattle moved again in the spring [of 1864] and continued until the end of the war. By war's end at least 75,000 head had been delivered to the government, while untold numbers had been traded covertly."[26]

Three small battles in the opening months of 1865 brought the war in the southernmost state sputtering to a close. On February 13, a USCT regiment sallied out of Cedar Key in an attempt to halt the collection of beeves in Levy County. Capt. E. J. Lutterloh's unit, reinforced by J. J. Dickison horse soldiers, fought the black soldiers at Station Number Four and, despite being outnumbered and short of ammunition, the rebel cavalry drove the enemy back to their base. A week later rebel Maj. William Footman led two hundred members of the Cow Cavalry through a pouring rain in an attack on the Union stronghold at Fort Myers. The Rebels bungled the operation from beginning to end and retreated during the night, having accomplished nothing. About three weeks later a strong Union infantry force debarked at Newport, a small town on the Gulf south of Tallahassee, and marched north in an attempt to capture Florida's Capital. Despite several determined attacks by USCT units, a ragtag rebel assemblage of militia, a few regulars, and Florida Seminary cadets turned back the bluecoat's advance at Natural Bridge, making Tallahassee the only Confederate capitol east of the Mississippi River not captured by the Federals.[27]

The surrender of the Southern armies at Appomattox Court House and Durham Station essentially ended the Civil War. Most of the people of Florida had long since wearied of the hostilities. Tired of the sacrifice, death, and destruction, and the economic and political chaos that the conflict engendered, most citizens of the southernmost state greeted the news of defeat with resigned acceptance. Several "renegade bands of deserters and Confederate irregulars continued to pose a threat in certain areas of the state for some time to come . . . [but] by mid-June 1865 all recognized Confederate units in Florida had capitulated."[28]

Despite the reluctance of the Davis Administration to condone the use of shadow warriors, the abandonment of the southernmost state left rebel sympathizers with few other options. Ill-equipped and almost always outnumbered, the rebel partisans made three significant contributions to the goals of the short-lived Confederate nation. A J. J. Dickison biographer noted: "From Cedar Key to Smyrna and Tampa to the Georgia line . . . [the graycoated guerrillas] kept Florida Confederate territory until the end of the war." In the process, their exploits and victories encouraged and kept hope alive for the Southern men, women, and children on the home front. More importantly, when the fall of Vicksburg made cattle from the Land of Flowers essential to the survival of Confederacy, the irregular units collected and herded the beeves to the railhead in Georgia, despite intense pressure from the Federals to halt the flow of meat on the hoof.[29]

Notes

1. Mark F. Boyd, "The Apalachicola or Chattahoochee Arsenal of the United States," *Apalachee* 4 (1956): 29–43; Dale Cox, "Historic Apalachicola Arsenal—Chattahoochee, Florida," http://www.exploresouthernhistory.com/arsenal1.html; Omega G. East, "St. Augustine during the Civil War," *Florida Historical Quarterly* (henceforth *FHQ*) 31 (1952): 75–77; David J. Coles, "Ancient City Defenders: The St. Augustine Blues" in *Civil War Times in St. Augustine*, ed. Jacqueline K. Fretwell (Port Salerno: Florida Classics Library, 1988), 68–69; US War Department, *The War of the Rebellion: A Compilation of the Official Records of the Union and Confederate Navies* (Washington, DC: Government Printing Office, 1894–1927) (henceforth *ORN*) vol. 12, 207–8; Rodney E. Dillon Jr., "'A Gang of Pirates': Confederate Lighthouse Raids in Southeast Florida, 1861," *FHQ* 67 (1989): 441–57.

2. J. D. P., "King Cotton," Macon *Telegraph*, October 3, 1861, 2. "Mymidours" is apparently a misspelling of a word from the "Iliad," meaning "mighty warriors."

3. Jerry McDowell King, "Shadow Warriors of the Confederacy" (unpublished MA thesis, University of South Florida, 1990), 4–5; James A. Ramage, *Rebel Raiders: The Life of General John Hunt Morgan* (Lexington: University Press of Kentucky, 1986), 54–66; Daniel E. Sutherland, *A Savage Conflict: The Decisive Role of Guerrillas in the American Civil War* (Chapel Hill: University of North Carolina Press, 2009), 26–32; "County Name Origins," www.flheritage.com/facts/reports/names/county.cfm.

4. *The War of the Rebellion: A Compilation of the Official Records of the Union and Confederate Armies* [henceforth ORA] (Washington, DC: Government Printing Office, 1880–1901), 52, 2, 489; King, "Shadow Warriors of the Confederacy," 28–30; Sutherland, *A Savage Conflict*, xi. Regarding the bushwhacker conflict, see generally, Sean Michael O'Brien, *Mountain Partisans: Guerrilla Warfare in the Southern Appalachians, 1861–1865* (Westport, CT: Praeger, 1991).

5. "Lincolnites Captured," Augusta *Chronicle*, October 22, 1861, 1; David James Coles, "Far from Fields of Glory: Military Operations in Florida during the Civil War" (unpublished PhD diss., Florida State University, 1996), 9–14; Robert A. Taylor, *Rebel Storehouse: Florida in the Confederate Economy* (Tuscaloosa: University of Alabama Press, 1995), 91. (See generally, Joe A. Akerman and J. Mark Akerman, *Jacob Summerlin: King of the Crackers* (Cocoa: Florida Historical Society Press, 2004).

6. *ORA* 6, 429; Daniel L. Schafer, *Thunder on the River: The Civil War in Northeast Florida* (Gainesville: University Press of Florida, 2009), 47–49; East, "St. Augustine during the Civil War," 78–79. See generally, John E. Reiger, "Florida After Secession: Abandonment by the Confederacy and its Consequences," *FHQ* 50 (1971): 128–42.

7. Shafer, *Thunder on the River*, 65–66; Zack C. Waters, "Florida's Confederate Guerrillas: John W. Pearson and the Oklawaha Rangers," *FHQ* 70 (1991): 136–39; Mellen C. Greeley, "Musings of Mellen Clark Greeley, Written in his Anec-Dotage," P. K. Yonge Library of Florida History, University of Florida, Gainesville.

8. *ORA* 53, 233–34; *ORA* 13, 224–26, 369; *ORN* 13, 369; Waters, "Florida's Confederate Guerrillas," 136–39.

9. "Movement and Spirit of the War," Richmond *Enquirer*, March 19, 1862, 2; "More Arms," [Atlanta] *Daily Constitutionalist*, March 19, 1862, 3; "Slaughter of the Enemy near St. Mary's, Georgia," New Orleans *Times-Picayune*, March 23, 1862, 5; Schmidt, Lewis G., *The Civil War in Florida: Florida's East Coast; A Military History* (Allentown, PA: n. p., 1991), 477.

10. East, "St. Augustine during the Civil War," 84–85; "War News," Boston *Herald*, September 15, 1862, 4; Florida Report to Provost Marshal, dated January 4, 1865, No. 14356 (G. W. Long).

11. Schafer, *Thunder on the River*, 81; Zelia Wilson Sweett, *New Smyrna, Florida in the Civil War* (New Smyrna Beach, FL: Volusia County Historical Commission, 1963), 5–6; "Naval Officer Killed by a Rebel Desperado," (Washington, DC) *Evening Star*, June 17, 1862, 3; "The Great Rebellion," *National Tribune*, December 29, 1892, 5.

12. Richard P. Weinert, "Dickison—the Swamp Fox of Florida," *Civil War Times Illustrated* 5 (December 1966): 4–11, 48–50; Mary Elizabeth Dickison, *Dickison and His Men: Reminiscences of the War in Florida* (facsimile reproduction, Jacksonville, FL: San Marco, 1962); John J. Koblas, *John J. Dickison: Swamp Fox of the Confederacy* (St. Cloud, MN: North Star Press, 2000).

13. "Letter from Corinth," Philadelphia (PA) *Inquirer*, November 6, 1862, 2. A veteran of Lee's army described the new arrivals from Florida as "[having] not received many clothes—only what their mothers and wives had spun or woven them. . . . They carried the Florida trademark." David R. Geer, "Memories of the War," [Lake City] *Florida Index*, February 2, 1906, 1.

14. "Jim Lanes' Manifesto," [Atlanta, GA] *Southern Confederacy*, June 28, 1862, 2; "Affairs in Florida," Philadelphia *Inquirer*, November 1, 1862, 3; Schafer, *Thunder on the River*, 131–41; *ORA* 14, 226; Richard Nelson Current, *Lincoln's Loyalists: Union*

Soldiers from the Confederacy (Boston: Northeastern University Press, 1992), 107–10; T. W. Higginson, "Negro Soldiers: Gallant Conduct Under Fire," [New York, NY] *Evening Post*, February 10, 1863, 1.

15. George E. Buker, *Blockaders, Refugees, and Contrabands: Civil War on Florida's Gulf Coast, 1861–1865* (Tuscaloosa: University of Alabama Press, 1993), 79–97.

16. Ira Berlin, ed., *The Destruction of Slavery* (New York: Cambridge University Press, 1985), 805–6; Joe Knetsch, "Forging the Florida Frontier: The Life and Career of Captain Samuel E. Hope," *The Sunland Tribune: Journal of the Tampa Historical Society* 20 (November 1994), 31–40.

17. *ORN* 17, 290–91; Buker, *Blockaders, Refugees, and Contrabands*, 44–45; Joe Knetsch, "Armed Boats Off Crystal River: A Chapter of the Civil War in Citrus County," *At Home: Citrus County Historical Society* 18, (2001): 1, 6.

18. Waters, "Florida's Confederate Guerrillas," 139–43; Zack C. Waters, "Tampa's Forgotten Defenders: The Confederate Commanders at Fort Brooke," *Sunland Tribune: Journal of the Tampa Historical Society* 17 (1991): 3–12; "A Yankee Raid on Tampa, Florida," Richmond *Examiner*, June 7, 1864, 3 (includes a short account by a Tampa citizen). Bowen served as a colonel of the Fourth Florida, Pearson as a lieutenant-colonel of the Ninth Florida, Turner as a major of the Eighth Florida, and Westcott as a major of the Tenth Florida.

19. Robert A. Taylor, "Rebel Beef: Florida Cattle and the Confederate Army, 1862–1864," *FHQ* 68 (July 1988): 16–17. See generally, Buker, *Blockaders, Refugees, and Contrabands*, 115–43; and, Robert A. Taylor, *Rebel Storehouse: Florida's Contribution to the Confederacy* (Tuscaloosa: University of Alabama Press, 2004).

20. Taylor, "Rebel Beef," 19–20; Robert A. Taylor, "Cow Cavalry: Munnerlyn's Battalion in Florida, 1864–1865," *FHQ* 60 (1986): 196–214; *ORA* 35, 1, 406.

21. Allen W. Jones, "Military Events in Florida during the Civil War, 1861–1865," *FHQ* 39 (July 1960): 42–45; Taylor, "Rebel Beef," 27; Taylor, "Munnerlyn's Cow Cavalry," 211; "Florida and Beef," Cleveland (OH) *Plain Dealer*, February 29, 1864, 2, states the Olustee expedition "is said to be for the purpose of cutting off the beef supply of the Southern Confederacy."

22. *ORA* 35, 1, 117–18, 334–35; *ORA* 35, 2, 15; Coles, "Far from Fields of Glory," 196–202; Zack C. Waters and James C. Edmonds, *A Small but Spartan Band: The Florida Brigade in Lee's Army of Northern Virginia* (Tuscaloosa: University of Alabama Press, 2010), 119–24.

23. Coles, "Far from Fields of Glory," 198–201; *ORA* 35, 1, 368–69; Schafer, *Thunder on the River*, 204–5.

24. Coles, "Far from Fields of Glory," 207–14; Koblas, *John J. Dickison*, 79–93; Schafer, *Thunder on the River*, 212–16, 234–37.

25. Buker, *Blockaders, Refugees, and Contrabands*, 98–114; *ORA* 35, 2, 348–49; 53, 320–21; William T. Cash, "Taylor County History and Civil War Deserters," *FHQ* 27 (1948): 28–58.

26. Coles, "Far from Fields of Glory," 248–76; Taylor, "Rebel Beef," 25–31; Jeff Cannon, "The Brooksville-Bayport Raid and the Civil War in Hernando County," http://www.pascocemeteries.org/Brooksville_bayport_raid.html.

27. Coles, "Far from Fields of Glory," 233–39; Koblas, *John J. Dickison*, 125–30; Rodney E. Dillion Jr., "The Battle of Fort Myers," *Tampa Bay History* 5 (1983): 27–36; Irvin D. Solomon, "Southern Extremities: The Significance of Fort Myers in the Civil War," *FHQ* 72 (1993): 129–52; Robert Bruce Graetz, "Triumph Amid Defeat: The Confederate Victory at Natural Bridge" (unpublished bachelor's honor's thesis, Florida State University, 1986); Dale Cox, *The Battle of Natural Bridge: The Confederate Defense of Tallahassee* (Fort Smith, AK: Self-published, 2007).

28. Coles, "Far from Fields of Glory," 387–92.

29. Vince Murray, *Dixie's Land* (Ocala: Florida Focus Publications, 1992), 16.

5

Embattled Executive

Governor John Milton's Civil War

R. Boyd Murphree

John Milton's governorship of Florida began and ended in violence. Two days after his inauguration, on October 9, 1861, Confederate forces attacked Union troops on Santa Rosa Island in an attempt to capture Fort Pickens. On April 1, 1865, in the midst of Confederate collapse, Milton killed himself at his plantation home near Marianna, Florida. As governor, Milton worked tirelessly to manage the state's affairs in the face of economic deprivation, Confederate manpower and supply demands, Unionist unrest, and Northern invasion. Although he often expressed his opposition to such Confederate policies as economic impressment and the suspension of habeas corpus, he was one of the most loyal supporters of Jefferson Davis among the Confederate governors and, as witnessed by his suicide, steadfastly refused any compromise peace with the North during his years as Florida's wartime governor.[1]

Like his four predecessors in office, Milton, who became Florida's fifth governor under statehood on October 7, 1861, was born outside of the state. He was born on April 20, 1807, in Jefferson County, Georgia, near Louisville, the former capital. His grandfather and namesake, John Milton, was a prominent officer in the South during the Revolutionary War, served as Georgia's first secretary of state, and was elected mayor of Augusta. Milton's father, Homer Virgil Milton, was a colonel and regimental commander during the War of 1812, a Georgia state senator, and a brigadier general in the Georgia militia. John attended the Louisville Academy in Jefferson County, read law, and established his first law practice in Louisville. On February 9, 1826, he married Susan Amanda Cobb, a cousin of the prominent Georgia politician Howell Cobb. They had four children, one boy and three girls, only one of whom, William Henry Milton, survived to adulthood.[2]

Figure 3.
Portrait of John Milton, Florida's Civil War governor,
courtesy of State Archives of Florida, Florida Memory

The most controversial period in Milton's early political life occurred in Columbus, Georgia, where he moved in 1831 to expand his law practice and speculate in Creek Indian land in neighboring Alabama. He entered politics as an independent, pronullification candidate in the congressional election of 1832, and his first political campaign and its aftermath were disastrous. He polled last in the election and created a number of political enemies in Columbus, including Major Joseph T. Camp, whom Milton believed was responsible for writing a scurrilous attack on his personal honor in one of the local newspapers. After publishing an accusatory and defamatory reply to Camp's supposed letter, Milton heard rumors that Camp, a well-known and practiced duelist, was intent on killing him. On August 12, 1833, notified that Camp was looking for him, Milton decided to strike first. He ambushed and killed Camp on a Columbus street in broad daylight, shooting him in the back with one barrel of a shotgun and unloading the other barrel into the man as he lay bleeding in the street. Camp may have been armed, and he may have even been looking to fight Milton, but the killing was no "duel" as some writers have suggested—it was murder. However, in a result that stunned people across Georgia and the nation—the national press reported on the "Milton-Camp Affair," as the killing was called—Milton was brought to trial and acquitted on grounds of self-defense. The jury reportedly believed testimony that Camp was on his way to kill Milton, who merely protected himself by shooting Camp first.[3]

After the trial, Milton resumed his legal practice in Columbus, but his political future in Georgia was over. He was too controversial to run for office within the state. In 1835, he decided to move his family and legal practice to Mobile, Alabama. Over the next ten years, Milton lived and worked in three states—Alabama, Louisiana, and Texas—before settling in Florida permanently in 1845. During those years, he remained politically active as a civic leader and popular Democratic orator but refrained from running for political office. An outspoken proponent of slavery and a slave owner in his own right, Milton also engaged in two other controversial antebellum policies: Indian removal and support for Texas. While living in Alabama, he served as a militia officer in the Second Creek War of 1836 and participated in the removal of the defeated Creeks from the state. In 1842, after years of aiding the cause of Texas independence, Milton moved to Texas, where he served as a volunteer in a militia company organized in response to an incursion of Mexican forces led by General Ráfael Vásquez.[4]

There is a gap in Milton's record from his service in Texas in 1842 until his second marriage in 1844, but sometime after June 1842 he returned to Alabama to resume his legal practice and business interests, especially in buying and selling cotton, which had long been part of his commercial pursuits. Four years after losing his first wife, Susan, who died in New Orleans in 1840, he married Caroline Howze of Marion, Alabama, on April 28, 1844. They would have ten children, three sons and seven daughters. Milton relocated for the last time in 1845, when he and his young bride—Caroline was nineteen when they married—moved the family to Jackson County, Florida.[5]

Milton's move to Florida was prompted by an opportunity to acquire land and stability. His maternal cousins, the Robinsons, owned extensive plantation lands in Jackson County, which in 1845 was part of the rich cotton belt of counties in Middle Florida, stretching from the counties along the Apalachicola River in the west to the Suwannee River in the east. Milton inherited and purchased land from the Robinsons and built a plantation home, which he named "Sylvania" (forest land), close to the Robinson's plantation about ten miles from Marianna, the county seat. His lands in Jackson County eventually included fourteen thousand acres, and he also owned fifty-two slaves by the time he was elected governor in 1860.[6]

His journey to that office began soon after his move to Jackson County. The Robinsons were a prominent Democratic family in Jackson County, which was a political stronghold of the Whigs. They encouraged Milton, a fellow Democrat, to become active in local and state Democratic politics. More than a decade had passed since his killing of Camp, and Milton's reputation as a skillful attorney and eloquent speaker made him the logical choice to lead the Jackson County Democrats against the Whigs. Although he lost his first bid for state office, in 1847, the race for a state senate seat was a close one. Milton used the support and publicity he gained in the campaign to win election to the position of major general of the First Division of the Florida militia, which comprised all the militia units west of the Suwannee River. Now known as "General Milton," a title that remained with him until his election as governor, he won a seat in the Florida House of Representatives in 1850.[7]

Although his party renominated him in 1852, Milton refused to run for another term in the Florida House. After losing a race for the state senate in 1854, he did not run for state office again until 1860. Since Milton's personal papers no longer exist, there is no documentation about his political thinking between 1854 and 1860. His reluctance to seek office may have been due to illness—he caught typhoid in 1855—or frustration with the continued dominance of the Whigs in Jackson County, "the banner county of Whiggery in the State," or it may have been a desire to focus on business and family matters: he and his oldest son, William H. Milton, maintained an active law practice in Marianna, in addition to the family's interests in land, cotton, and slaves.[8]

Milton returned to politics in 1860. He was chosen to lead Florida's delegation to the fateful Democratic presidential convention in Charleston, South Carolina, in April 1860. When it became clear that the Northern Democrats would not support the Southern demand for the unrestricted introduction of slavery into territories, Alabama led a walkout of nine slave states, including Florida. On his return to Florida, Milton spoke to a crowd in Fernandina that had gathered to welcome home the delegation. He told the people that the division at the convention was inevitable given "the profound difference in public opinion [between] North and South." His role at the Charleston convention and his prominence in Democratic politics in West Florida (the counties to the west of the Apalachicola River) made him a potential gubernatorial nominee at the state Democratic convention in Quincy on June 4, 1860. When the balloting for a nominee began, it became apparent that the delegates could not agree on a nominee to replace outgoing Governor Madison Starke Perry. Milton had the solid support of the Jackson County delegation as well as the Democrats from West Florida; however, it took twenty-three ballots for him to secure the nomination.[9]

He began his campaign by presenting his views on the sectional crisis in an acceptance letter to the Democratic Party. Published in newspapers across the state, the letter urged the Southern states to organize themselves in reaction to what he saw as the Republican threat to the unity of the nation. Milton endorsed the Southern states' withdrawal from the Charleston convention and their subsequent nomination of John C. Breckinridge and Joseph Lane as the South's Democratic ticket for president and vice president. He blamed the Republicans for destroying the "National Conservative" consensus in the North, where, as a result, a majority of the people now opposed the South. Milton advised the Southern states to present a united front to the North by adopting "decisive measures" that would prove to the North and the world the South's determination to stand up for the constitutional rights of free men living in sovereign states and in the territories. Such determination would encourage the North to reflect on the political, social, and economic consequences of disunion, the necessity of which he deplored as he had never been a "Disunionist." In a warning to those in the South who might support the Douglas Democrats (supporters of Northern Democratic nominee Stephen A. Douglas) and the Constitutional Union Party in the upcoming election, Milton urged Southerners to put aside their "petty differences" and unite against the Republicans, who would win if the South were divided. Such an outcome, he predicted, would mean civil war. "Disunion," he warned, "will be proclaimed amid streams of blood."[10]

Even though the Southern Democratic ticket enjoyed more potential support in Florida than their opponents—a majority of Florida newspapers, for example, supported Breckinridge and Lane—Milton had to wage a vigorous campaign. His proclamation that he was no "Disunionist" may have been a strategy to appeal to Whigs and moderate Democrats who were uneasy about secession. The Douglas Democrats had little or no support in Florida, but the Constitutional Unionists and their gubernatorial candidate, Colonel Edward Hopkins, enjoyed support in traditionally Whig West Florida and the Unionist portions of East Florida, which consisted of Jacksonville and the northeast coastal counties.[11]

Milton ended up beating Hopkins in the October election by 1,712 votes; he won in Jackson County and all the cotton belt counties of Middle Florida, except Gadsden. While Hopkins carried most of the counties in West Florida, Milton won a majority of the votes in the eastern and southern counties of the state. Milton would be Florida's next governor, but it would be another year before he could assume office. Governor Perry was elected in October 1856 but began his four-year term in October 1857. When Milton was elected in October 1860, Perry still had a year left in his term.[12]

During that year, Florida and the nation were transformed by secession, the creation of the Confederate States, and civil war. Florida was the third state to leave the Union, behind South Carolina and Mississippi. On January 10, 1861, Florida severed all connections with the United States in an ordinance of secession that declared the state to be a "Sovereign and Independent Nation." The next day, the secession convention delegates proceeded to the east portico of the state capitol to sign the ordinance. Governor-elect Milton officiated at the signing ceremony, standing in for Governor Perry, who was ill. Milton had accepted the inevitability of secession since the Republican victory in November. He now supported secession as the only alternative to Southern submission to the North. Although he would rather have seen all the Southern states leave the Union together, he realized that the states were going to act individually. This being the case, it was better for his home state to leave the Union sooner rather than later, so that Florida could play a role in the creation of a Southern confederacy. Following the signing of the ordinance, Milton presented the delegates with a flag for the new "nation," a white silk banner with three blue stars, which ladies from East Florida had created for the occasion. With this flourish the secession ceremony came to an end.[13]

Milton's year as governor-elect must have been one of the most frustrating periods of his life. The state had 1,350 miles of coastline to defend and few resources to do so. When the war began on April 12, 1861, the Union maintained control of Fort Pickens at the mouth of Pensacola Harbor, Key West, and Fort Jefferson on the Dry Tortugas. Although Governor Perry had succeeded in getting the legislature to raise state regiments, there was too little money in the treasury to provide enough arms for them. Florida also had the smallest population of the Confederate States. It was unrealistic to think that the state could defend itself without substantial manpower and material aid from the Confederate government, which, with the exception of Pensacola, saw little strategic utility in expending its limited resources on defending a state that the Union was unlikely to invade. Given this state of affairs, Governor Perry adopted a policy of full military cooperation with the Confederacy.[14]

During these months between the beginning of the war and the day of his inauguration on October 7, 1861, Milton devoted much time to thinking about, writing on, and observing Florida's preparations for defense. What he learned horrified him. While it was true that by June 1861, Confederate general Braxton Bragg commanded a sizeable army at Pensacola, the rest of the state was virtually defenseless. Two poorly equipped Florida Confederate infantry regiments had the responsibility of defending the two most likely areas of a future Union invasion: the Third Florida Infantry at Amelia Island on the Atlantic coast and the Fourth Florida Infantry on the Gulf coast from Apalachicola to Tampa. Even though he had no constitutional authority to intervene in the state's military affairs, Governor-elect Milton could not refrain from action. As early as April 24, 1861, he telegraphed Confederate president Jefferson Davis and Confederate secretary of war Leroy P. Walker to request that Florida troops remain in the state. While there is no evidence that either Davis or Walker responded, the telegram is an early indicator of the energy and initiative that Milton would display as governor. He refused to stand by or ignore policies and actions he believed were detrimental to the security and well-being of his state. A restless "prince-in-waiting," Milton spent much of the summer of 1860 inspecting military preparations in Florida. In July, he arrived in Pensacola, where Private William D. Randolph reported that Milton attended a dress parade, inspected artillery, and stayed for "two days" to "look around generally."[15]

The impressiveness of the Confederate troop concentration at Pensacola stood in stark contrast to the pitiful state of Florida's overall defensive preparations. After inspecting Gulf defenses in and around Apalachicola in August, Governor-elect Milton wrote Secretary Walker that Apalachicola "is in a condition almost defenseless" and urged that "now is the time to prepare for its defense." He told Walker that the most likely spot for a Union landing was along the shore between St. Joseph's Bay and Apalachicola. Milton pointed out that after inspecting the terrain between the bay and the city he concluded that the "grounds are very favorable for defense by artillery, cavalry, and infantry." He recommended that Walker should place an expert artillerist at Apalachicola to ensure the proper placement and use of cannon and promised that soon after he became governor he would ensure that state troops reinforced any Confederate forces in the area. Walker thanked Milton for his concern but politely dismissed any possibility of a Union attack on Apalachicola as "the enemy will, doubtless, find employment elsewhere." He made it clear to the anxious governor-elect that the Confederacy, not Florida's governor, would direct the defense of the state by informing Milton of the appointment of Brigadier General John B. Grayson as commander of the newly created Department of Middle and East Florida, which was responsible for the defense of Florida from the Apalachicola River in the west to the Atlantic in the east. Walker's remarks did not reassure Milton, who continued to warn Confederate officials of the "most deplorable condition" of Florida's defenses in the days leading up to his inauguration.[16]

After his inauguration at the state capitol in Tallahassee on October 7, 1861, Milton set to work immediately. Now that he was finally governor, he told General Grayson's executive officer that he was resolved to bring order out of chaos: "By god sir, I intend to have all these things straight—trust me for that." Beginning only an hour after his inaugural ceremony, Milton undertook a grueling work schedule of eighteen-hour days, sometimes writing all night. He believed such effort was required to undo the damage done to Florida's defense by his predecessor, Governor Perry, whom Milton blamed for the disorder of the state's military affairs. Upon taking office, Milton found the executive departments in "utter confusion." He was especially appalled by the inaction of Perry's adjutant and inspector general, whose official papers were absent of any "useful or important facts."[17]

Milton condemned Perry for commissioning incompetent officers in the Third and Fourth Florida regiments. He had received reports of drunkenness among the officers of the Third Regiment and complaints about the poor leadership of the Fourth Regiment, whose commanding officer, Colonel Edward Hopkins, he believed was making a mess of the defenses of Apalachicola. Hopkins had removed guns from Apalachicola to reinforce a distant battery on Saint Vincent's Island, which could be easily isolated by Union warships, and was uncooperative with the state troops assigned to defend the port. Colonel Hopkins, according to one of his own officers, was so incompetent that "he cannot even drill a squad of men." Other officers in

Hopkins's regiment enjoyed similar reviews. A Tampa resident bemoaned that the city had been "exceedingly cursed in having damned fools sent here as commanders to protect us."[18]

Many of the actions and dispositions of Florida's recently formed regiments deserved criticism, but then inexperienced officers and men on both sides of the war made poor choices and lacked discipline. The problems were not unique to Florida units but common to green regiments, whether they were wearing blue or gray. While some of Milton's criticisms were valid, many of his critical reports to Richmond were based on politics and a failure to recognize that the Confederacy, faced with a critical shortage of weapons and ammunition, was not going to waste precious military resources on the defense of Florida, a sparsely populated state on the periphery of the new Confederate nation. In his study of Florida Confederate officers and men, Jonathan Sheppard points out that many of Milton's criticisms of Confederate officers, at least in the first months of his administration, were based on politics as much as on their lack of professional skill. For example, Colonel Edward Hopkins, whom Milton criticized for incompetence at Apalachicola, had been the Constitutional Unionist candidate against Milton in the gubernatorial election in 1860. Milton also attacked Lieutenant Colonel W. G. M. Davis, another Whig, and the commander of the First Florida Cavalry Regiment, as a man who had received a prominent Confederate commission despite having been a lukewarm secessionist.[19]

Milton not only attacked Davis the man but also objected to the existence of Davis's cavalry regiment, which he believed to be both wasteful and unnecessary. He told President Davis that the creation of cavalry units took horses away from more pressing agricultural uses, were too expensive to equip, and were not useful for coastal defense. Instead, he argued for a defensive plan based on batteries of heavy guns manned by well-trained Confederate officers and crews, who would defend the most important ports. The ports would be connected by an extensive coastal warning network of small boats and teams of dispatch riders; the boats and riders would signal the approach of the enemy in time for combined arms teams of state troops to react to the invasion. Milton emphasized that his plan would require relatively small numbers of men, who could be maintained at much less expense than the large numbers of cavalry companies being mustered into Confederate service. He could personally vouch for the effectiveness of such a defense. Just days after becoming governor, he led a state force of light artillery from Tallahassee to Saint Marks in reaction to reports that Union troops were about to land and seize the local fort and lighthouse. Although the reported invasion turned out to be false, Milton was proud of the readiness of his state troops, who rushed to defend the coast; they remained on guard until relieved by Confederate troops, who did not arrive for several days due to the unresponsiveness of the local Confederate commander.[20]

Obviously, Milton's plan of defense ignored realities. The Confederacy did not have the resources or the intention to implement a comprehensive defense of Florida. In addition, given the great distances between Florida's ports, cavalry, which could react quickly to Union incursions, was better suited for the state's defense than were concentrations of infantry and artillery. The underlying point of much of Milton's military correspondence with Richmond, however, was not this or that strategy but the fact that the Confederate government left Florida to largely fend for itself. Focused on the main fronts in Virginia and Tennessee, Richmond could not be concerned about such distant outposts as Apalachicola and Amelia Island. True, thousands of Confederate troops remained stationed in a standoff with Union troops at Pensacola, but even that city had been largely forgotten by the spring of 1862, as the Confederacy transferred most of General Bragg's regiments to reinforce Confederate troops in Tennessee after the fall of Forts Henry and Donelson. Lacking Confederate support, Milton believed that Florida must rely on state troops to defend its shores. He would devote much of his time as governor trying to create and maintain a reliable force of state troops and to focus the state's limited military resources on the defense of Middle Florida and portions of West Florida.[21]

Milton believed that Apalachicola was the key to the region's defense. He was obsessed with the protection of the town and the security of the Apalachicola River throughout his governorship. The port had once been Florida's most prosperous city, a center of the cotton trade for Florida, Georgia, and Alabama Counties located along the Apalachicola, Flint, and Chattahoochee Rivers. Although its portion of the cotton trade dropped substantially with the coming of the railroad to Columbus, Georgia, in the 1850s, a massive cotton crop in 1860 gave the town new life. In 1861, the port remained the principal exporter of cotton from West and Middle Florida, especially in Milton's home county of Jackson, which contained some of Florida's most productive cotton land. Milton had a personal stake in the security of Apalachicola. A Union blockade of the port would end local cotton shipments, while Union capture of the city could lead to an invasion of Middle and West Florida, the occupation of Jackson County, and a Union thrust up the Chattahoochee to Columbus. The economic impact of such a scenario would be devastating for the economy of the tristate region and personally for Governor Milton, whose cherished Sylvania might be lost to Yankee rule. To avoid this outcome, Milton continually stressed the need for a proper defense of Apalachicola, lobbying each successive Confederate secretary of war, President Davis, neighboring governors, Confederate commanders in Florida, and just about anyone else who would listen.[22]

Unfortunately for Milton, the Confederate government never saw Apalachicola as a defensive priority, even in Florida, which was at the bottom of Richmond's strategic concerns. Besides Pensacola, which was so isolated from the rest of the state that it constituted an independent front, the Confederate Army focused on the defense of Amelia Island on the Atlantic as the most likely target of any Union attack. Just north of Jacksonville, the island would make a good base for Union operations in northeast Florida and was vulnerable to naval assault. By the end of 1861, most Confederate troops in northeast Florida were concentrated on Amelia Island. Despite Milton's efforts to lobby Brigadier General James H. Trapier, who replaced General Grayson as the commander of Middle and East Florida following the latter's death from consumption, to focus instead on the defense of Apalachicola, the Confederate government refused to change its defensive priorities, although Milton did succeed in getting Trapier to establish his headquarters in Tallahassee rather than in East Florida.[23]

Although in November 1861 his military concerns increased after a Union flotilla captured Port Royal, South Carolina, and consequently threatened the coasts of Georgia and Florida, Milton faced a more immediate threat to his own political future. At the end of December 1861, the state's secession convention was called back into session to address financial problems that had occurred as a result of discrepancies between financial laws enacted by the legislature and financial ordinances passed by the state convention. An important part of the convention's financial investigation was to determine whether Milton had mistakenly or intentionally contributed to the financial woes of the state by using funds that he was not authorized to spend. The convention required that Milton report on the financial affairs of his administration, including details about the organization, mission, and expenses of the state troops. While financial investigation was the official reason for the reappearance of the convention, politically aware Floridians knew that the convention had also assembled for the "purpose either of deposing his Excellency or limiting his power."[24]

Milton's enemies in the convention were joined in their criticism of the governor by much of the Florida press. Comparing Milton to a physician guilty of malpractice, Tallahassee's *Florida Sentinel* said Florida was dying after being "purged, vomited, bled, [and] blistered to death by Milton's ministrations." The *Sentinel* was not alone in its negative assessment of Milton's actions. With the exception of the *Marianna Patriot*, Milton's hometown paper, by 1862 it was hard to find one newspaper in the state that supported his administration. Milton created much of the bad press himself during his first legislative session as governor when he denounced all newspapers that criticized his administration, especially those owned by natives of the North, and called for laws that would ensure that "no Yankee of doubtful character be permitted to edit a public journal at the South." Not surprisingly, the press did not favor such legislation. The *Monticello Family Friend*, one of the "Yankee-owned" newspapers, denounced Milton as a "corrupt demagogue and pretended patriot" who "would have every press in Florida that dares to speak free and untrammeled, suppressed—so that his evil deeds may escape scrutiny."[25]

Opponents of Milton's military policies used the convention to attack his support of General Trapier and the militia. The convention passed resolutions against Trapier for having his headquarters in Tallahassee rather than on Amelia Island, the most "threatened and exposed point in the State." The resolutions questioned Trapier's manhood, suggesting the general was too soft to endure the hardships of camp life and too cowardly to place himself in proximity to the enemy. After condemning Trapier, and by implication Milton for supporting the general, the convention moved against Milton's cherished state troops. Arguing that the state could no longer afford the state troops, which were superfluous since the Confederacy had assumed responsibility for the defense of Florida, the convention moved to deny Milton use of the state militia, the most tangible evidence of his authority as commander in chief. On January 27, 1862, the convention passed an ordinance requiring the governor to transfer all state troops into Confederate service by March 10, 1862; any troops remaining in state service after that date would be disbanded.[26]

The same day the convention voted to disband the militia, a majority of the delegates voted to create a new executive body for Florida. Potentially the most damaging blow to Milton's authority, the Florida Executive Council was designed to act as a check on Milton's power. The convention had previously authorized Governor Perry to appoint "Counsellors of State," who were to consult and advise the governor on policy. The idea for the new council, however, was inspired by South Carolina's convention, which, in opposition to Governor Francis W. Pickens, created a powerful executive council that acted in all respects as a true committee of public safety, planning and managing the state's war effort. Florida's executive council was supposed to have similar authority: it consisted of four members entrusted with the same powers as the governor, who was supposed to cooperate with them in carrying out such duties as declaring martial law, maintaining the police, procuring arms for war, and appointing state officials.[27]

Fortunately for Milton, Florida's executive council never enjoyed the status or power obtained by the South Carolina executive body, whose members ran the executive departments and were some of the state's most prominent citizens. While all of Florida's four executive councilmen were members of the convention, only one of them, Mariano D. Papy, had achieved statewide distinction: he served as Florida attorney general from 1853 to 1860. Governor Milton was not impressed. He made it clear he did not recognize the convention's right to legislate or revise the state constitution by creating a new executive authority. While he did not recognize their right to exist, Milton said that for the sake of harmony he was willing to work with the council, but he would meet with them only when he considered their "attendance necessary at the Capitol." The council members seemed to have been too unsure of their own authority to voice much opposition to Milton's objections. They met with the governor only five times during the council's existence and usually agreed to endorse Milton's policies. These included many military related measures: empowering local officials to collect any state arms still in private hands; allowing the governor to employ the state coast guard when needed; expropriating private telegraph equipment to construct a telegraph line from Tallahassee east to Baldwin; approving Confederate troops requisitions; and even endorsing Milton's nomination of his son, William H. Milton, to the position of adjutant and inspector general.[28]

These cooperative actions had no impact on the immediate military crisis in the state, however. On March 4, 1862, Union troops occupied Fernandina on Amelia Island and were soon in control of Jacksonville, while Union gunboats pushed up the St. Johns River. As the clock ticked toward the March 10 termination date for Florida's state troops, the nervous council members approved Milton's request that it allow the state troops in Apalachicola to remain in place past March 10 to maintain the city's defenses in the face of what Milton believed was imminent Union invasion. The executive council even resolved to reestablish the state militia, but continued political and press opposition eventually defeated these measures: the state troops disbanded, Apalachicola was left undefended, and the militia remained inactive. Apalachicola remained a no-man's-land for the rest of the war, visited occasionally by a Union warship, Confederate irregulars, or the odd blockade-runner.[29]

Although the loss of Apalachicola was a tremendous blow for Milton and his contention that Confederate neglect, disloyal citizens, and the selfish interests of state politicians had put Florida in "a hopeless position," the governor's belief in the Confederate cause and his willingness to sacrifice for ultimate victory seem to have been strengthened by the military crisis in the spring of 1862. He told Confederate Secretary of War Judah P. Benjamin that he was willing to see his state sacrificed "if the sacrifice of Florida is necessary to secure the sacred rights claimed by the people of the Confederate States." Shaken by recent Confederate defeats in Tennessee and the attack on his own state, Milton recognized that Florida could secure its independence only if the Confederacy as a whole prevailed in the war.[30]

One way to realize this goal was to tie Florida closer to the military and economic resources of the Confederate States, especially to Georgia, which was second only to Virginia in industrial strength. At the beginning of the war Florida had no direct rail links to either of its neighboring states, Alabama and Georgia. In May 1861, the Alabama and Florida Railroad completed a connection between Montgomery and Pensacola, but there was no link between Pensacola and the rest of the state across the Panhandle. When Milton became governor in October 1861, Florida's Pensacola and Georgia Railroad was constructing a connection between its line at Live Oak, Florida, and Georgia's Atlantic and Gulf Railroad at Lawton, Georgia, but the project stalled on the Florida side due to the Pensacola and Georgia's lack of iron rails. Milton tried to obtain a loan from the Confederate government to purchase the rails from the Florida Railroad Company, which controlled a line that ran across the state from Cedar Keys on the Gulf to Fernandina on the Atlantic. When the Confederate Congress ignored his loan request, Milton used the Union attack on Amelia Island and Fernandina in March 1862 as an excuse to begin the removal of a portion of the Florida Railroad before the valuable iron fell into Union hands. Since the Union had already captured Cedar Keys in January 1862, Milton believed their capture of Fernandina made the remaining miles of track between the two ports largely useless for military or economic purposes. In 1863, he resolved to secure the remaining track for use in completing the line from Live Oak to Lawton and to build another extension from Quincy, Florida, to the Apalachicola River, which would provide an additional avenue of transportation between Georgia and Florida.[31]

To achieve these objectives, Milton had to contend with the opposition of the powerful owner of the Florida Railroad, former US senator David Levy Yulee, who was determined to keep his railroad intact. Throughout 1863 and into the summer of 1864, Milton fought Yulee for control of the rails. In months of correspondence, the two men argued the legal, military, and political merits of government versus private ownership of the railroad's iron in time of war. Milton had the support of the Confederate War Department, President Davis, and General P. G. T. Beauregard, commander of the Department of South Carolina, Georgia, and Florida, who all agreed with Milton's plan to confiscate Yulee's railroad for Confederate military use. In March 1864, with the Union preparing to invade Georgia, the Confederacy wanted to complete the Live Oak to Lawton connection to facilitate the transportation of beef and other agricultural goods from Florida into Georgia.[32]

When the War Department ordered the army to remove the Florida Railroad iron to build the connecting line, Yulee turned to the state courts and obtained an injunction to stop the army's confiscation of the rails. In an interesting turn of events, which showed his innate tendency to support states' rights, Milton supported the court's injunction. He said the Confederate government could not ignore the authority of a state court. Milton wanted the Confederacy to have the iron, but he wanted the transfer done according to civil procedures, not martial law. The Confederate government insisted it had the right to the rails under congressional impressment laws passed in 1863. If a state court could deny the confiscation of the rails, it could deny the Confederacy the use of other property and goods as well. Although Milton supported the Confederate position when it came to conscription and the need for the interstate rail link, he had been a staunch opponent of the impressment laws due to the terrible effect of the operation of impressment on Florida's economy and the morale of its citizens. The Florida Railroad case entered the jurisdiction of the Confederate District Court for the Eastern District of Florida in the summer of 1864. The district court ruled in favor of the army, which now had the authority to finally possess Yulee's rails. Delays in construction, however, prevented the opening of the

Live Oak to Lawton connection until March 1865, too late to affect the war in Florida or anywhere else in the Confederacy.[33]

Although Milton expressed unreserved distaste for the impressment laws in 1863, he had already made a name for himself in the Confederate press as one of the staunchest gubernatorial supporters of President Davis and one of Davis's most controversial policies: conscription. Inoffensively titled "An Act to Provide for the Further Public Defense," the Conscription Act or "Conscript Act," which became law in the Confederate States on April 16, 1862, authorized the president to draft all able-bodied white male residents of the Confederate States between the ages of eighteen and thirty-five for three years of military service. To encourage initial recruitment, the Conscription Act allowed those men not currently in service who were eligible for the draft to volunteer in the period before actual enrollments began. By volunteering before being drafted, men could avoid the stigma the public attached to conscripts, whose courage and patriotism were called into question because they had not volunteered to fight. Those men eligible for conscription were given the option of furnishing a substitute should they choose not to serve. The president could obtain the consent of the governors for the use of state officers as conscription or enrolling agents. If that consent was not forthcoming, the president could use Confederate officers to enroll the men. Once enrolled, the secretary of war assigned the men to units from their own state.[34]

The unprecedented nature of conscription—there had never been a national draft in America before 1862—roused public debate about its necessity and constitutionality. Newspapers in Florida reflected opinions on conscription that were found in newspapers across the Confederacy. Editorial opponents of the draft denounced conscription as a violation of individual and states' rights, calling it "the devil's own invention for the subjugation of liberty," and warned that by stripping the governors of their military powers, conscription made the states the "creatures of the Confederate Government." Southerners hated conscription. They believed it demeaned patriotism by pressuring men to serve instead of relying on their willingness to volunteer. And they resented the inequities of the draft, which allowed the wealthy to avoid service by hiring substitutes and placed more value on those who practiced certain trades and professions by exempting those men from service while forcing other less fortunate or less skilled men to fight. Despite the draft's unpopularity, however, most Southerners and newspapers seemed to recognize the necessity for conscription in the midst of the recruitment crisis that confronted the Confederacy in the spring of 1862. Conscription might not be popular, the *Tallahassee Florida Sentinel* observed, but "imperious necessity ensured its passage."[35]

Governor Milton agreed with the *Sentinel*'s assessment. In his annual message to the General Assembly on November 17, 1862, he addressed the legitimacy of the Conscription Act. He told the lawmakers that while he would have preferred for the states to have enacted conscription, now was not the time to question its constitutionally. Such a debate should be left to the courts. Congress had enacted the laws out of military necessity. It was therefore essential "during the existence of the war, to watch and baffle the purposes of the enemy, than with skeptical apprehensions to criticize and defeat the purposes of the Government of our choice, administered by statesmen of our own selection."[36]

Milton was more selective in his endorsement of Confederate exemption practices. He criticized the Exemption Act of October 11, 1862, for extending conscription exemptions to such occupations as millers, tanners, and salt makers without any state supervision of the individuals engaged in those pursuits. Milton was especially concerned that many of the men who claimed to be salt makers were really draft evaders; he received reports that Floridians and men from neighboring states had descended on the Panhandle coast ostensibly to make salt but in fact were trying to avoid conscription. He argued that if salt makers and others engaged in business were to be exempted, they should be forced to sell their goods at reasonable prices to prevent them from reaping profits at the expense of less fortunate citizens. When the Union began to conduct raids to disrupt the production of the saltworks, Milton supported legislation to force the salt workers to defend themselves rather than appealing to the Confederacy to defend men who may have been avoiding military service. The legislation authorized the governor to appoint three officers to organize the salt workers for coastal defense. All able-bodied men engaged in salt making had to participate or they could not continue their occupation, and nor would the state compensate them for their service.[37]

The governor was not as critical of exemptions that applied to his own planter class. He supported the provision in the October exemption act that called for the exemption of one white male of draft age for supervision of plantations containing twenty or more slaves. Milton believed the act was crucial to prevent slave escapes and slave rebellions and to maintain agricultural production for the benefit of the fighting men's families at home. He maintained support for the "Twenty Nigger Law," despite receiving troubling information about its unpopularity with poor and lower-middle class whites, who resented the idea that the rich would be allowed to stay home while they fought and died.[38]

Milton had reason to be apprehensive about domestic unrest. By 1864, with so many of its men of military age on service out of state, its agricultural resources at the mercy of Confederate impressment officers, and its ports closed by the Union naval blockade, Confederate Florida was in an increasingly vulnerable and perilous condition. The Union took advantage of this situation in February 1864, when its forces occupied Jacksonville for a fourth time—Union troops had occupied the city for brief periods in 1862 and 1863—and launched an attack toward Lake City that culminated in the Battle of Olustee on February 20. Although Olustee was a Confederate victory that blocked further Union advances from the east, Milton remained preoccupied with the defense of the area from Jackson County along the Apalachicola to Tallahassee, which he maintained was the most vulnerable and likely target for a Union invasion.[39]

His concern for this region's defense was compounded in 1864 by the growing threat posed by bands of deserters and draft dodgers, or "lay outs," in West and Middle Florida. Ethelred Philips, a physician and farmer living in Marianna, wrote to his brother in North Carolina that "the country for fifty miles between here and the Gulf is now infested with hundreds of deserters in communication with the Blockaders." Milton reported to General Beauregard that Jackson, Washington, Calhoun, and Holmes Counties were swarming with deserters from Florida and other states. The deserters had joined forces with Unionists in the area and were in constant contact with enemy ships along the Gulf. Treasonous bands equaled the number of loyal troops, and fifty-two men from one of the best companies in the district had deserted with their arms in hand. Milton told Beauregard that he had already asked the Confederate government to send General Edward A. Perry's Florida Brigade from Virginia to Florida to fight deserters and gather new recruits to make good the losses the regiment had sustained in 1863.[40]

The situation had become so bad that Milton received information from Chattahoochee, Florida, that a hundred deserters were planning to ambush and capture him as he traveled between that town and his plantation in Jackson County. Captain James F. McClellan, stationed in Marianna, suggested that Milton suspend the writ of habeas corpus in the region to suppress the traitors. Milton rarely addressed the question of suspending habeas corpus. In response to McClellan's request, he told Beauregard that he believed the governor had the constitutional authority to suspend the writ, but he believed that the Confederate court judge in Marianna would insist upon the writ. While Milton thought that suspension of the writ might "excite alarm, increase dissatisfaction, and produce no decisive and beneficial result," he urged that something had to be done to address the desertion crisis. He recommended that it might be necessary to have the president declare martial law in the region. Milton asked Beauregard to submit his views to the president through the secretary of war.[41]

The Confederate Army did take action against the deserters along the Gulf, but Richmond did not see fit to return Perry's Brigade to Florida, suspend the writ of habeas corpus, or declare martial law. Instead, in March 1864, Confederate forces moved against the deserters and disaffected citizens in Taylor and Lafayette Counties but were able to capture only a couple of suspects. The deserters enjoyed support from the local communities. It was impossible to track down the large number of men now hiding in swamps and forests along the Gulf. Desertion and disaffection only increased as Confederate military fortunes waned. In September 1864, Henry W. Feilden, a visitor from South Carolina, wrote to his wife about the deserters taking refuge in Florida: "Throughout this state but especially on the coast there are large numbers of deserters and desperadoes who have fled from our armies and hid themselves in these almost inaccessible wilds. They issue out from their strongholds at times and commit all sorts of depredations, aided and abetted by their Yankee allies." The Confederacy managed to return only 220 Florida men to military service out of the more than 2,219 Florida soldiers the army had recorded as deserters.[42]

Milton's support for tough measures against deserters was not unusual. Every Confederate governor waged war against deserter bands in their respective states. One area where Milton differed with many of his fellow governors was in his rejection of any blockade-running not sanctioned by the Confederate government. In February 1864, the Confederate Congress passed a bill giving the president the power to regulate all foreign trade. The president could control the exportation of cotton, tobacco, military and naval stores, rice, sugar, and molasses. Luxury items were specifically prohibited as items of import. On March 5, Davis, Secretary of War James A. Seddon, and Secretary of the Treasury Christopher G. Memminger approved regulations that included a provision making it illegal for any owner of a vessel to refuse the Confederate government the use of one half of the vessel's tonnage on both the outward and homeward voyage. Vessels not in compliance would not be allowed to leave Confederate-controlled ports.[43]

Georgia Governor Joseph E. Brown opposed the regulation, which forced vessels to devote half of their cargo space to Confederate property. The most outspoken opponent of Jefferson Davis's leadership and policies among the Confederate governors, Brown had been especially critical of conscription. He saw the tonnage regulation as another example of Richmond's interference in state affairs: the regulation meant that the states would be forced to sacrifice half of the cargo space on state-chartered vessels to the Confederate government. Brown asked Milton and the governors of Mississippi, Alabama, North Carolina, and South Carolina to support him in asking Congress to repeal the cargo space restriction.[44]

Milton refused Brown's request. He did not think it proper for governors to ask Congress to legislate on a particular subject. If a governor disagreed with an act of Congress, Milton said the proper way to address the matter was for the state legislature to pass a resolution asking the state's congressional delegation to take action on the subject. He feared that if each state sought to supply its citizens at home and in the military independently of the Confederate government, "the result would be alike disastrous to the Confederate States and the several States." Separate state action during the war would "endanger the stability of the Confederate Government, if not entirely destroy it." Milton told Brown the states should try "to avoid all conflicts and competition between the State and Confederate authorities for political power, or commercial privileges, at all events during the existing war." After the Confederacy had won its independence, it would then be proper for the states and the Confederate government to address constitutional issues, including states' rights.[45]

By January 1865, it was clear that the goal of Confederate independence was becoming less likely with each passing day. Milton was deeply pessimistic about the war's progress. He wrote to Representative R. B. Hilton, one of Florida's Confederate congressmen, about Florida's desperate straits: "Cut off as Florida is, from all reliable sources for help, infested with tories and deserters, and threatened by the enemy—having but few troops in the State and no ready means of concentrating them—under existing circumstances, our prospects are indeed gloomy." Milton was worried that a portion of General William Tecumseh Sherman's victorious Union Army in Savannah might be diverted for an invasion of Southwest Georgia and Middle Florida.[46]

Although he was reluctant to bother President Davis, who was concerned "with much more important matters," Milton believed it was his duty to offer Davis a four-point plan of action for the defense of the region: assign responsibility for the defense of Southwest Georgia to the Military District of Florida; keep the Confederate reserves and militia in the counties for defense; remove the rail from the Albany and Gulf Railroad near Savannah to prevent the enemy's use of the railroad to transport their forces to Thomasville, Georgia; and construct a railroad from Thomasville to Albany, Georgia, and from Quincy, Florida, to the Apalachicola River. Milton told Davis that with the cooperation of the militia and reserves of Florida and Georgia, and with the help of Governor Brown, the region could be defended against a relatively large Union force. The Florida governor's plan made some sense on paper, but there was no chance of its implementation. Given the hopeless military situation facing the Confederacy by 1865, Milton might just have well have urged Davis to lead a march on Washington instead of asking the president to build new railroads in a forgotten corner of the war amid the South's military and economic devastation.[47]

The final threat to Confederate Florida did not come from the north through Georgia but from the south through the Gulf. On March 6, 1865, Confederate and Union forces met south of Tallahassee at the Battle of Natural Bridge, where the Confederates halted the Union advance and forced their retreat to the coast. Governor Milton had some responsibility for this victory, which thwarted a possible Union capture of Tallahassee and proved to be one of the last Confederate victories of the war. Ever since the secession convention had disbanded the state troops in March 1862, Milton had urged the General Assembly to reconstitute a state defense force. In July 1864, the legislature finally agreed to create a new state militia consisting of those seventeen-year-olds and men between the ages of forty-five and fifty able to carry arms. These requirements matched those of the Confederate reserve forces organized in each state. It was the reserves and the militia that constituted most of the force that defeated the Union troops at Natural Bridge.[48]

Celebration of the victory in Tallahassee was short-lived, however. It was clear that the South would still lose the war despite the individual bravery of men and boys. The strain of the last few months of war and the prospect of certain defeat darkened Milton's outlook and caused a marked deterioration of his physical and mental health. As he saw the troops off to Natural Bridge, among whom was his young son, John Milton Jr., the governor looked "overworked and ill." Milton had always been concerned for his family's safety during the war. Although he visited home as often as possible, Milton worked in Tallahassee, while Caroline and the children remained at Sylvania in Jackson County, which the governor believed was more secure from the threat of attack. His was particularly distressed when the Union raided the county in September 1864, briefly capturing Marianna after a short but bloody fight. Worried about his family, exhausted from work, and depressed about the looming defeat of the Confederacy, Milton returned to Sylvania for the last time on April 1, 1865. Not long after he arrived, he entered his study and killed himself using a family shotgun.[49]

With his suicide, Milton became the only prominent Confederate political or military leader to take his own life: Edmund Ruffin, the fire-eating Southern nationalist, but non-office holder, killed himself at war's end wrapped in the Confederate flag. Some historians view Milton's manner of death as a final act of loyalty to the Confederate cause. In support of this theory, they often cite his last annual message to the General Assembly in November 1864, in which he said that "death would be preferable to reunion." While it is more likely that his suicide was the result of mental and physical exhaustion, the loyalty theory does point to his unwavering support for Jefferson Davis and the Confederacy throughout his governorship.[50]

By his actions, Milton reinforced his belief that Florida's fate was tied to the victory or defeat of the Confederate States: he did nothing to hinder conscription and even made sure that more Floridians were available for military service by limiting state exemptions; he was unceasing in his advocacy of cooperation between the states as long as that cooperation was in support of Confederate government policies and not a design to criticize and hinder Richmond; and he would not countenance independent wartime trade by the states, endorsing instead Confederate restrictions on private and state-supported blockade-running. Even when he did criticize the Confederate government, Milton never let his negative opinions of Confederate policies interfere with his high regard for President Davis.[51]

Milton's faith in Davis's leadership never wavered. He took full advantage of Davis's early invitation to establish a frequent and open correspondence between them. Milton poured out his concerns, frustrations, achievements, and loyalty in his letters to Davis. For Milton, any popular sense of Confederate nationalism among the people of the South was unthinkable without the leadership of Jefferson Davis: "The Confederacy was more truly his creation than many guessed; his spirit compelled it, his devotion gave it purpose." If Davis remained strong, the Confederacy would too. At least this was the belief of Milton and other loyalists of the president. Despite his serious concerns about aspects of conscription, impressment, and the Confederate government's continual neglect of Florida's defenses, Milton remained a steadfast promoter of Confederate unity and Davis's leadership. Although he maintained his belief in the doctrine of states' rights and was always ready to defend the sovereignty of his state, Milton was a pragmatic loyalist who was able to put aside his constitutional concerns about Confederate policies, such as conscription, in order to strengthen the Davis administration and the war for Southern independence.[52]

Notes

1. The only published biography of Milton is John Adams, *Warrior at Heart: Governor John Milton, King Cotton, and Rebel Florida 1860–1865* (Victoria, British Columbia: Friesen Press, 2015). Another study of his governorship is Ridgeway Boyd Murphree, "Rebel Sovereigns: The Civil War Leadership of Governors John Milton of Florida and Joseph E. Brown of Georgia, 1861–1865" (PhD diss., Florida State University, 2006).

2. For Milton's family history and his early years, see Murphree, "Rebel Sovereigns," 1, 3–4, and William Lamar Gammon, "Governor John Milton of Florida, Confederate States of America" (MA thesis, University of Florida, 1948), 1–20.

3. Murphree, "Rebel Sovereigns," 4–8.

4. Ibid., 8–9.

5. Ibid., 9.

6. Ibid.

7. See Gammon, "Governor John Milton," 20–21, 30, 38–42, and Daisy Parker, "John Milton, Governor of Florida 1861–1865" (MA thesis, University of Virginia, 1940), 38–40, for Milton's political career before 1860.

8. Murphree, "Rebel Sovereigns," 11–13.

9. Ibid., 13–14.

10. Ibid., 14–16; For Milton's letter accepting the Florida Democratic nomination for governor, see "Acceptance of Gen. Milton," *Tampa Florida Peninsular*, August 4, 1860.

11. Sydney J. Weinburg, "Slavery and Secession in Florida" (MA thesis, University of Florida, 1940), 171–73.

12. Parker, "Governor John Milton," 53–55.

13. Murphree, "Rebel Sovereigns," 26–27.

14. For Florida's economic and military status at the beginning of 1861 and Perry's direction of the state's defense, see Murphree, "Rebel Sovereigns," 32–34, 37–38.

15. Ibid., 58–60; William Duval Randolph to Arthur Moray Randolph, July 23, 1861, Randolph Family Papers, M75-86, State Archives of Florida, Tallahassee, mentions Milton's visit to inspect the defenses at Pensacola.

16. John Milton to Leroy P. Walker, August 16, 1861, *The War of the Rebellion: A Compilation of the Official Records of the Union and Confederate Armies*, series 1, vol. 1 (Washington, DC: Government Printing Office, 1880–1901), 471–72 (hereinafter cited as *Official Records)*; Leroy P. Walker to John Milton, August 30, 1861, *Official Records*, ser. 1, vol. 1, 473; John Milton to Stephen R. Mallory, October 2, 1861, *Official Records*, ser. 1, vol. 6, 287–88.

17. There is no copy of Milton's inaugural address. For references to his inauguration, see "Gen. John Milton," *Monticello Family Friend*, October 12, 1861, and the *Columbus Daily Sun*, October 12, 1861. Confederate first lieutenant Charles Wood attended the inauguration and had several conversations with Milton. See Wood's diary on Milton's determination to reorganize Florida's administration and defenses: Charles Wood Diary, October 18, 1861, MS 2734, Hargrett Rare Book and Manuscript Library, University of Georgia. Milton speaks of his dismay over the condition of Governor Perry's military administration in John Milton to Stephen R. Mallory, November 2, 1861, Territorial and State Governor's Letterbooks, vol. 6, John Milton, October 1861 to November 1863, Record Group (RG) 101, Series 32, State Archives of Florida, Tallahassee, Florida (hereinafter cited as Milton Letterbook, 1861–1863; this letterbook is a photocopy of the original, which is located at the Florida Historical Society, Alma Clyde Field Library, Cocoa, Florida).

18. John Milton to Stephen R. Mallory, October 2, 1861, *Official Records*, ser. 1, vol. 6, 287–88; John Drysdale to John Milton, October 31, 1861, and James Gettis to H. V. Snell, October 25, 1861, in Letters Received by the Confederate Secretary of War, RG 109, Microcopy 437, Roll 14, National Archives, Washington, DC.

19. Jonathan C. Sheppard, *By the Noble Daring of Her Sons: The Florida Brigade of the Army of Tennessee* (Tuscaloosa: University of Alabama Press, 2012), 28–29, 32–34; Murphree, "Rebel Sovereigns," 61.

20. John Milton to Stephen R. Mallory, November 2, 1861, Milton Letterbook, 1861–1863; John Milton to Jefferson Davis, October 18, 1861, *Official Records*, ser. 1, vol. 6, 290–91; John Milton to J. Wayles Baker, October 17, 1861, Milton Letterbook, 1861–1863.

21. Murphree, "Rebel Sovereigns," 64, 74–75.

22. Ibid., 64–66.

23. Ibid., 68–70.

24. William C. Havard, "The Florida Executive Council, 1862," *Florida Historical Quarterly* 33, no. 2 (October 1954): 77–96; Unknown to Edward L' Engle, December 22, 1861, Edward L'Engle Papers, MS 425, Southern Historical Collection, University Library, University of North Carolina, Chapel Hill, North Carolina.

25. "Health of Florida, and Gov. Milton as Physician of the State," *Tallahassee*

Florida Sentinel, January 21, 1861; Special message of the Governor, December 5, 1861, *Journal of the Proceedings of the House of Representatives of the General Assembly of the State of Florida at its Eleventh Session, begun and Held in the City of Tallahassee, on Monday, November 18, 1861* (Tallahassee, FL: Office of the Floridian and Journal, 1861), 182–83; "Gov. Milton's Special Message and Ourself," *Monticello Family Friend*, December 14, 1861.

26. Resolutions relative to Brig. Gen. J. H. Trapier, *Journal of the Convention of the People of Florida* (Tallahassee, FL: Office of the Floridian and Journal, 1862), 44–45 (hereinafter cited as *Convention Journal)*; Ordinance on State troops, *Convention Journal*, 103.

27. Havard, "Florida Executive Council," 1862, 77–96.

28. Murphree, "Rebel Sovereigns," 73.

29. Ibid., 74.

30. John Milton to Judah P. Benjamin, March 5, 1862, *Official Records*, ser. 1, vol. 6, 402–3.

31. Murphree, "Rebel Sovereigns," 120–26.

32. Ibid.

33. Ibid.

34. Ibid., 78–79.

35. "Military Conscription, *Savannah Daily Morning News*, April 10, 1862; "The Conscription Law," *Tallahassee Florida Sentinel*, May 5, 1863.

36. Message of the Governor of Florida, November 17, 1862, *Journal of the Proceedings of the House of Representatives of the General Assembly of the State of Florida* (Tallahassee, FL: Office of the Floridian and Journal, 1862), 11–13.

37. Murphree, "Rebel Sovereigns," 103

38. Ibid., 103–4.

39. Ibid., 153–54.

40. E. Philips to James J. Philips, January 14, 1864, James Jones Philips Papers, M972, Southern Historical Collection, University Library, University of North Carolina, Chapel Hill, North Carolina; John Milton to P. G. T. Beauregard, January 29, 1864, Territorial and State Governor's Letterbooks, vol. 7, John Milton, November 1863 to May 1865, Record Group (RG) 101, Series 32, State Archives of Florida, Tallahassee, Florida (hereinafter cited as Milton Letterbook, 1863–1865).

41. Luke Lott to John Milton, February 4, 1864, Milton Letterbook, 1863–1865; J. F. McClellan to John Milton, January 20, 1864, Milton Letterbook, 1863–1865; John Milton to P. G. T. Beauregard, February 4, 1864, Milton Letterbook, 1863–1865; John Milton to P. G. T. Beauregard, February 5, 1864, *Official Records*, ser. 1, vol. 35, part I, 563–64.

42. John E. Johns, *Florida during the Civil War* (Gainesville: University of Florida Press, 1963), 160–69; Henry W. Feilden to My Darling, September 1, 1864, Henry Wemyss Feilden Papers, 1851–1949, MS 1015, Box 11, Folder 25, South Carolina

Historical Society, Charleston, South Carolina; John F. Reiger, "Deprivation, Disaffection, and Desertion in Confederate Florida," *Florida Historical Quarterly* 48, no. 3 (January 1970): 279–98.

43. Murphree, "Rebel Sovereigns," 158.

44. Ibid., 159.

45. John Milton to Joseph E. Brown, April 14, 1864, Allen D. Candler, compiler, *Confederate Records of the State of Georgia*, vol. 3 (Atlanta: Charles P. Byrd State Printer, 1909–1910), 497–500.

46. John Milton to R. B. Hilton, January 9, 1865, Milton Letterbook, 1863–1865.

47. John Milton to Jefferson Davis, January 17, 1865, Milton Letterbook, 1863–1865.

48. Johns, *Florida during the Civil War*, 201–5.

49. Ibid., 205; For the role of the West Florida cadets and John Milton Jr. at Natural Bridge, see David J. Coles, "Florida's Seed Corn: The History of the West Florida Seminary During the Civil War," *Florida Historical Quarterly* 77, no. 3 (Winter 1999): 283–319; Gammon, "Governor John Milton of Florida," 255–58.

50. Murphree, "Rebel Sovereigns," 165–66.

51. Ibid., 166.

52. Ibid., 166–67. Milton named one of his sons after the Confederate president.

6

"The Church Did Not Die"

Religion in Florida during the Civil War

David B. Parker

On Thursday, January 3, 1861, sixty men met in Tallahassee to decide Florida's future course. Abraham Lincoln, "a wily abolitionist," had been elected president of the United States, and the state's legislature called for a special convention of the people to answer the question on everyone's mind: Should Florida follow South Carolina's lead and leave the Union? John C. Pelot, of Alachua County, opened the convention by noting that "the eyes of the world are upon us." He acknowledged that differences of opinion existed among the members of the convention but said, "We . . . must stand shoulder to shoulder in the great work before us."[1]

Pelot's phrases bring to mind the words of another leader preparing his people for the creation of a new society—John Winthrop, in 1630, preaching to the Puritans onboard the *Arbella*: "We must be knit together, in this work, as one man. . . . The eyes of all people are upon us." The New England setting for Winthrop's words might make Pelot's surprising, but the religious rhetoric at the Florida convention should surprise no one. Secession was not a religious act, but it was often couched in religious terms.

On December 8, 1860, under the headline "Bible Enjoins Secession from Abolitionists," a Tallahassee newspaper simply quoted 1 Timothy 6:1–5, a well-known passage that began with St. Paul laying down the duty of servants to obey their masters and ended with the following: "If any man teach otherwise . . . he is proud, knowing nothing. . . : from such withdraw thyself." Governor Madison Starke Perry, an Episcopalian, in a letter addressed to the members of the General Assembly shortly after the state seceded, used an Old Testament image: "It is manifest that the inhabitants of the non-slaveholding States are hardening their hearts against all signs and evidences which justify our exodus from among them, and that like

Egyptians of old, they are not willing that we should depart in peace from our state of bondage, but in the spirit of the oppressor, they seek to tighten their grasp upon a people who have been to them an abundant source of profit and advantage, and are preparing their host to follow after and to return us to a captivity, the latter end of which must be worse than the first."[2]

On August 26, 1861, John DuBose, a Presbyterian minister, spoke to the soldiers of the newly formed Company M (the Howell Guards) of the Second Florida Infantry Regiment as they prepared to leave Tallahassee for the battlefield. Like Governor Perry, Rev. DuBose saw the situation in Old Testament terms. He compared the soldiers to "the grand army of Israel," who, under Joshua, captured Canaan. "Entire families were exterminated" during this campaign, the preacher noted; "cities were destroyed, and lands laid waste." But in all this, "we can behold the people of the Lord engaged. They were accomplishing the double purpose of achieving their own independence, and of administering retributive justice to their enemies and the Lord's." DuBose then made the comparison explicit: "In the ordinary dispensation of Divine Providence, we perceive repeated instances of a nation affecting its destruction by the corrupt administration of its own affairs. . . . To no nation can we point as a more striking illustration, than the one from which we but recently withdrew." While circumstances might cause the Confederate soldier "to shed much blood and to be the agent in producing much suffering," he must remember that he, like Joshua, will "be guiltless before God."[3]

Historian James W. Silver noted that, "as no other group, Southern clergymen were responsible for a state of mind which made secession possible, and as no other group they sustained the people in their long, costly and futile War for Southern Independence."[4] This was certainly true in Florida. In November 1860, a couple weeks after Lincoln's election, the annual meeting of the Florida Baptist Convention approved a resolution that "this Convention (though assembled solely for the purpose of promoting the progress of the Redeemer's Kingdom on earth), in view of the mighty events which are now transpiring, and which must of necessity affect to an incalculable extent the Christian, as well as the political welfare of our whole population, and more especially of our slaves, deems it proper at once to express their cordial sympathy with, and hearty approbation of those who are determined to maintain the integrity of the Southern States, even by a disruption of all existing political ties."[5]

Baptist leaders the following year called for prayer "that our country be speedily delivered from threatened despotism, war and bloodshed, and that peace and good will may abound throughout our Southern Confederacy and the world."[6] In Key West, which remained in Union hands throughout the war, a federal officer suspended habeas corpus a month after the attack on Fort Sumter; in response, "a Methodist preacher-militant invoked Heaven against the Federal government, and was promptly arrested."[7]

The religious imagery was not confined to the secessionist perspective. After the convention's vote to leave the Union, Richard Call, former territorial governor of Florida (and an Episcopalian), told prosecession revelers: "You have opened the gates of Hell, from which shall flow the curses of the damned which shall sink you to perdition!" In a published letter to "John S. Littell, of Germantown, Pennsylvania," Call wrote hopefully that the secessionists "may retire to the idolatrous worship of their local and sectional divinities, but the American heart will love and worship the God of our fathers; it will continue to beat in the American bosom, in the centre of the American Union; its warm blood will continue to circulate on both sides of the line of slavery, binding together, in national bonds, the kindred affections of one race in different communities."[8]

In his historical overview of religion in Florida, Samuel S. Hill noted that, because of the state's newness (statehood in 1845), "religious life in Florida is described as functioning in discrete units. What was happening in one area had relatively little bearing on what was happening in other places." Spanish Catholicism had been displaced decades earlier, but Baptists did not have their first church until 1821, Presbyterians in 1824, and Episcopalians a year later. Methodists began organizing as societies and classes in the early 1820s, some years before their first church. The first Jewish congregation was organized in 1874, a decade after the Civil War ended. In 1860, Christians, and especially evangelical Protestants, made up the largest part of Florida's population. The five largest groups were Methodists, with 30,360 members; Baptists, 20,325; Presbyterians, 9,580; Catholics, 4,350; and Episcopalians, 3,175.[9]

Methodists, the largest group, belonged to a denomination that, a year after Florida statehood, had split over the issue of slavery. John Wesley, the founder of the Methodist movement (though not himself a denominationalist—he stayed within the Anglican Church), spoke out against slavery, calling it "that execrable sum of all villainies," but by the early nineteenth century, the national church, in deference to Southern white members, was largely silent on the issue. With the rise of abolitionism in the 1830s, the two sides became vocal (the Georgia Annual Conference in 1837 resolved, without a dissenting vote, that "slavery, as it exists in the United States, is not a moral evil"), and in 1845, southern Methodists withdrew from the national church.[10]

A decade and a half later, Florida Methodists were preparing to secede again. Rev. John C. Ley, a minister in Micanopy, wrote that "the Church in all its operations sympathized with the excitement" of secession and the coming war. When some of his neighbors prepared to volunteer, they asked Ley to go with them as chaplain. His congregation approved, and Ley was off to Fernandina and Fort Clinch. He remained there until March 1862, when Confederates evacuated the fort. Simon Peter Richardson, a Methodist preacher in Gadsden County, told a similar story. "Regiments were being formed," he wrote, and "the brethren were anxious for me to go as chaplain. I jestingly told them to elect me major, and I would command them and preach too. I had no idea of going to war. . . . But to my astonishment they met and elected me major, and I had to go." Ley and Richardson were not alone; according to a local historian, "Methodist ministers . . . played leadership roles in at least three military units identified with Holmes County."[11]

Methodist churches suffered during the war, more often as a function of economic dislocation than of military action. In Madison County, Cherry Lake Methodist Church discontinued regular services for lack of attendance. In Ocala, the Marion Circuit had reported Sunday Schools "in prosperous condition" in 1860, but by 1865, to a question at a quarterly conference about Sunday schools, the response was "None, there being no schools." And so it went. The war "soon assumed dimensions of magnitude greater than any had conjectured," wrote George Gilman Smith, minister and historian of Florida Methodism, "and family after family gave up its best loved. They went to the field of battle and many of them fell. There was but little religious prosperity at such a time as this." By the end of the war, a correspondent to the *Christian Advocate and Journal* reported that "[Methodist] clergymen should not come here [to Florida] to labor without having some provision made for their maintenance," as "the people [have] no way of supporting them." Rev. Ley reported the somber mood at the annual meeting of the Florida Conference in November 1865: "We scarcely dared contemplate the future. How could we meet the actual necessities of wives and children and yet serve the Church, when that Church was bankrupt in purse and almost despairing in mind?"[12]

We often say that Baptists, like Methodists, split over the issue of slavery, but that is not strictly true; unlike their Wesleyan brothers, Baptists did not have a national denominational structure (in fact, the emphasis on congregationalism was a hallmark of American Baptists), but they did have a couple national missionary organizations and a national tract society. When the General Convention of the Baptists' Home Mission Society met in Philadelphia in April 1844, the two sides, North and South, were becoming firmer in their positions and less likely to yield (as we saw with Methodists at the same time). Delegates from Alabama demanded an "avowal that slaveholders are eligible, and entitled, equally with non-slaveholders . . . to receive any agency, mission, or other appointment." The convention board responded, "If . . . any one should offer himself as a missionary, having slaves, and should insist on retaining them as his property, we could not appoint him." A year later, Baptists from the slaveholding states met in Augusta, Georgia, to form the Southern Baptist Convention. (Although claiming to represent the slaveholding South, 241 of the 293 delegates at Augusta were from the two states of Georgia or South Carolina.) "As the meeting drew to a close," noted C. C. Goen, the historian of mid-nineteenth-century denominational schisms, "they all joined hands and sang 'Blest Be the Tie That Binds.'"[13]

Baptists varied in their perspectives on the coming war (as indeed they did over many things, including membership in the Southern Baptist Convention). Primitive Baptists, also called Old School Baptists, were a conservative group that, on biblical principles, opposed instrumental music, organized missionary efforts, Sunday schools, and theological seminaries, and favored foot washing and baptism by immersion. Their beliefs also led them to distance themselves, or at least their religion, from the politics of the day—"the Kingdom of Christ is not of this world." John G. Crowley, in a study of South Georgia and Florida, found few partisan statements from Primitive Baptists in the years leading up to and including the Civil War. In 1854, the Suwannee River Association passed a resolution against the "clergymen of New England who have threatened our Congress with the vengeance of Almighty God upon the passage of the Nebraska Bill," but Crowley noted that "this resolution is the only overt antebellum political statement made by the Primitive Baptists of the region."[14]

Not all Baptists were Primitive, of course, and many in Florida no doubt agreed with their neighbors just over the state border to the north. A writer in the *Christian Index*, a publication of Georgia Baptists, noted that newly inaugurated Abraham Lincoln and the "blockheaded blundering of a Black Republican Cabinet" would take the nation to war; it seemed, the *Index* reported the next year, that "the money-loving mercenary Yankee means to enslave us, . . . with his bayonet at our heart, and his foot upon our neck."[15] When the Southern Baptist Convention met in Savannah in May 1861, the nation had already split, as the denomination had two decades earlier. "The fanatical spirit of the North has long been seeking to deprive us of rights and franchises guaranteed by the Constitution," began a series of resolutions approved by the convention; "after years of persistent aggression, they have, at last, accomplished their purpose." The convention resolved "that we most cordially approve the formation of the government of the Confederate States of America" and "that we will assiduously invoke the divine direction and favor in behalf of all those who bear rule among us, . . . not only in seeing these Confederate States prosper under their administration, but in contributing to the progress of the transcendent kingdom of our Lord Jesus Christ."[16]

Historian Jack P. Dalton noted that "as a loyal Southern organization," the Florida Baptist Association "instructed its treasurer to use the Association's funds to purchase Confederate Bonds." But there were other economic issues on the minds of the state's Baptists. In 1863, the Bethlehem Baptist Association resolved "that we are firmly of the opinion that a corroding canker, in the form of speculation and extortion, is now sapping the vitals of our country's cause. . . . It is a lamentable fact, that many inconsiderate brethren are engaged in this unholy trade, from which, for the sake of our Master's cause, for the sake of our country, as also for the sake of humanity, we cannot too strongly urge every brother to desist and repent of this evil practice and forsake it."[17]

Presbyterians split in 1837, several years before Baptists and Methodists, over doctrinal issues arising out of the Second Awakening. "New School" Presbyterians, concentrated in Ohio and New York, included most of the denomination's abolitionists, and many "Old School" traditionalists were Southern slaveholders; still, the debate at the time centered on revivalism, missionaries, and ecumenism rather than slavery.[18] In any case, the Presbytery of Florida, separated from the Presbytery of Georgia in 1841, remained small at the beginning of the Civil War, with only sixteen ministers and thirty-three churches.[19]

In November 1860, having just returned from the Presbytery meeting at Gainesville, a participant offered the following report: "It is painful to speak of the state of political feeling among us. In all sections, our citizens are organizing, drilling and arming for defence against any measure of the General Government to coerce them into an acquiescence in the rule of the incoming administration. The Union is virtually at an end. Agitators North and South have won the day. The die is cast. The fearful experiment of secession must be tried. The event is in God's hands." The reporter also described the Sunday morning service at the host church, with particular attention to the administration of the Lord's Supper. "After the white communicants were served," he noted, "the colored people surrounded the tables. Would that all the brethren of the North who say such hard things of Southern christians, could have witnessed the scene, and heard the simple but touching words of welcome, exhortation and encouragement, that were addressed to these humble sons and daughters of Ham."[20]

A Presbyterian Unionist in St. Augustine complained that, early in the war, "a daily prayer meeting was held, ostensibly for *peace*; but alas! The great burden of the prayers then offered was success to Southern arms." The writer noted, with more approval, that with the Federal occupation of the city, the church was used by soldiers from Connecticut for meetings and services.[21]

The Catholic Church had a more convoluted history in Florida. In 1763, the Treaty of Paris ended the Seven Years' War and two centuries of Spanish rule in Florida. As it took over the territory, England promised religious freedom to Spanish Catholics there, but practically all fled (most to Cuba). In 1783, another Treaty of Paris ended the American Revolution and two decades of Florida as an Anglican land. Spain regained control, but this iteration of Spanish Florida was much weaker, from both a governmental and an ecclesiastical standpoint. When the Adams-Onís Treaty gave Florida to the United States in 1821, there was little of an organized Catholic presence, and Florida was attached to the See of Savannah after its establishment in 1850.

Florida received its first bishop in 1858: Augustin Verot, a French-born prelate who was known as a man of great compassion. In the summer of 1860, he was in Key West when a captured slave ship was brought in. "I cannot describe the distressing sight which these poor people presented," Verot wrote in a letter to the Propagation of Faith office in Paris. "It was a cargo of boys and girls between the ages of ten and eighteen. They were piled one upon the other in the hold of the ship, all in a state of complete nudity." Verot condemned "this hideous commerce" and went on to discuss the "spiritual misery" he found among slaves he had encountered in the American South. "Marriage is scarcely known among them. . . . Masters do not care about having their slaves educated. . . . Masters do not like for us to preach to these Negroes."[22] But while Verot condemned the slave trade and owners who did not properly care for their slaves, he did not speak out against slavery itself. In fact, a few months after writing this letter, he preached one of the most famous sermons of the Confederacy.

On January 4, 1861, the day proclaimed by President Buchanan as a day of prayer and fasting, Bishop Verot delivered a sermon in the old Spanish Church in St. Augustine on "Slavery and Abolition." He said, "Slavery is the origin of the present disturbances, and is the fatal sand-bank upon which the Ship of State has already made a total or partial shipwreck. . . . I wish to show, on the one side, how unjust, iniquitous, unscriptural, and unreasonable is the assertion of Abolitionists, who brand Slavery as a moral evil, and a crime against God, religion, humanity, and society; whereas, it is found to have received the sanction of God, of the Church, and of Society at all times, and in all governments. On the other side, I wish to show the conditions under which servitude is legitimate, lawful, approved by all laws, and consistent with practical religion and true holiness of life in masters who fulfil those conditions."[23]

Michael V. Gannon, the bishop's chief biographer, describes Verot's discussion of slavery in the first part of the sermon as "the common American Catholic opinion on the subject." In the second part, Verot, "in the strongest language used by any American prelate prior to the Civil War," proceeded to "shew the conditions upon which this state of things receives the sanction of justice, of God himself, and of the church"—that is, the proper Christian approach to slavery. "A man, by being a slave, does not cease to be a man, retaining all the properties, qualities, attributes, duties, rights and responsibilities attached to human nature, or to being endowed with reason and understanding, and made to the image and likeness of God."[24]

According to Verot, among "the various conditions which must accompany a legitimate possession of slaves" was, first, that the slave owner must repudiate the slave trade, which is "absolutely immoral and unjust." Second, that "the rights of free colored persons [must] be respected." Third, "that the whites do not take advantage of the weakness, ignorance, dependence, and lowly position of colored females, whether slaves or not." Fourth, "that matrimonial relations be observed among slaves, and that the laws of marriage be enforced among them." Fifth, "that husband and wife are joined together until death parts them." ("There ought to be, therefore, a provision made and sanctioned by the civil law, . . . that families shall never be separated.") Sixth, "that the master must really and in good faith provide food, clothing, and dwelling for his servant." Finally, "that servants must be provided with the means of knowing and practicing religion." Verot concluded by noting that if the Southern Confederacy "is meant to be solid, durable, stable and permanent, it must rest upon justice and morality."[25] Verot's sermon, in which he justified slavery but demanded fair and moral treatment of slaves, was widely reprinted and cited, in the South as well as the North. He did not explicitly call this a covenant, but that was basically his argument: God would allow the South to continue and prosper, if Confederates accepted and followed God's demands.

Verot was in Jacksonville on March 29, 1863, when, during the Federal evacuation of Jacksonville, a fire destroyed much of the city. A correspondent for the *New-York Tribune* described the events of the day: "Yesterday the beautiful little cottage used as the Catholic parsonage, together with the church, was fired by some of the soldiers, and in a short time burned to the ground. Before the flames had fairly reached the church, the soldiers had burst open the door and commenced sacking it of everything of value. The organ was in a moment torn to strips and almost every soldier who came out seemed to be celebrating the occasion by blowing through an organ pipe." The bishop's biographer writes that "this sacrilege would live in Verot's memory all the rest of his life."[26]

Unlike other mainstream Protestant churches, Episcopalians did not split in the 1840s. Rather, the denomination remained unified until secession divided the nation and, therefore, the Episcopal Church in the United States. At a meeting in Montgomery, Alabama, in July 1861, church officials resolved "that the secession of the States . . . from the United States, and the formation by them of a new government, called the Confederate States of America, renders it necessary and expedient that the Dioceses within those States should form among themselves an independent organization."[27] The Protestant Episcopal Church of the Confederate States of America, formed a few months after the war began by the necessity of the political division of the nation, ended a few months after the war ended, and in February 1866, Florida "renewed" its connection with the national church.

The church's unity, though, did not mean that all Episcopalians opposed secession. On November 18, 1860, William J. Ellis, rector of St. John's Episcopal Church in Tallahassee, preached a sermon in which he addressed recent events, including the presidential election. "Our duty is plain," he said: "to look evil in the face; to oppose against it courtesy, love, justice, courage—a clear head and a sound heart, and a strong arm nerved up by convictions of right and the consciousness that the Lord of Hosts is with *us*—that *our* cause is in truth the cause of humanity, and that our defeat will be the knell of human liberty." He ended by noting that the congregation should pray that God will "enlighten the minds and change the hearts . . . of our brethren at the North . . . , enabling them to perceive the truth and turn themselves from their course of folly and ruin."[28]

Francis Huger Rutledge, a native of Charleston, had been appointed the first bishop of Florida in 1851. In December 1860, when South Carolina approved its Ordinance of Secession, Rutledge said that, as Christians, "we cannot contemplate this dismemberment of the Union without deepest regret." But "it is," he added, "in the hand of Providence." Bishop Rutledge was present in Tallahassee when Florida's secession convention opened on January 3, 1861. Following John Pelot's opening remarks, McQueen McIntosh, a delegate from Apalachicola, addressed the assembly. "With nations as with men there is a Providence that fashions their destinies," said McQueen. "It is the blessing of that Providence to direct us in our future deliberations that we should now implore." McQueen moved that Rutledge be allowed to lead the convention in prayer. The bishop asked God to "enlighten direct and strengthen" the delegates so that they "may, in counsel, word and deed, aim supremely at the fulfilment of their solemn duty, at the promotion of thy glory and the advancement of the welfare of their country."[29]

The convention did not meet the next day. President James Buchanan, facing the threat of Southern secession, had ordered January 4 to be a day "set apart for Humiliation, Fasting, and Prayer throughout the Union." Edmund Ruffin, the Virginia secessionist who was in Tallahassee to observe the proceedings, was disgusted by the proclamation, which he saw as "a rebuke & censure to the seceding states, & of their cause, & of the very action which this Convention is assembled to consummate," and he refused to attend the church services for the day. Rutledge, who had told Ruffin that in his heart he had already seceded with his native state, also refused to attend. As it happens, the rector at St. John's "preached a strong disunion sermon in favor of immediate secession."[30]

Bishop Rutledge was silent when the convention resumed its debates on January 5 (at least as far as the convention's *Journal* records), but on January 8, a communication from the bishop was read into the convention's proceedings: "The undersigned promises to pay into the Treasury of the State of Florida, on demand, the sum of five hundred dollars, towards defraying the expenses of government for the year eighteen hundred and sixty-one, whenever by ordinance she shall be declared an independent Republic. (Signed,) FRS. H. RUTLEDGE."[31] Two days later, after the convention passed an ordinance of secession, Rutledge invoked God's continued guidance and protection for the delegates "to consummate a work which Thou hast given them to perform—a work in which we trust they have been directed by Thy counsel, and which has been effected in accordance with Thy will: a work which is intended to be for the advancement of Thy glory—the good of Thy church—and the safety, honor and welfare of this people, in time to come."[32]

Episcopalian churches seemed to have suffered more physical damage than others during the war. According to Joseph Cushman, the "first ecclesiastical casualty of the war" was St. John's Church in Warrington. The church's steeple was hit by a shell on November 22, 1861, as artillery at Union-held Fort Pickens opened fire on Fort Barrancas and the naval yard in Warrington. The church, completed only in 1860 and still not consecrated, caught fire and was destroyed. John Jackson Scott, rector at St. John's (and the only priest in Florida to serve as a chaplain in the Confederate Army), recorded his great disappointment in the loss of the church: "In a brief space all our cruel enemy left us of this house we had built for the good of man and the glory of God, was a heap of ashes."[33]

Rev. Scott was also rector at Christ Church in Pensacola, which survived the war but suffered when it was used as a barracks for Federal soldiers in 1862. A visitor to the church in November 1862 reported that he found "both doors wide open, the vestry room floor broken down, the table of the altar missing (it was afterwards found, used as a soldier's mess table,) the walls much discolored with tobacco juice, the windows very foul, and some lights broken, and the organ used as a plaything and very much out of order. The whole appearance of the building was sad in the extreme. But the surroundings were worse. The church-yard fence torn down and burned, the shade trees abused, the parish school-house smoked and greased and used as a military kitchen, all spoke of ruin, neglect, abuse."[34]

In Jacksonville, as Federal troops departed in the spring of 1863, a fire broke out that burned much of the city. According to one historian of the event, among the departing regiments was one that was predominantly Catholic and one that was Protestant. "For reasons unknown, dislike and hatred existed between them to such an extent that vandals in the Protestant regiment set the Catholic church on fire, and in retaliation, the Episcopal Church was burned by members of the Catholic regiment." However the fire began, it spread quickly. Alfred Walton, a medical officer with a Maine regiment, wrote in his diary of the destruction. "I ran into St. James," he wrote, "and groping through the smoke and fire I took from the altar a large guilt-bound prayer-book with the inscription on the cover 'St. James Episcopal Church, Jacksonville.'" Walton returned the prayer book to the church in 1866.[35]

In Palatka, Union soldiers used St. Mark's Church as a barracks. They moved the church bell to the sanctuary, where they placed it in an aisle. According to a history of the church, "Every time the bell was rung for service it would be the gathering place for all the children of the neighborhood who would come to see it." As Federal troops withdrew, someone took the bible; "a number of years later, the officer, who had been in charge of the troops, . . . sent another bible to replace it."[36]

When the war began, the Diocese of Florida seemed to be on solid ground for continued growth, with fourteen parishes (some with new churches), twelve priests, and well over a thousand congregants. At the first diocesan conference after the war, only three churches were represented.[37] The diocese was poor, disorganized, and understaffed (in terms of rectors). Recovery would come, though, and within a quarter century, the diocese found that it had to split in two to cover the state adequately.

Religion played an important role in the lives of many Floridians outside of church, of course. Winston Stephens, a planter from Waleka who served as an officer to a Confederate cavalry unit stationed in Northeast Florida, frequently mentioned God in his letters home to his wife, Octavia. "I think our cause a just one," he wrote in the spring of 1862, "and I believe that the God of battles will yet crown our arms with more and greater Victories and that the cause will yet prosper." Near the end of 1863, Winston wrote that "we hear they are fighting in Chattanooga and I do hope God will give us the Victory," but a few months later he seemed to sense the coming defeat: "I pray God to avert the awful calamity and to shield us from the threatened danger and I believe he will do it." He told Octavia that sometimes he was despondent, but "other times I think God will see fit to have it stoped [*sic*] and at no distant day, then I feel cheerful."[38]

Amy Suzanne Parker, in a study of marriages involving Florida's Civil War soldiers, noted that "women, deemed the moral sex in contemporary gender constructions, were supposed to influence their husbands in their religious devotion." "You must pray for me," wrote soldier Robert Tate to his wife, Lizzie, "for the good book says the prayers of the righteous shall be answered." Michael Raysor wrote his wife, "Sallie you know that I have never been converted that is feel that my sins were forgiven but fell deeply convicted of my sins & I do humbly pray God to pardon them for me. You my Dear Wife must pray for me that God in his infinite mercy might pardon and forgive me sins. I have made up my mind to give my heart to God." Hugh Black told his wife, Mary, "Let your prayers constantly assend to the throne of heavenly grace for us That is all you can do for me—but we are assured the fervent effectual prayer availeth much."[39]

Tracy Revels described similar letters in her study of Florida's Civil War women. Isaac Auld wrote to his mother, "It is a great comfort to me to know that I have such a good mother at home praying for me while enduring the hardships of soldering. I am sorry to inform you that I lost my little testament," he added, "but I got another out of a Yankee knapsack which I will try to keep." Sarah Fletcher's letters to her sons Malcolm and John showed her concern for their spiritual well-being. "Let me beg of you to watch and pray lest you fall into bad practices, let me urge you to make it your first chief concern to seek religion there is no safety without it. . . . Of all men the soldier has the greatest need of Piety, under the privations and hardships of Camp Life he needs the consolations that nothing but 'grace' can give." Thomas J. Clark begged his wife to "pray for me that I may return hom from the front lein. . . . I don't know whether I will ever see you agin in this world." On Christmas Day 1863, Dallas Wood reminded his sister that if he did not return home alive, "we all have the cheering assurance of a blissful home in Heaven where there will be no war and no parting again."[40]

Death was a constant concern—and not just on the battlefield. In January 1863, Winston Stephens was worried about his month-old daughter, Rosa, whom he had never seen and who was very ill. "If I should lose her," he wrote to his wife, "I shall think it a punishment because I have ben so much taken up with my Dear family that I have not paid the devotion to him that I should." As it happens, Rosa had died a few days before he wrote; when Winston learned of her passing, he wrote that "his will *must* be done and we have to submit. I know that he knows best, he saw proper to take our darling notwithstanding my prayers for oh if any poor mortal prayed I did, that she might be spared to us, from the bottom of my heart and incessantly."[41]

The correspondence of Winston and Octavia Stephens reveals another aspect of religion in Civil War Florida. Winston warned from the field that the slaves might attempt an uprising and told her "the guns must be loaded." "I hope the negroes will not try what you wrote about," Octavia replied. "Last Sunday Mother had them . . . all up here and read a chapter in the Bible etc and intends continuing it. They have not given the least trouble so far." White slave owners often used religion as a means of social control. Historians of Marion County wrote that "on Sunday afternoons Bible instruction was given to the children of the servants," an event that was likely repeated across the state. Robert L. Hall writes that "Florida Methodists concurred with the judgement of the South Carolina Conference of the Methodist Episcopal Church, South, that slave missions had considerable value in 'securing the quiet and peaceful subordination of these people.'"[42]

This is a common theme in the ex-slave narratives gathered by the Works Progress Administration in the 1930s. "Slaves were not told about heaven," said "Aunt Bess" Hilyard; "they were told to honor their masters and mistresses and of the damnation which awaited them for disobedience." Another reported a white preacher who told slaves not to steal, lie, or run away and to "be sure and git all dem weeds outen dat corn and your master will think a heap of you." Margrett Nickerson, an ex-slave from Leon County, remembered that "we had church wid the white preachers and dey tole us to mind our masters and missus and we would be saved; if not, dey said we wouldn't."[43]

African Americans in Florida and throughout the South no doubt considered religion as something other than a means of social control, and they practiced their own version of religion—sometimes, notes Larry Rivers, "in the presence of unsuspecting whites." Amanda McCray, a former slave living in Florida, recalled that her master allowed "a Negro minister" to preach on the plantation any time he wished, "so long as he did not interfere with the work of the other slaves." The slaves heard news of the Civil War from this minister, who "held whispered prayers for the success of the Union soldiers." In Jackson County, Henry Call, a Methodist slave preacher, held plantation prayer meetings on Thursday nights. "At the conclusion of the meetings slaves engaged in a general handshaking that meant to them that they had joined the 'African Methodist Episcopal' Church. Call asserted that he and three companions had organized an A.M.E. church 'while the overseer looked on unaware of anything more than a prayer meeting or a handshaking was going on.'"[44]

As soon as the disruptions of the war allowed it, African Americans formed their own congregations and churches—St. Mary's Primitive Baptist in Tallahassee in June 1861, for example, and First Baptist in St. Augustine in March 1864. Breaking away from white churches and forming their own congregations was "one of the major symbolic actions taken by free persons to signify their new status." They continued this with a new momentum after the war, often aided by Northerners and national organizations.[45]

For African Americans in Florida, the end of the war brought hope for a new beginning, and their religious life reflected that hope. Many white Floridians were not as sanguine. On May 21, 1865, a week after the postwar Union occupation of Tallahassee began, Rev. William Ellis, the rector at St. John's Church who four and a half years earlier had called for prayer that God would "enlighten the minds and change the hearts . . . of our brethren at the North," ended a service without the usual prayer for the president of the United States. Such an omission would have been expected during the war; now, it was time to return to the old form. Union General Edward M. McCook, who had been assigned the reestablishment of Federal control in Florida, sent Rev. Ellis a message. "It may be inconsistent with your personal feelings to offer this prayer," the general noted, but it "is part of the formula prescribed by the bench of bishops. . . . I must request that in the future you either include this customary prayer or the church be closed." General McCook reported that Ellis "prayed for the President that afternoon." As Lee Willis noted, "The ecclesiastical resistance to Union authority, which had been critical in launching Florida into the Confederacy four years earlier, ended grudgingly."[46]

But not always grudgingly. In the summer of 1866, Bishop Verot, who had prayed for Confederate victory, urged Catholics to accept the situation, to "put away all prejudice, all dislike, all antipathy, all bitterness against their former servants. Away with all feelings to bickerings, envy or jealousy which could only bespeak a narrow mind and the lack of noble and elevated feeling."[47]

The war had brought disruption and destruction to Florida's churches. George Gilman Smith, the historian of Methodism in Florida who had himself lived through the conflict, described the postwar prospects of religion in Florida. "There were not a few hearts which failed then for fear," he said, "and who declared firmly that the days of Southern Methodism were numbered. Yet the Church did not die."[48] No doubt those twin emotions of fear and relief were shared by many.

Notes

1. *Journal of the Proceedings of the Convention of the People of Florida, Begun and Held at the Capitol in the City of Tallassee on Thursday, January 3, A.D. 1861* (Tallahassee: Office of the Floridian and Journal, 1861), 3–4. Pelot's "wily abolitionist" remark is on p. 3.

2. *Floridian and Journal*, December 8, 1860, 2; *A Journal of the Proceedings of the House of Representatives of the General Assembly of the State of Florida, at Its Tenth Session, Begun and Held at the Capitol, in the City of Tallahassee, on Monday, November 26, 1860* (Tallahassee: Office of the Floridian and Journal, Printed by Dyke & Carlisle, 1860), 252. Perry's letter was dated February 2. Lee L. Willis III described Perry as a "parishioner" of Tallahassee's St. John's Church. "Secession Sanctified: Bishop Francis Huger Rutledge and the Coming of the Civil War in Florida," *Florida Historical Quarterly* 82, no. 4 (Spring 2004): 431.

3. John E. DuBose, *[Sermon to] Capt. Parkhill's Company, "The Howell Guards," on the Eve of Their Departure for the Seat of War, August 26, 1861* (Tallahassee, FL: Office of the Floridian and Journal, 1861), 3–5.

4. James W. Silver, *Confederate Morale and Church Propaganda* (New York: W. W. Norton, 1957), 101.

5. Quoted in John Leonidas Rosser, *A History of Florida Baptists* (Nashville, TN: Broadman, 1949), 48.

6. *Minutes of the Annual Session of the Bethlehem Baptist Association, 1861* (N.p.: 1861), 9. The Bethlehem Association included parts of western Florida.

7. William Watson Davis, *The Civil War and Reconstruction in Florida* (1913; reprint, Gainesville: University of Florida Press, 1964), 248.

8. Herbert J. Doherty Jr., *Richard Keith Call: Southern Unionist* (Gainesville: University of Florida Press, 1961), 5, 158; *Union.—Slavery.—Secession: Letter from Governor R. K. Call, of Florida, to John S. Littell, of Germantown, Pennsylvania* (Philadelphia: C. Sherman & Son, Printers, 1861), [3].

9. Samuel S. Hill, "Florida," in *Religion in the Southern States: A Historical Study*, ed. Samuel S. Hill (Macon, GA: Mercer University Press, 1983), 61–63, quotation on 63. Church numbers, from the Eighth Census, are cited on John E. Johns, *Florida during the Civil War* (Gainesville: University of Florida Press, 1963), 238n70. Lutherans and Universalists followed the top five, each with about six hundred adherents.

10. C. C. Goen, *Broken Churches, Broken Nation: Denominational Schisms and the Coming of the American Civil War* (Macon, GA: Mercer University Press, 1985), 78–90 (quotes on 79, 80). That same year, 1845, the Florida Conference of the Methodist Episcopal Church, South was formally organized, having been split from the Georgia Conference the year before. Geo. G. [George Gilman] Smith Jr., *The History of Methodism in Georgia and Florida, from 1785 to 1865* (Macon, GA: Jno. W. Burke & Co., 1877), 387, 400.

11. John C. Ley, *Fifty-Two Years in Florida* (Nashville: Publishing House of the M. E. Church, South, 1899), 88–89; Simon Peter Richardson, *The Lights and Shadows of Itinerant Life: An Autobiography* (Nashville: Publishing House Methodist Episcopal Church, South, 1900), 173; E. W. Carswell, *Holmesteading: The History of Holmes County, Florida* (Tallahassee, FL: Rose Printing Company, 1986), 39.

12. Elizabeth H. Sims, *A History of Madison County, Florida* (Madison FL: Madison County Historical Society, 1986), 44; George A. Foster, Mrs. Roy F. Thomas, and Jennie C. Weaver, *The First United Methodist Church of Ocala, Florida, 1844–2000* (Ocala, FL: First Impressions Printing, n.d.), 18–19; Smith, *History of Methodism in Georgia and Florida*, 407; "Florida Correspondence," *Christian Advocate and Journal* 40, no. 41 (October 12, 1865): 326; Ley, *Fifty-Two Years in Florida*, 96.

13. Goen, *Broken Churches, Broken Nation*, 90–98 (quotations on 95).

14. John G. Crowley, *Primitive Baptists of the Wiregrass South: 1815 to the Present* (Gainesville: University Press of Florida, 1998), 86, 88–89.

15. *Christian Index*, April 17, 1861, and February 25, 1862, quoted in Jack P. Dalton, "A History of Georgia Baptists" (PhD diss., University of Florida, 1952), 596.

16. Quoted in [Samuel Boykin], *History of the Baptist Denomination in Georgia* (1881; reprint, Paris, AR: Baptist Standard Bearer, 2000), 1: 226.

17. Dalton, "A History of Georgia Baptists," 71; *Minutes of the Bethlehem Baptist Association, Held with the Belleville Church, Conecuh County, Ala., on the 26th, 27th, and 28th of September 1863* (Montgomery, AL: Memphis Appeal Book and Job Printing Office, 1864), 5.

18. Goen, *Broken Churches, Broken Nation*, 68–78. Goen suggests that while many Southern Presbyterians would have naturally been Old School, the growing presence of abolitionism among the New Schoolers "aroused the Presbyterians of the South" (69).

19. Ernest Trice Thompson, *Presbyterians in the South*, vol. 1: *1607–1861* (Richmond, VA: John Knox, 1963), 423.

20. "Florida Presbytery," *New York Observer and Chronicle* 38, no. 48 (November 29, 1860): 378.

21. "A Loyal Church in Florida," *New York Observer and Chronicle* 45, no. 33 (August 17, 1865): 1.

22. Quote in Kenneth J. Zanca, ed., *American Catholics and Slavery, 1789–1866: An Anthology of Primary Documents* (Lanham, MD: University Press of America, 1994), 239–42.

23. Augustin Verot, *A Tract for the Times: Slavery & Abolition, Being the Substance of a Sermon, Preached in the Church of St. Augustine, Florida, on the 4th Day of January 1861, Day of Public Humiliation, Fasting and Prayer* (New Orleans: Catholic Propagator Office, 1861), 3.

24. Michael V. Gannon, *Rebel Bishop: The Life and Era of Augustin Verot* (Milwaukee: Bruce Publishing Company, 1964), 32–44; Verot, *A Tract for the Times*, 9–10.

25. Verot, *A Tract for the Times*, 10–14.

26. *New-York Tribune*, April 8, 1863, quoted in Gannon, *Rebel Bishop*, 72.

27. Joseph Blount Cheshire, *The Church in the Confederate States: A History if the Protestant Episcopal Church in the Confederate States* (New York: Longmans, Green, 1911), 37.

28. [Tallahassee] *Floridian and Journal*, December 15, 1860.

29. Quoted in Cheshire, *The Church in the Confederate States*, 12, 14; *Journal of the Proceedings of the Convention of the People of Florida*, 4–5.

30. Quoted in Gannon, *Rebel Bishop*, 30; Dorothy Dodd, "The Secession Movement in Florida, 1850–1861: Part II," *Florida Historical Quarterly* 12, no. 2 (October 1933): 60. Ruffin said in his diary that he was "much pleased with the venerable old minister [Rutledge], & with his ardor & patriotic sentiment." Quoted in Willis, "Secession Sanctified," 432.

31. *Journal of the Proceedings of the Convention of the People of Florida*, 20.

32. Ibid., 33. Rutledge began the prayer by noting that "Thou hast nourished and brought us up as children, but we have rebelled against Thee" (32).

33. Joseph D. Cushman Jr., "The Episcopal Church in Florida during the Civil War," *Florida Historical Quarterly* 38, no. 4 (April 1960): 295–96. The perception of the disproportionate destruction of Episcopalian churches could be simply a function of reportage.

34. "A correspondent of the *Church Journal*," quoted in *New York Observer and Chronicle* 41, no. 27 (July 2, 1863): 211.

35. Thomas Frederick Davis, *History of Early Jacksonville, Florida: Being an Authentic Record of Events from the Earliest Times to and Including the Civil War* (Jacksonville: The H. & W. B. Drew Company, 1911), 183–84; T. Frederick David, *History of Jacksonville, Florida, and Vicinity, 1513 to 1924* ([St. Augustine]: Florida Historical Society, 1925), 132.

36. *History of St. Mark's Church, Palatka, Florida* [St. Augustine, FL: The Record Company, 1920], 7. I am grateful to Stephen Bartlett for providing this source. J. H. Haughton, a druggist from Palatka, told the story differently in a 1939 interview: "During the Civil War the Federal troops used St. Mark's Church as a barracks and when they went away they carried off the Bible and a number of prayer books. In 1906, as clerk of the church, I received a letter from T. W. Downs of Bridgeport, Conn., telling me the books were in his possession and asking how we wanted them mailed, as he wished to return them. A short time later, Mr. Downs sent the Bible and the books back here and they are again in the possession of the Church." Quoted in Brian E. Michaels and the Putnam County Action '679 Heritage Task Force historical manuscript Subcommittee, *The River Flows North: A History of Putnam County, Florida* (Palatka, FL: Putnam County Archives and History Commission, 1976), 89.

37. Cushman, "The Episcopal Church in Florida during the Civil War," 294–95, 300.

38. Winston Stephens to Octavia Stephens, March 13, 1862, in *Rose Cottage Chronicles: Civil War Letters of the Bryant-Stephens Families of North Florida*, ed. Arch Frederic Bailey, Ann Smith Leinhart, and Winston Bryant Stephens Jr. (Gainesville: University of Florida Press, 1998), 106; November 30, 1863, 288; February 2, 1864, 313.

39. Amy Suzanne Parker, "Love Is a Battlefield: The Marriages of Confederate Soldiers and Their Wives in Florida during the Civil War" (Honors thesis, Florida State University, 2009), 70; Robert Tate to Lizzie Tate, May 6, 1864, in "Love Is a Battlefield," 71; Michael Raysor to Sallie Raysor, May 17, 1863, in "Love Is a Battlefield"; Hugh Black to Mary Black, October 15, 1863, in "Love Is a Battlefield," 72.

40. Isaac McQueen Auld to Mother, September 22, 1862, quoted in Tracy J. Revels, *Grander in Her Daughters: Florida's Women during the Civil War* (Columbia: University of South Carolina Press, 2004), 54; S. A. Fletcher to "Dear Sons," May 6, 1861, in *Grander in Her Daughters*, 54; Thomas J. Clark to Martha Ann Law Clark, transcribed in Janice Cox Brown, "Thomas J. Clark and James A Clark, CSA," *Magazine of the Jefferson County Historical Society* Vol. LXXI (December 2005): 97; Dallas Wood to sister, December 25, 1863, in *Grander in Her Daughters*.

41. Winston Stephens to Octavia Stephens, January 27, 1863, and January 31, 1863, in *Rose Cottage Chronicles*, 195, 197.

42. Winston Stephens to Octavia Stephens, December 22, 1861, in *Rose Cottage Chronicles*, 80; Octavia Stephens to Winston Stephens, January 6, 1862, in *Rose Cottage Chronicles*, 90; Eloise Robinson Ott and Louis Hickman Chazal, *Ocali Country, Kingdom of the Sun: A History of Marion County, Florida* (Ocala, FL: Perry Printing Company, 1966), 67; Robert L. Hall, "'Yonder Come Day': Religious Dimensions of the Transition from Slavery to Freedom in Florida," *Florida Historical Quarterly* 65, no. 4 (April 1987): 413.

43. Federal Writers' Project of the Works Progress Administration for the State of Florida, *Slave Narratives: A History of Slavery in the United States from Interviews with Former Slaves*, vol. 3: *Florida Narratives* (Washington, DC: N.p., 1941), 54, 68, 242.

44. Larry Eugene Rivers, *Slavery in Florida: Territorial Days to Emancipation* (Gainesville: University Press of Florida, 2000), 114; Larry Eugene Rivers and Canter Brown, Jr., *Laborers in the Vineyard of the Lord: The Beginnings of the AME Church in Florida, 1865–1895* (Gainesville: University Press of Florida, 2001), 17; *Slave Narratives*, 214; Hall, "Yonder Come Day," 414–15, 418.

45. Robert L. Hall, "Tallahassee's Black Churches, 1865–1885," *Florida Historical Quarterly* 58, no. 2 (October 1979): 185–96.

46. *The War of the Rebellion: A Compilation of the Official Records of the Union and Confederate Armies* (Washington, DC: Government Printing Office, 1880–1901),

Series 1, Vol. 49 (Part 2): 862, 945. In his official report, McCook wrote: "The pastor of the Episcopal Church in his public service omitted the customary prayer for the President of the United States. I thought it my duty to Christianize him, if possible, and succeeded in convincing him of the error of his way" (945). Susan Bradford Eppes told a similar story of Rutledge: "He was a Southerner of Southerners, and for four years his whole heart had gone up in prayer for Jefferson Davis," and he ended the prayer, "We beseech Thee with Thy favor to behold and bless Thy Servant The President of the Confederate States." "Realizing his mistake," Eppes wrote, "the poor old head fell low on his breast as he retrieved himself, and in a faltering voice repeated" the prayer, this time for "the President of the United States and all others in authority." Susan Bradford Eppes, *Through Some Eventful Years* (Macon, GA: J. W. Burke Company, 1926), 341. Lee L. Willis, *Southern Prohibition: Race, Reform, and Public Life in Middle Florida, 1821–1920* (Athens: University of Georgia Press, 2011), 79.

47. Quoted in David T. Gleeson, "'No Disruption of Union': The Catholic Church in the South and Reconstruction," in *Vale of Tears: New Essays on Religion and Reconstruction*, ed. Edward J. Blum and W. Scott Poole (Macon, GA: Mercer University Press, 2015), 177.

48. Smith, *History of Methodism in Georgia and Florida*, 410.

7

Civil War and Florida's New Legal Paradigm

Chris Day

As the echoes of cannon fire from Fort Sumter rolled across Florida, the thunderous call for abolition soon followed, but the willfulness of emancipation would be met with equal resistance from those who owned the enslaved. Although initially Abraham Lincoln clearly articulated that it was a war for the maintenance of the Union, eventually the question of slavery had to be answered on the battlefields of the South as well as of Florida. Louisiana sugar plantation owner Babillard La Branche allegedly stated, "The Yankees are king here now, and that they, the slaves, must go to their king for food and shelter."[1] Even though La Branche was not a Floridian, his words are no less prophetic. The status of the enslaved was in question, and the answer would not be given over unceremoniously. It was clear what would happen if the Confederacy was victorious, but what would be the lot for the enslaved if the Union were victorious? How would the transition from slavery to freedom operate, and how would the status of property ultimately be removed? The Civil War would not last forever, but an enslaved Texan advised his son, "Our forever was going to be spent living among the Southerners, after they got licked."[2] This sentiment would dominate the civil rights movement in Florida for more than a century.

How would the Civil War in Florida impact not only the civil rights movement but also the formerly enslaved and descendants of the enslaved? Would emancipation grant true freedom or merely remove the status of property? When the enslaved were emancipated, were they truly free or merely the subjects of a new king, or master, as La Blanche supposedly alluded? This quandary did not start with the Civil War, but it would be answered because of it. The war placed the status of the enslaved into a state of flux. Historians such as Larry Rivers and Steven Hahn have argued that the war was the largest slave rebellion in history.[3] They buttress their arguments by discussing the role of African American troops and their participation in ending enslavement. While this conclusion provides the most agency for African Americans, it does fail to take into consideration the legal ramifications of slavery. This failure is evident in the difficulty the Union had in determining the status of the enslaved. Their position was tied to the South and its institutions, which may or may not be protected by the Constitution. How was the law going to interpret this, and how did the events of the war influence this?

These questions are vexing when placed into the lexicon of the civil rights movement. The current historiography of the civil rights movement has focused on the origins of the modern movement of the 1950s and 1960s, in what Jacquelyn Dowd Hall has called the "Long Civil Rights Movement."[4] She argues that the modern movement was defined by direct action, and it was necessary to find earlier forms of direct action to determine the origins of the modern movement. The concept of the Long Movement fails to understand the process of civil rights activism. Historians have typically compartmentalized African American history into the antebellum period and post–Civil War struggle for equality. The distinction typically made is that slaves because of their status were not citizens afforded civil rights. When citizenship was bestowed on African Americans following the Civil War, they had to fight to define that citizenship in an increasingly hostile society. This idea misrepresents the movement. First, citizenship was not bestowed on African Americans; it was earned. The definition of citizenship was not fully realized until the enslaved, in seeking their freedom, challenged the lack of a definition. That definition was haunted by the *Dred Scott* decision, and lawmakers wanted to negate all vestiges of Roger Taney's "legal argument." Historians could avoid this issue by calling this process the quest for freedom, but that is also short-sighted, because the argument could be made that the attainment of freedom occurred with the passage of the Thirteenth, Fourteenth, and Fifteenth Amendments. This is a complicated issue that requires historians to break out of the simplistic compartmentalization of history, creating monographs so focused on specific issues they fail to understand the historical contexts.

The experience of African Americans in Florida is appropriate in the furthering of civil rights history. State studies are not unusual in African American history and have yielded diverse views of the black experience, and the events that transpired on the national level had a considerable impact on African Americans in Florida. The Civil War and its legacies would influence civil rights activism in the state. Enslaved African Americans worked tirelessly to remove the shackles of property, and the status solidified during the antebellum period would not simply erode as the result of its contact with blood or ink. These issues can be gleaned from court cases filed in the Florida State Supreme Court. Unfortunately, emancipation was not enough to truly realize freedom for the enslaved. The status of property would be attached to the formerly enslaved with a vigorous tenacity. Antebellum jurisprudence, along with *Dred Scott*, was not easily dismissed during the Civil War, nor after. As will be evidenced in *Luke v. Florida*, the legal wrangling used to support slavery was unparalleled in its time, and the results of this case would have an impact even after abolition.

Luke v. Florida dealt with the dominance of the master and questioned where the will of the master stopped and the intellect of the slave began. Historian Craig Buettinger addressed whether slaves could have free will in a system that denied them the thinking ability of a human being, in lieu of being a dominated slave.[5] Buettinger may have oversimplified whether a slave could commit a crime in the eyes of the law, as the question about whether they could consciously commit a crime fails to recognize the law. It was obvious that a slave could make the decision to commit a crime; the question was whether the law allowed the overt act to be acknowledged and whether that acknowledgement weakened the dominance of the master. Perhaps historian Thomas D. Morris has a clearer view of this subject. He writes, "The more absolute the power of the master in theory, the more recognition of the slave's humanity."[6] The dominance of the master was in direct response to the will of the slave, so the free will of the slave is not in question because the law reflects that will. At this point the question then becomes who was responsible for the criminal act, because if the courts say it was the slave, then the master loses control, and if the courts say the master, then the slave cannot commit a crime, and therefore slave codes were irrelevant because slaves can never be held responsible. This was quite a conundrum for the court system to deal with and the following case will bear this out.

Luke v. State originated in St. Johns County on November 3, 1851, when Luke was charged with maliciously wounding an animal. He allegedly killed two mules, worth $300, owned by Joseph M. Hernandez on July 20, 1851.[7] Luke had complained to his master, Andrew DuPont, about mules getting into his garden enclosure. When Luke asked what he should do, DuPont responded that he should shoot the mules. Adam, Hernandez's African American slave driver, found the mules, determined they had been shot, and followed the blood on the ground back to DuPont's plantation. Adam asked Luke if he knew who shot the mules and Luke said he did it at the behest of his master, because they had been menacing DuPont's plantation and he wanted to get rid of the nuisance.[8]

The case was brought before Judge Thomas Douglas of the Eastern District Court. Luke's attorney, McQueen McIntosh, asked the judge to instruct the jury that the crime was not malicious because Luke was under the control of his master; Judge Douglas declined. Luke was convicted and sentenced to three months in the St. Johns' County jail and ordered to pay the costs of his prosecution. After the trial, McIntosh moved to arrest the verdict based on Douglas's overruling the requested charge not to hold the slave responsible because of the control of the master. Luke's master, along with four other men, put the necessary bond of $1,000 each to free Luke until his appeal was heard.[9]

In the appeal, McIntosh argued that Luke could not be prosecuted under the act of February 10, 1832, because the punishment proscribed was for free white persons. He stated that the legislature never intended to fine a slave. He said the eighth section proved this, because it was the outlined exception that proved the rest of the statute was for free persons. Since there were two codes of punishments, the legislature's intentions were clear. He noted that sections nineteen and twenty in *Thompson's Digest* outlined separate punishments for slaves.[10] McIntosh argued, "It might be contended that the act under which the prisoner was indicted is general in its terms, when it says, 'if any person shall maliciously,' &c. Yet it would be in contravention of the spirit of the law to apply to slaves such portion of it as relates to bigamy, adultery, &c., wherein the same phraseology is used. The prisoner, acting at the instigation and under the control of his master, was incapable of committing the offence charged in the indictment. There was the absence of will, without which there was no malice, the essence of the crime, and what must be proven. The slave is a chattel in law, and has no volition to disobey a master."[11] His arguments caused problems for the laws binding slaves within Florida's society. If a slave did not have free will, then a separate code was meaningless, because the master would be the only person held accountable for their actions. This issue was not lost on John P. Sanderson, who argued the case for the state.

Sanderson outlined that since Florida statutes did not distinguish between persons acting under the direction or command of the master, he turned to the legal relationships between husband and wife and parent and child. He argued they are not excused for committing a crime if the husband or father commanded it. He concluded that Luke was alone and not under the direct control of his master and was therefore responsible for his crime. "The principles of common law are held to be applicable to the slave—not as a slave—but as a reasonable being."[12] He further articulated that the slave was recognized as a person and protected by Florida law. "Humanity—self-preservation—public policy and necessity, enforce and demand that the ruling of the court below be sustained."[13]

Justice Leslie A. Thompson wrote the majority opinion of the court. He stated that the jury found Luke guilty under the fifty-ninth section of the act of February 10, 1832. It had been argued that Luke could be convicted not under the fifty-ninth section of the statute but under the sixty-first section of the act of November 21, 1828.[14] Thompson ignored this with the explanation that there was not enough time to provide the proper legal consideration for this issue. He said that the Act of 1832 was the only law in force. It was the state's intention to provide separate punishments for free whites and slaves. Thompson noted that the statute for assault provided whites with a punishment of a fine. If a slave committed the same crime they received thirty-nine lashes, and if the intent of the assault was to kill, they received a death sentence. The difference in severity was proof of the slave's inferior status. "Although in the absence of the Act of November 21, 1828, the punishment of that inferior caste of persons who are either slaves or free, might be inflicted under the general laws, yet as the Legislature has provided other and different modes and degrees of punishment for them, the latter must be observed."[15] The Legislature did intend to disrupt the distinction made between whites and slaves with the passage of the Act of 1832. The distinction made by the Act of 1828 was still enforced. On slavery, Thompson wrote:

> The perpetuation of the institution, indeed the common safety of the citizens during its continuance, would seem to require that the superiority of the white or Caucasian race over the African negro, should be ever demonstrated and preserved so far as the dictates of humanity will allow—the degraded caste should be continually reminded of their inferior position, to keep them in proper degree of subjection to the authority of free white citizens. And thus there is an obvious propriety in visiting their offences with more degrading punishment than is inflicted on the white citizens, while the humanity of the law is demonstrated by securing to them the same forms of law in making defense—a trial by jury—compulsory process for their

> witnesses—the aid of counsel—and indeed, as full, fair, and impartial trial, as can or may be claimed by a white person.[16]

Thompson concluded by stating that the indictment should have been for the sixty-first section of the Act of November 21, 1828, and not the fifty-ninth section of the Act of February 10, 1832. This was an error and therefore the judgment of the lower court was reversed, vacated, and set aside.

Thompson's section about the inferiority of the slave and its reflection in the punishments for crimes is quite telling. Thompson was from Middle Florida, where South Carolinian attitudes impacted the views of the people. According to historian Daniel L. Schafer, they had a rigid view of race relations compared to the more progressive views of Eastern Florida.[17] Even though Thompson tried to ignore the section about free will, his opinion did not support that omission. If he allowed for the idea of free will, then he was equating slaves with whites, who, in his opinion, had a free will. He did not avoid the idea; he shut it down and maintained the notion of African American inferiority. The concept of free will was not the issue in this case; it was the implication created by accepting that concept. Buettinger did question why the justices skimmed over the free will portion of the defense. He believed the courts did so because of time constraints and decided to rule on procedural law and not the applicability of common law. The simple assumption was that Justice Thompson understood that by arguing free will, they had to legally accept the humanity of the slave, which could complicate property laws. Florida lawmakers and jurists worked diligently to maintain the status of property. They understood that the only way to protect slavery was to codify its restraints on slaves, masters, free white citizens, and free blacks. Had they legally recognized Luke as a human with free will who could have committed a crime without compulsion, how was the judicial system going to reconcile property and humanity? It was not possible. Luke's participation in the court system forced Florida jurists to solve this quandary. Had he not been granted a jury trial, this could not have occurred, and this small access to civil rights forced the court to define the humanity of the slave within the dominance of slave society.

In antebellum Florida, cases such as *Luke v. Florida* provide insight into the difficulties created by the legal codification of enslaved property and the tenacity employed to maintain that status for the enslaved. The State Supreme Court cases that deal with enslaved property explain that the status of property, coupled with dehumanization, would not be easily dismissed in Florida. While the national debate over slavery raged throughout the 1850s, Florida continued to cement the enslaved's status as property. The forthcoming war would ultimately crack that monolith, but it would take persistence to demolish it.

The journey began in 1860 with the election of Abraham Lincoln. The governor of South Carolina, William Henry Gist, asked other Southern states if they would secede from the Union if South Carolina did so after Lincoln's election, and many Southern states agreed that they would follow South Carolina. South Carolina subsequently held a convention and voted unanimously to secede from the Union. Mississippi, Florida, Alabama, Georgia, Louisiana, and Texas followed and Arkansas, Tennessee, North Carolina, and Virginia seceded after the fall of Fort Sumter in 1861. In the months following these events, Congress tried to come up with another compromise to help keep the Union together, but it was clear that the time for compromise had passed and question of the future of the institution of slavery must be answered once and for all on the blood-soaked battlefields of America.

The impending epoch created by the war was not lost on abolitionists. Frederick Douglass wrote, "They have exposed the throat of slavery to the keen knife of liberty, and have given a chance to all the righteous forces of the nation to deal a death-blow to the monster evil of the nineteenth century."[18] Not everyone shared this characterization of the war. In 1861, the Civil War was not a war of emancipation. Lincoln understood that he would not have the support he needed to keep the Union together if the loyal slave states thought they were fighting for emancipation. The border states of Missouri, Kentucky, Maryland, and Delaware were important to maintain. Lincoln needed to keep these states in the Union if victory was to be achieved, but the question of freeing the slaves became apparent as early as 1861.

From the onset, many slaves thought their freedom would be granted if they escaped to Union camps. Some slaves were granted freedom, but this was not always the case. Concerned about keeping the border states in the Union, military officials were especially protective of slavery. This issue was in the decision-making of General John C. Fremont in Missouri. On August 30, 1861, Fremont put Missouri under martial law, confiscated the property of rebels, and proclaimed, "Their slaves, if any they have, are hereby declared freemen."[19] Only a few months into the conflict and Fremont was already trying to free the slaves. Considering the political climate of the time, Fremont's act was premature, and only a few days later Lincoln made Fremont rescind his declaration. Lincoln said, "It would alarm our Southern Union friends and turn them against us; perhaps ruin our rather fair prospect for Kentucky."[20] Lincoln understood the theater in which his political moves were being played out. The enslaved participated in a debate that affected the rest of their lives and they did not have a direct political voice in it. Their political voice may not have been direct in the traditional sense, but their active resistance was no less effective.

Fremont's declaration was an extreme measure of dealing with slaves coming over to Union lines during the war. Many of the Union officers were not interested in freeing the slaves and many were sent back to their masters. The justification was much broader than that they felt slaves should remain enslaved. The debate at the time was whether the states that seceded could do so constitutionally. Did the fact that they decided to leave Union mean that they could legally leave? If not, were they still under the protection of the Constitution? The Union officers had to enforce the Fugitive Slave Act if they were still under the protection of the Constitution. For example, during an attack on Cedar Key in Florida, Naval Commander George F. Emmons had three slaves escape from their master and board his ship. Emmons sent the slaves back, which brought praise from the Confederates.[21] Another example of officers returning slaves occurred in Virginia, where General Robert C. Schenck ordered that slaves of loyal citizens be surrendered when demanded by their owners, and Colonel Dixon S. Miles sent ten slaves belonging to John A. Washington, an officer in the Confederate Army, back to their plantation.[22] Miles believed that even though Washington was fighting against the Union, he was entitled to the rights guaranteed him under the Constitution. The political landscape of the time and the reading of the law made the prospect of a fair future for slaves a difficult goal to achieve, because of all the different forces acting upon the direction of the path.

At Fort Monroe in Virginia, General Benjamin Butler needed to decide how to treat the fugitive slaves migrating to the fort. He was faced with the same political problems the other generals encountered. Butler was a Democrat, and before he was stationed at Fort Monroe he had offered to help Governor Thomas H. Hicks of Maryland suppress a threatened slave uprising.[23] It was clear that Butler was not an abolitionist. Three slaves of Confederate Colonel Charles K. Mallory, commanding officer of the 115th

Virginia Militia, escaped to Fort Monroe. The slaves were building Confederate batteries with Mallory's permission.[24] The slaves, who were the private property of Mallory, were being used as labor for the rebellion against the Union, and the fact that they were building military batteries proved this. The next day Major M. B. Cary of the Virginia volunteers appeared at Fort Monroe, for Colonel Mallory, and said: "In accordance with the terms of the Fugitive Slave Act the slaves must be returned. You say we cannot secede, and so you cannot consistently detain the Negroes. Confronted with this dilemma, Butler rebutted, but you say you have seceded, so you cannot consistently claim them. I shall hold these Negroes as contraband of war."[25] Butler created a new path for the enslaved, which moved them from being property of the Southern plantation owners to "contraband of war." This was a transitory term, because it continued the inherent status of property while allowing the Union to eventually free runaway slaves. This was not an enormous step, but it was the first step in an exceptionally long journey toward a positive outcome.

The simple use of the word "contraband" alleviated many of the problems created by Fremont's declaration and Miles's return of slaves to a Confederate soldier. By not immediately emancipating the slaves, the border states did not feel that the fight for the Union was a fight to end the institution of slavery, and by not returning the slaves immediately, abolitionists felt that slavery might eventually be abolished. As Edward L. Pierce, Butler's superintendent of contraband labor, observed, there was "often great virtue" in such technical phrases as "contraband of war" for shaping public opinion.[26] Pierce was correct in his observations, as both sides were content with the state of the slave question. The use of the word "contraband" was evidence of the Union balancing on a political tightrope that placed them between keeping the border states loyal and assisting them in the war, on the one hand, and losing their loyalty and possibly losing the war, on the other.

The debate over refugee slaves was another step toward freedom, because without such debate civil rights could not be achieved. The plight of the enslaved, from bondage to freedom, had to commence with an initial step, and as insignificant as it sounds that first step was being labeled "contraband." The label did not erase someone's identity as personal property, but it did allow those who were someone's personal property to begin chipping away at that shackle and eventually free themselves from bondage. It is also important to note that not all slaves were considered contraband.

Many slaves escaped from their master's plantations near Union lines, but many also existed in the South as property of other living souls. Ultimately, General Butler's new status for fugitive slaves did create a chance for liberation within a political and wartime environment that resisted the complete abolition of slavery.

The political climate of the United States was changing in 1862, as the tide of the Civil War shifted in favor of the Union. General Ulysses S. Grant achieved sizable victories in Tennessee, and Union forces pushed back General Robert E. Lee at Antietam. President Lincoln believed the time was ripe to begin the process of emancipation; the pendulum had swung and the Confederate cause was now in doubt. A slave of the North Carolina planter who joked at the outbreak of war that he would be back by dinner said, "He went away and it wuz four long years before he c[ome] back to dinner."[27] The basis of their "superiority" was now considered contraband and confiscated by the United States. During this time, Lincoln sent a message to Congress proposing a gradual abolition of slavery. He resolved "that the United States ought to co-operate with any State which may adopt gradual abolishment of slavery, giving such State pecuniary aid, to be used by such State in its discretion, to compensate for the inconveniencies, public and private, produced by such a change of system."[28] This was a calculated move on Lincoln's part because he was not forcing abolition of slavery but promoting the idea of it through government aid. Lincoln remarked, "In my judgment gradual and not sudden emancipation is better for all."[29] It is unclear exactly who "all" encompasses, but the welfare of the enslaved had to be on his mind. The idea that Lincoln wanted to create a gradual emancipation shows that he was not a man who wanted to abolish slavery with a simple government proclamation.

In September 1862 Lincoln announced the preliminary Proclamation of Emancipation. This was not like his proposal in which states would receive aid if they abolished slavery. The Proclamation stated that slaves held in states still in active rebellion against the United States were to be set free on January 1, 1863. The former slaves could now move from slaves to contraband to freedmen. The act of emancipation was more than just freeing those slaves who were used to perpetuate the Confederate cause and extended to all slaves in the South. The decision was difficult for Lincoln. He still had to contend with the issue of the border states, but he also had to deal with abolitionists. Lincoln called a border-state congressman to the White House to discuss gradual emancipation, which he had proposed earlier in 1862. Lincoln said, "If the border-states did not make a decision at once to emancipation gradually . . . the institution in your states will be extinguished by mere friction and abrasion—by the mere incidents of war . . . and you will have nothing valuable in lieu of it."[30] Historian James McPherson wrote that "even this blunt warning fell on deaf ears."[31] Lincoln also found opposition in Congress. In a minority report against the emancipation of rebel slaves, W. Noell wrote, "This sudden and unnatural process of emancipation would put an end for the next twenty years to the production of cotton, sugar, rice, and tobacco in the Southern States."[32] Lincoln finally decided to pursue a more radical stance and emancipated slaves in the insurrectionary states. It was the next logical step within the war and the future of slaves was an important matter at hand. This step was accomplished when the final Emancipation Proclamation took effect on January 1, 1863.

The release of slaves from bondage began with Lincoln's preliminary announcement of the proclamation. Leon Litwack writes: "Against background of military setbacks, mounting casualty lists, and unfilled recruitment quotas, President Lincoln issued in September 1862 a preliminary Proclamation of Emancipation which stipulated that on January 1, 1863, in those states or portions of states still engaged in rebellion, the slaves would be forever free."[33] Was emancipation merely a result of wartime necessity? Historian Louis Gerteis contends, "By the end of 1863 the government's policy was clear. 'The fortunes of war,' Secretary Stanton told Congress, burdened the government with the care and support of large numbers of dependent blacks. However bothersome to Union troops, these refugees represented a greater loss to the enemy."[34] The use of African American troops is an interesting case study, but for the purposes of this discussion it will be touched upon only as part of the journey toward freedom. The call for African American soldiers came after the formalization of the Emancipation Proclamation in 1863, and the formation of colored units was not an acceptable avenue of enlistment until after that time. Initially, most were used for menial labor and did not fight often. As the war progressed, the situation changed and former slaves became active participants in the Civil War. In Florida, refugees who fled to the Union Navy were used to destroy saltworks along the coast.[35] When Colonel Thomas Wentworth Higginson, an abolitionist, was asked, "Do you think that, as preparation for the life of a citizen, the organization of Negroes into military bodies is important?" Higginson answered, "I should say of unspeakable value."[36] He believed that enlistment in the army could assist the freedmen in their new life of citizenship. The organization of African American troops marked a change in political temperament toward the slave question. The government was now willing to arm them, which a year earlier they were not ready to do. Emancipation was not solely a wartime measure. It was a benefit to the army to strip Confederates of labor, which would, in turn, not free up as many men for battle. The Union was capable of calling up more men than the South because of their population advantage. Lincoln seized upon the opportunity presented by the Emancipation Proclamation to begin the process of abolition.

The Emancipation Proclamation increased the influx of refugees to Union lines. Some historical scholarship has concluded that many slaves were mere children when it came to dealing with their freedom. Historian Stanley Elkins hypothesized that "North American slavery was so absolutely closed that its inmates, the slaves, were forced to become sambos."[37] The slaves, according to Elkins, were imprisoned not only in body but in mind as well. These were the typical products of the system: individuals utterly infantilized, docile, and dependent upon their masters for their ideas, values, and existence.[38] During the Civil War, many whites thought African Americans were unable to fend for themselves and would not survive without help from white people. It may be true that they needed help in the beginning to adjust to their new providence, but the assistance given to them was needed not because they were incapable of survival. It was because even after their liberation many whites sought to oppress and enslave them once again. Abolitionist groups felt that it was important for the government to have a plan to deal with the transition of slaves to free citizens. The Emancipation League wrote a memorial concerning this issue on December 12, 1862. It stated: "In view of the emancipation of so many of these people, it becomes of the highest importance to inquire what are the best regulations for their new condition, and what has been the experience of other times and nations in similar emergences. There is at present great ignorance on these points among our people and among even our civil and military officers. To remedy like ignorance in England, France, and Russia, in Denmark and Holland, the government of those countries have instituted committees of parliament, grand commissions, and similar bodies, which have accumulated facts of the greatest value to guide the action of these governments. Your memorialists, therefore, respectfully and earnestly urge upon Congress the importance of the immediate establishment of a

Bureau of Emancipation."[39] The question of the needs of the freedmen was to be answered by the American Freedmen's Inquiry Commission.

Charles Sumner, a senator from Massachusetts, was an abolitionist and willing to take up the cause of the freedmen. Sumner wrote in a letter, "This war is nothing unless it finishes Slavery, & our State must lead."[40] His resolve was strengthened after South Carolina Congressman Preston Brooks attacked him and beat him with a cane, which forced Sumner to leave the Senate for a time. His "vacant chair" became a symbol of the South's uncompromising need to hold on to slavery as a part of their lives. On March 16, 1863, Sumner asked Secretary of War Edwin M. Stanton to create the American Freemen's Inquiry Commission, to "investigate the condition of the colored population and to report what measures will best contribute to their protection and improvement, so that they may defend and support themselves."[41] Stanton commissioned social reformer Robert Dale Owen and abolitionists James McKaye and Simon Gridley Howe to lead the commission.[42] Howe was also one of the authors of the memorial for the Emancipation League. The report compiled by the commission was integral to determining what was needed from the government to assist the freedmen.

After the commission decided what questions they needed to ask and how they wanted to ask them, they traveled to Virginia and North Carolina and gave a preliminary report on the condition of the freedmen in those areas. The report dealt primarily with the economic condition of the freedmen and how it reduced some of them to stealing.[43] The commission was also concerned with the marital practices of the freedmen. This issue was unimportant given the context, that is, of dealing with the survival of a group of people. The commission did state, "Sufficient evidence is before us that the colored refugees in general place a high value both on education for their children and religious instruction for themselves."[44]

The commission felt that the two economic systems of enslavement and free compensated labor were too divergent and that four million people could not make that change undirected. This was keen insight on the part of the commission. Various potential employers who understood African Americans only as slaves would not be able to adjust to them as wage laborers. The direction was not only for the freedmen but also for the potential white employers. The commission wrote, "They must feel themselves treated as freemen before they can fully realize the fact that they are and will forever remain as such."[45] In an almost naive view of race relations, the commission argued that the only way for freedmen to feel truly free was to be treated as citizens. It would have been more accurate to state that freedom could only be achieved when the American populace was willing to protect their civil rights, but the social reformer and the two abolitionists did not utter this language.

After they finished traveling to contraband camps, the Freedmen's Inquiry Commission issued its final report, on May 15, 1864. The final recommendation of the commission was that a temporary agency be created to aid people's transition from slavery to freedom. The commission felt that it was necessary to make the institution temporary because "the sooner they shall stand alone and make their own unaided way, the better for both their race and ours."[46] This was a simplistic solution to a complex problem. Allowing former slaves to stand alone could not erase two hundred years of bondage. Both races would need time and energy to deal with this social change. The commission also dealt with the need to protect the freedmen from becoming forcibly enslaved again. Emancipation would not become synonymous with independence.[47] The commission wrote in this regard, "Secure to them, by law, their just rights of person and property; relieve them, by fair and equal administration of justice, from the disgraceful prejudice; above all, guard them against the virtual restoration of slavery in any form, under any pretext, and then let them take care of themselves."[48] This report was the precursor to the formation of the Freedmen's Bureau.

Massachusetts Congressman Thomas Eliot first introduced the formation of the Freedmen's Bureau, which passed the House by a slim margin and went to the Senate, where Charles Sumner chaired the Senate Select Committee on Slavery and Freedmen.[49] The bill sat in Sumner's committee for almost a year while they debated whether the bureau should be under the Treasury or the War Department. The American Freedmen's Inquiry Commission felt that any bureau should be under the direction of the War Department, as did Eliot. Sumner felt it belonged under the Treasury Department because it controlled the confiscated lands. In the end, the Bureau of Refugees, Freedmen, and Abandoned Lands came under the umbrella of the War Department.

House of Representatives Bill #51 was titled "An act to establish a bureau of freedmen's affairs." The Freedmen's Bureau, as it came to be known, was the next step in the journey toward African American civil rights. Thousands lacked the essentials of life; they had been uprooted, and they flocked to towns and cities to enjoy their newfound freedom only to find they did not have the means to support themselves.[50] The Freedmen's Bureau was established for this purpose. Thomas Eliot wrote, "The shackles have been loosened from the slave, but conquering armies would leave the defeated free to weld them on again with bolts that could not be stricken off."[51] HR 51 formed the agency to aid African Americans in their adjustment to freedom, but it also helped with the transition from slave to free labor. The Freedmen's Bureau was the last step taken during the Civil War in the slaves' journey to freedom. The bureau and the national discourse about freedom were evidence of the changing paradigm of civil rights, but this change was not fully realized in Florida's court system until after the war and abolition.

During the war, the Florida Court system still functioned on a limited basis. The State Supreme Court heard a smaller number of cases that dealt with slaves, but the cases adjudicated were significant. Most of them dealt with slaves as property and ignored their humanity in favor of their profitability. For example, *McLeod v. Executor of B. M. Dell*, *Stephens v Orman*, and *Smith v. Hines* dealt with African Americans as property in probate disputes, as they had in the antebellum period.[52] Enslaved African Americans were still barred from participating in commerce, as evidenced in *Donaldson v. The State*.

Emily Donaldson was the widow of William S. Donaldson, a forty-five-year-old carpenter from Maine living in Jacksonville whose estate was insolvent by 1855. Probate Judge Felix Livingston published a notice dated June 20, 1855, stating the terms the court required for the debts to be paid. Florida Attorney General John B. Galbraith tried the case with Judge J. Wayles Baker presiding.[53] Emily Donaldson was indicted during the 1859 spring term of the Eastern Circuit Court in Duval County on two counts of trading with a slave. One count was for receiving grain from a slave who did not have a permit to offer grain, and the other count was for purchasing grain from a slave. The name of the slave and the exact crop purchased were not provided in the record. Donaldson pleaded autrefois convict, which means a person cannot be tried or convicted for the same crime twice: double jeopardy.[54] Donaldson's plea was overruled and she changed her plea to not guilty. Donaldson was tried in October 1859 and the original trial ended in a hung jury. The case was tried again the following day with a new jury empanelled, which found Donaldson guilty of all charges. They recommended clemency, and the court assessed a twenty-five-dollar fine. This may have occurred because Donaldson's husband's estate was insolvent and she was facing financial hardships. Samuel L. Burritt, Donaldson's attorney, made a motion for a new trial but was overruled, and therefore a writ of errors was filed with the Florida State Supreme Court.[55]

The state's high court concluded that the autrefois convict plea was the right plea and should have been upheld. It also contended that the court erred in its charge, as "the permit to a slave to sell or dispose of grain must be in writing."[56] The court did not argue the above points brought up by Burritt and instead looked at the law code itself; the court said that section eight of the code, which regulated the trade between slaves and whites, had been repealed by the act of February 14, 1835, as stated in section nine of *Thompson's Digest*.[57] The amended portion of 1851 did not include Duval County and therefore Donaldson could not be held liable. The case was reversed, but the intent of the law was to continue to exclude the enslaved from participating in commerce. Were they allowed to participate in the economy, their status as property would be challenged.[58] Even though Donaldson was the focus of the case, the actions of the enslaved, and that challenge to their status as property, led her to the courtroom.

The *Donaldson* hearing was typical of the cases brought before the court during the war. It focused on the enslaved as property and the application of law to sustain that status. The court rarely adjudicated on cases that directly challenged bondage. The State Supreme Court record mentions only one manumission suit, in 1864, and it was the result of a probate dispute over the last will and testament of Thomas G. Gaskins of Wakulla County. James M. Gaskins, Thomas G. Gaskins's son, filed suit against Charles K. Miller because he felt Miller did not abide by the terms of the will. According to Thomas G. Gaskins's will, he bequeathed two slaves, Sarah, thirty-five, and William Henry, sixteen, to Miller. The enslaved were put into a trust for him to manage, and he was supposed to allow Sarah to go to a free state if she wanted. Miller was to be given $100 from the estate to help her travel to a free state, and William Henry was to be bound out to a useful trade until he was twenty-one. Miller was to "allow Sarah and William Henry to enjoy such privileges and freedom as is consistent with law," but he was to "have sole control and management of them for the purpose herein expressed, without account to any one."[59] It was argued that Miller was not supposed to be vested with ownership of the slaves but merely to facilitate their manumission when necessary. The court stated the bequest was void because it was contrary to law. Slaves were not allowed to be partially free or to trade as free persons. They could not live on a plantation without a white person. Sarah was not allowed to decide whether she would go to a free state, because she was a slave.

In the original case before the Middle Circuit Court, James Gaskins argued that the property, Sarah and William Henry, belonged to himself, Edward Barco, and Allen Felkel. Gaskins asked Alfred Barco to start proceedings to find Sarah and William Henry, but he refused to do so, citing that the will had been executed legally. All debts were paid and property was distributed. Judge J. Wayles Baker ordered an injunction to keep Miller from taking Sarah and William Henry out of the court's jurisdiction. Both slaves were to be handed over to the Leon County Sheriff Richard Saunders until the matter was resolved. Baker also required Gaskins to provide a $5,000 bond made payable to the defendant, Miller, in case of damages. The injunction was not to be enforced until the bond was paid. Gaskins received help with the bond from S. B. Ferrell and H. H. Walker. Bond was paid on April 15, 1863.[60]

Thomas G. Gaskins died June 13, 1862, in Wakulla County. He had three children, Christina, William G., and James M. Christina died before the testator and was survived by two infant children, Allen Felkel and Edward Barco. In the original will, William was granted nine slaves and 620 acres in Wakulla County. James was given eight slaves; Edward received three slaves and land in Leon County.[61] William G. Gaskins also died before Thomas Gaskins. Alfred T. Barco, Edward's father, was the executor of the will. It was alleged Miller took possession of the slaves with the permission of the executor, Barco. It was also alleged that Sarah was living in Florida as a free woman without any restraints, payment of wages to Miller, or subjection to him as a master. She was left to take care of herself at large in the city of Tallahassee as if she was a free person. "It further states she threatens to run off . . . if an opportunity is afforded or she has a chance."[62] William Henry was in Miller's possession working as a slave for Miller. He was being treated "with great severity."[63] Miller responded by denying that Sarah was given her freedom and that William Henry was treated with severity. On July 18, 1864, in the Middle Circuit Court, Judge Baker ruled that Miller had violated the terms of the will, making the clause in the will void. The slaves were to be confiscated and sold at auction with the proceeds going to Thomas Gaskins's estate.[64]

Miller appealed the judgment to the Supreme Court and Justice David Shelby Walker wrote the court's majority opinion.[65] He argued it was important to understand the true intention of the testator. He stated, "It is the first and great rule in the exposition of wills, and to which all other rules must bend, that the intention of the testator expressed in his will shall prevail, provided it be consistent with the rules of law."[66] Walker noted that in every other part of the will slaves bequeathed were specifically stated as being slaves and owned by those mentioned in the document. When it came to Sarah and William Henry they were not listed as slaves and therefore were not intended to be held by Miller as such. Walker argued the will gave Miller the power to protect Sarah and William Henry from "laws enacted against free negroes, and against all persons who should attempt to interfere with them."[67] He continued, "There is no evil against which the policy of our laws is more pointedly directed than that of allowing slaves to have any other status than that of pure slavery. By our act of 1828, the master or employer of a slave is forbidden to allow such slave to go at large and trade as a freeman."[68] The language evoking the concept of evil expressed the fear many in the South had of freed slaves. This case was heard in 1864, when the tide of war had turned in favor of the Union. Walker explained the necessity of the legal control over the disposition of enslaved property as yielding a private right to the public good. He did not believe Sarah had the right to decide whether she could be free or not, and her status as a slave did not provide her with that choice. He stated that Florida law recognized only absolute freedom or absolute slavery, nothing in between. Walker determined that the sixth clause of Gaskins's will was null and void and that the slaves were still part of the estate, therefore upholding Baker's judgment.

In Florida, the above cases proved that the law was unwilling to view slaves as anything other than property. This viewpoint not only impacted the enslaved but also the free black population. Until the law was amended to create a new vantage point, it proved difficult for African Americans to continue their quest for freedom. As much as the war assisted in the emancipation of the slaves, legal precedent played a greater role. The Emancipation Proclamation initially did little to free the entire slave population and had no real impact on free black people in the South. The legal status of slaves had to change to benefit all African Americans, because they were seen as property first and this made it difficult for them to fight for civil rights. As in *Dred Scott*, because of the legacy of slavery jurists did not believe that African Americans belonged to the body politic. If this is accurate, then the only way for all African Americans to become involved in the body politic was to remove the property status of the enslaved. This would change the discourse, because no longer could the courts use property rights to support exclusion; they would have to deal with African Americans' humanity and the protection of law. Where did this change emanate from, the state or the federal level? The Civil War provided a unique opportunity to finally deal with the contradiction that had plagued the Republic since its inception: slavery and freedom. While there were great strides taken for abolition, Floridians continued to fight for the profit of enslaved property after the cessation of conflict.

The Thirteenth Amendment was designed toward the war's end to codify Lincoln's proclamation. The historical scholarship on the Thirteenth Amendment is scant at best. The most in-depth study on the debate over the amendment is by Michael Vorenberg, in *Final Freedom: The Civil War, the Abolition of Slavery, and the Thirteenth Amendment*, in which Vorenberg discusses the politics of the amendment and its legacy. He writes, "One of the monumental legacies of the Thirteenth Amendment, then, was its signal to later generations that the Constitution could be amended to enact social reforms rejected or unimagined by the framers."[69]

Typically, the Fourteenth Amendment overshadows the Thirteenth Amendment, but its impact should not be ignored. The Thirteenth Amendment changed the nature of labor relations and the status of African Americans. Whether the Thirteenth Amendment freed the slaves is debatable. While their status as citizens was not fully determined by the amendment, their status as property under the law no longer applied. Even with the amendment's failure to define their citizenship, this was an important step in ending the legal codification of slavery. From its ratification on, African Americans could never legally be recognized as property. Vorenberg stated, "In the same way that Republicans could not yet fathom and articulate all the rights that inhered in freedom, they were unable to express with clarity the related issue of citizenship."[70]

The specter of *Dred Scott* was not fully felt in the proceedings in Congress. Senators such as Charles Sumner discussed African Americans and civil rights in the same breath, while others refused to accept them as equal citizens. The fact that citizenship was not fully defined was not an error on the part of lawmakers; it was a calculation. Much like abolitionists of the time, politicians may have wanted to end slavery, but they were not in agreement about life after slavery. Prejudicial and paternalistic attitudes plagued logic and reason and created a shortsighted view of liberty that protected white supremacy.

Vorenberg argues that some politicians were afraid to alter the Constitution for fear of destroying it. He tends to ignore the nature of racism in the nineteenth century. What they did struggle with was how to define citizenship in a way that satisfied *Dred Scott* and Frederick Douglass. In 1865, this compromise was the Thirteenth Amendment. Despite the criticism that can be heaped upon this legislation, it does allow for a few things to occur. It forced the people as a nation to redefine what it meant to be American. Vorenberg noted that after the amendment it was up to Americans "to work out the origins and meaning of freedom long after the measure was adopted."[71] Unfortunately, this was a parallel journey for white and black America. Former slaves were forced to define their freedom through action and sacrifice in the years following the war, while white America sought to maintain their position through codification and intimidation. This successive chapter in the civil rights movement found African Americans in a position of quasi-freedom that would define their citizenship and test their ability to protect what little rights they were granted. While the national stage witnessed the discussion of emancipation and its impact on property through the use of words like "contraband," the Florida Supreme Court tended to function as it had during the antebellum period. The era of Reconstruction would be a significant challenge for the movement, because of the promise of freedom and legal equality that would vanish with the Redemption of the South. The framers failed to define who was to be a citizen, but it was African Americans who forced the United States to review its ideals and realize that in a free society citizenship and freedom were synonymous.

The status of property was not easily removed, because it was connected to custom and paternalistic legal traditions. Historian Walter Manley exclaims, "The institution of slavery and defense of states' rights represented focal points of the war, while the ability to gather armies large enough to contest it formed another."[72] Within this mindset, it was difficult for white Northern lawmakers to advocate for equality, and they instead sought to simply end the institution. This was an opportunity for lawmakers to achieve the altruistic ideals of their predecessors, but this was not always in the politicians' forethought. Some did advocate revolutionary ideals, but it was merely rhetorical. Historian Michael Vorenberg writes, "Antislavery congressmen hauled out the writings of Patrick Henry and James Madison to prove that the natural sentiments of the founding generation were against slavery."[73] The war saw its fair share of revolutionary rhetoric from both sides of the battlefield. Northerners claimed to be fighting for the Constitution and the Union, while the South claimed they were fighting oppression as their forefathers had done. While these rhetorical and real battles raged on, slaves were simply doing all they could for freedom. They did not wait for it, and it was not bestowed upon them; it was earned. They fought for it on the plantations, in the cities, and in the courtroom. They continued to struggle on their battlefronts as others wringed their hands over ideas. In Florida, slaves were still challenging the law in the appellate court. These attempts to achieve freedom were ultimately rewarded with the close of hostilities, but not without a legacy. Manley stated that as the Civil War waged, Florida laws changed little and the Supreme Court interpreted the laws as they did before the war. The journey from slavery to freedom was only one portion of the fight, and African American participation in the military played a significant role, but the continued presence in courtroom would have a greater impact on the movement for civil rights in the years following emancipation. The status of property would not be removed with the stroke of a pen but with activism in the courtroom.

The first case to adjudicate on enslaved property after emancipation was *David S. Walker, Appellant v. James H. Gatlin, Appellee*. This 1867 Supreme Court case saw Walker briefly entertain the idea of using the Emancipation Proclamation to negate the sale of an enslaved man named George. The case did not fixate on the Proclamation but on the Thirteenth Amendment and abolition itself. The status of property was not easily shed in the court system or by constitutional amendment. *Walker v. Gatlin* spoke to this issue, and the Supreme Court had to explain the nature of private property and the discretion of the federal government to exert control over it.

This case originated in the Middle Circuit Court in Tallahassee on January 7, 1867, with Judge J. Wayles Baker presiding. According to Walker's complaint, James H. Gatlin signed his name as a surety for a promissory note issued by Joseph H. Alston. The note was for $300, to be paid on the first day of October 1862, with a penalty of 8 percent per annum. Around July 31, 1861, Walker "offered to said Gatlin in payment of said note the bills of this Pensacola & Georgia Railroad Company which were then usually received in payment of debts but said Gatlin refused to receive said bills." On March 28, 1864, Gatlin obtained a judgment against Alston and Walker for $305.83. When the judgment was executed on December 20, 1865, the Sheriff informed Walker that Alston did not have any property to levy and that he would have to pay the judgment. Walker "endeavored to settle with said Gatlin by offering him in payment a Comptroller's warrant on the State of Florida or a Treasury certificate or an execution against another person which [Walker] is advised and believes is perfectly good." He said Gatlin refused this type of payment.[74]

Walker wanted Judge Baker to determine whether he legally owed Gatlin any debt, because the note was for the payment for an enslaved man named George. The original price was $400, but the other $100 was paid at the time of purchase. Walker argued that the note was invalid because of the abolition of slavery, and Gatlin gave a warranty that George would be enslaved for life. "The question presented to your Honor is will the Government after having declared it unlawful for said Alston to own said property yet compel the surety of said Alston to pay for it."[75] Walker wanted an injunction against Gatlin's judgment until Baker could render a judgment on the question at hand. Judge Baker executed an injunction against Gatlin's judgment, and Walker paid a $600 bond for the injunction to take effect. During the injunction, Judge Baker would determine the legality of Walker's complaint. The injunction was filed on December 3, 1866, and the bond was paid on December 8, 1866.

Gatlin responded to Walker's complaint by stating that he did try to pay him through a variety of methods that Walker determined to be less than equitable. The bonds and notes offered did not equal the value of the enslaved property. In regard to abolition, Gatlin argued that this could not be used as a plea during the original trial in 1864 and had no bearing on the current proceedings. He believed that for the reasons outlined by his response the case of injunction should be dismissed. Gatlin offered a bill of sale as exhibit A in his plea. The exhibit showed that he had originally purchased a forty-five-year-old enslaved male named George for $596 from Joseph H. Alston on March 12, 1859. On January 7, 1867, Judge Baker dissolved the injunction, dismissed the bill, and ordered Walker to pay his debt to Gatlin along with the costs of the suit.[76]

After the judgment was rendered, Walker filed an appeal bond on January 10, 1867. John McDougall, commissioner of the City of Tallahassee Bank during the Civil War, and David Walker Gwynn provided security for the bond with Walker in the amount of $500. The case was heard before the Florida Supreme Court with Robert Benjamin Hilton and Alfred L. Woodward Sr., as Walker's counsel and James D. Westcott and Mariano D. Papy as Gatlin's.[77] The case brought before the court was an attempt to argue the nature of the Thirteenth Amendment. It was Walker's contention that the contract made with Gatlin was null and void because the guaranty of "slave for life" was not upheld because of emancipation. As a result, he did not believe he was legally obligated to pay the balance of the promissory note. The debate centered on the federal government's ability to confiscate property without due process of law. The judgment of the case had the potential to set a dangerous precedent, because it could effectively rule the Thirteenth Amendment unconstitutional regardless of its status as an amendment.

After hearing the facts of the case, Chief Justice Charles DuPont delivered the opinion of the court. He stated that this issue was unprecedented in American jurisprudence and that he did not believe there were any recent adjudications that were binding under stare decisis. DuPont argued that the contract making an African American "a slave for life" was commonplace under the institution. The parties involved dealt with each other as equals. He said, "The one agreed to transfer to the other his title in the property, and by clause of special warranty, to guarantee its *political status*."[78] The other agreed to pay the specified price for the transfer and title of the enslaved property. DuPont noted that the date of the contract was one month before the Secession Ordinances, and he wrote, "Can it for a moment be imagined, that at that interesting period, when all hearts were aglow with buoyant hopes of national independence, it ever entered into the mind of either party that the warranty given in the bill of sale was *intended* to provide against the possible contingency which has since happened—the defeat and overthrow of the Confederate Government, and the consequent abolition of the institution of negro [*sic*] slavery?"[79] DuPont argued that the warranty was not created to deal with the eventuality of emancipation but instituted to indemnify the status of the enslaved at the time. If the enslaved ran away to a "so-called free State" the warranty would have been broken. He also stated that if a slave escaped and was captured by the Union Army, the owner again would lose control of that property because they would be freed by their capture. "Thus subjecting the question to the test of *intention*, the Court is clearly of opinion that there has been no breach of the warranty contained in the bill of sale, and that consequently, the injunction which had been granted to stay the execution at law, was properly dissolved."[80]

He continued to discuss the concept of the covenant for "quiet enjoyment," which cannot be broken by any action of the state. He said it was "based upon the established right of 'eminent domain,' as defined in the books. This right finds its sanction in the idea that the ultimate title to all property resides in the government, and that its enjoyment by the citizen is held subservient to that limitation and condition."[81] The right of property rested on the sovereignty of the people, and the government had the right to take possession of that property as directed by the laws of the state set forth by their Constitution. DuPont stated, "The right of sovereignty has been applied to and exercised over the negro involved in this controversy, so as to alter his political status, as it existed at the date of the contract, from that of slavery to freedom, and we do not think that the vendor should be held responsible for the act; it is one over which he could exercise no control."[82] He said this was the first case to bring this issue to the court. The court affirmed the dissolution of the injunction, but the fight over payment for enslaved property in the court system was not over. This debate was significant, because the state courts still wanted to rule on the property rights of slave owners even when those rights had been removed by federal constitutional amendment. They wanted to slowly erode the authority of the Thirteenth Amendment to maintain the antebellum status quo. For African Americans, the new discourse on civil rights was in danger of being severely curtailed in favor of white supremacy.

The journey to freedom was a Herculean task assumed by black men and women. The last great surge toward freedom began with the firing on Fort Sumter. They took the initiative and escaped to the Union lines in the hope that they would be freed. By the end of the Civil War, slaves had acquired the status of freedmen. The war had freed them, and the federal government set up a bureau to help them cope with the change. The Thirteenth Amendment and the Emancipation Proclamation changed the civil rights discourse. Abolition was achieved, but the war was far from over. The ratification of the Thirteenth Amendment paved the way for the Fourteenth and Fifteenth Amendments, which were designed to further define citizenship and civil rights. The civil rights movement moved into its next phase: fighting for former slaves' rights as fellow American citizens. Roger Taney's illogical definition of citizenship could be ignored with regard to these amendments, but unfortunately this ideology did not disappear from the vernacular of jurisprudence. This, along with the invocation of state's rights as used by the Confederacy, not only dominated the Florida court system but also, eventually, the federal courts. The movement had new weapons at its disposal, but with them came new and more stringent responses that would plague the effort throughout the nineteenth century.

Notes

1. 37th Congress, 2nd Session, Senate Executive Document 67. *Instructions Given to Commanding Generals under Act of Congress August 6, 1861.* This was a quote from Babillard La Branche, a sugar plantation owner near Carrollton, Louisiana. Major Peck of Camp Parapet reported this on June 16, 1862, a short time after the firing on Fort Sumter.

2. Leon Litwack, *Been in the Storm So Long: The Aftermath of Slavery* (New York: Vintage Books, 1979), 63.

3. For further reading, see Steven Hahn, *The Political Worlds of Slavery and Freedom* (Cambridge, MA: Harvard University Press, 2009); Larry Eugene Rivers, *Rebels and Runaways: Slave Resistance in Nineteenth-Century Florida* (Urbana: University of Illinois Press, 2012); Larry Eugene Rivers, *Slavery in Florida: Territorial Days to Emancipation* (Gainesville: University Press of Florida, 2000).

4. Jacquelyn Dowd Hall, "The Long Civil Rights Movement and the Political Uses of the Past," *Journal of American History* 91 (2005): 1233–63.

5. Craig Buettinger, "Did Slaves Have Free Will? *Luke, a Slave, v. Florida* and Crime at the Command of the Master," *Florida Historical Quarterly* 83, no. 3 (Winter 2005): 241–57.

6. Thomas D. Morris, *Southern Slavery and the Law, 1619–1860* (Chapel Hill: University of North Carolina Press, 1996), 282.

7. *Luke v. State*, Florida State Archives, Record Group 1100, S49, Box 440, Wallet 773.

8. Mariano D. Papy, *Reports of Cases Argued and Adjudged in the Supreme Court of Florida, at Term Held in 1853, Vol. 5, No. 1* (Tallahassee: Office of Floridian & Journal, Charles E. Dyke, 1853), 185–88.

9. *Luke v. State*, Florida State Archives. The other men were Archibald Gould, Godfrey Foster, Peter C. Lylstra, and James Pellicer.

10. Leslie A. Thompson, Esq., *Manual or Digest of the Statute Law of the State of Florida, of a General and Public Character, in force at the end of the Second Session of the General Assembly of the State, on the sixth day of January 1847* (Boston: Charles C. Little and James Brown, 1857), 541. Section 19: "When any negro or mulatto slave shall be convicted of any felony not punishable with death, such negro or mulatto slave shall be whipped, not exceeding one hundred lashes, by the proper officer of the Court, and suffer such other corporal punishment as the Court shall think fit to inflict." Section 20: "If any negro or mulatto, bond or free, shall commit any other crimes or misdemeanors against the laws of this State, it shall be lawful for the jury convicting him of the same, to punish him by such number of stripes as they may award, not exceeding one hundred."

11. Papy, *Reports of Cases Argued and Adjudged in the Supreme Court of Florida, at Term Held in 1853, vol. 5, no. 1*, 188.

12. Ibid., 189.

13. Ibid., 190.

14. For more information, see *Thompson's Digest*, 541.

15. Ibid., 193.

16. Ibid., 195.

17. Daniel L. Schafer, "A Class of People Neither Freemen nor Slaves: From Spanish to American Race Relations in Florida, 1821–1861," *Journal of Social History* 26, no. 3 (Spring 1993): 587–609.

18. Michael Vorenberg, *Final Freedom: The Civil War, the Abolition of Slavery, and the Thirteenth Amendment* (Cambridge: Cambridge University Press, 2001), 23.

19. George Bentley, *A History of the Freedmen's Bureau* (Oxford: Oxford University Press, 1955), 3.

20. Ibid.

21. George Buker, *Blockade, Refugees, and Contrabands: Civil War of Florida's Gulf Coast, 1861–1865* (Tuscaloosa: University of Alabama Press, 1993), 43.

22. Bentley, *A History of the Freedmen's Bureau*, 3.

23. Ibid., 1.

24. Ibid., 2.

25. Ibid.

26. Louis Gerteis, *From Contraband to Freedmen: Federal Policy Toward Southern Blacks, 1861–1865* (Westport, CT: Greenwood, 1973), 15.

27. Litwack, *Been in the Storm So Long*, 5.

28. 37th Congress, 2nd Session, House Executive Doc. 69, *Message of the President.*

29. Ibid.

30. James McPherson, *Battle Cry of Freedom: The Civil War Era* (New York: Ballantine Books, 1988), 503.

31. Ibid.

32. 37th Congress, 2nd Session, House of Representatives Report 120, *Emancipation of Slaves of Rebels.*

33. Litwack, *Been in the Storm So Long*, 69.

34. Gerteis, *From Contraband to Freedmen*, 32.

35. Buker, *Blockade, Refugees, and Contrabands*, 58.

36. 38th Congress, 1st Session, Executive Doc. 53, *Report of the Freedmen's Inquiry Commission.*

37. Edward Magdol, *A Right to the Land: Essays on The Freedmen's Community* (Westport, CT: Greenwood, 1977), 5.

38. Ibid.

39. 37th Congress, 3rd Session, Misc. Doc. 10, *Memorial of the Emancipation League.*

40. Beverly Palmer, ed., *The Selected Letters of Charles Sumner, Volume II* (Boston: Northeastern University Press, 1990), 35.

41. David Herbert Donald, *Charles Sumner* (New York: Da Capo Press, 1996), 120.

42. Gerteis, *From Contraband to Freedmen*, 35.

43. 38th Congress, 1st Session, Senate Executive Doc. 53.

44. Ibid.

45. Ibid.

46. Ibid.

47. Gerteis, *From Contraband to Freedmen*, 32.

48. 38th Congress, 1st Session, Senate Executive Doc. 53.

49. Donald, *Charles Sumner*, 174.

50. John A. Carpenter, *Sword and Olive Branch* (Pittsburgh: University of Pittsburgh Press, 1964), 87.

51. Richard Finley, *From Slavery to Uncertain Freedom: The Freedmen's Bureau in Arkansas, 1865–1869* (Fayetteville: University of Arkansas Press, 1996), 6.

52. John B. Galbraith, *Reports of Cases Argued and Adjudged in the Supreme Court of Florida, at Terms Held in 1860–1861, Vol. 9* (Tallahassee: Office of Floridian & Journal, Dyke & Carlisle, 1861); John B. Galbraith, *Reports of Cases Argued and Adjudged in the Supreme Court of Florida, at Terms Held in 1864, 1865, 1866, & 1867, Vol. 11* (Tallahassee: Dyke & Sparhawk, 1867).

53. Justice Williams A. Forward was absent and Judge J. Wayles Baker of the Middle Circuit sat in for him.

54. Galbraith, *Reports of Cases Argued and Adjudged in the Supreme Court of Florida, at Terms Held in 1860–1861, Vol. 9*, 403.

55. Ibid., 402–3.

56. Ibid.

57. Leslie A. Thompson, Esq., *Manual or Digest of the Statute Law of the State of Florida, of a General and Public Character, in force at the end of the Second Session of the General Assembly of the State, on the sixth day of January 1847* (Boston: Charles C. Little and James Brown, 1857), 509.

58. The enslaved was not typically prosecuted for this offense. The statute places the criminal act on the buyer and not the seller. Lawmakers argued that the law was designed to reduce theft, but it did not delineate between stolen goods and rightfully obtained goods. The result was full exclusion from the marketplace. Enslaved persons were ultimately prosecuted for theft, although the record does not state whether this happened in the *Donaldson case*.

59. Galbraith, *Reports of Cases Argued and Adjudged in the Supreme Court of Florida, at Terms Held in 1864, 1865, 1866, & 1867, Vol. 11*, 73.

60. *Miller v. Gaskins*, Florida State Archives, Record Group 1100, Series 49, Box #780.

61. Galbraith, *Reports of Cases Argued and Adjudged in the Supreme Court of Florida, at Terms Held in 1864, 1865, 1866, & 1867, Vol. 11*, 73.

62. *Miller v. Gaskins*, Florida State Archives.

63. Galbraith, *Reports of Cases Argued and Adjudged in the Supreme Court of Florida, at Terms Held in 1864, 1865, 1866, & 1867, Vol. 11*, 74.

64. *Miller v. Gaskins*, Florida State Archives.

65. Walker was Florida's eighth governor, 1865–1868.

66. Galbraith, *Reports of Cases Argued and Adjudged in the Supreme Court of Florida, at Terms Held in 1864, 1865, 1866, & 1867, Vol. 11*, 75–76.

67. Ibid., 78.

68. Ibid.

69. Vorenberg, *Final Freedom*, 197.

70. Ibid., 105.

71. Ibid., 4.

72. Walter W. Manley II, E. Cantor Brown, and Eric W. Rise, eds., *The Supreme Court of Florida and Its Predecessor Courts, 1821–1917* (Gainesville: University Press of Florida, 1997), 195.

73. Michael Vorenberg, *Final Freedom*, 197.

74. *Walker v. Gatlin*, (1867), Florida State Archives, Record Group 1100, Series 49, Box #779.

75. Ibid.

76. Ibid.

77. Hilton was a member of the Confederate Congress and a state judge in 1867.

78. John B. Galbraith and A. R. Meek, *Reports of Cases Argued and Adjudged in the Supreme Court of Florida, at Terms Held in 1867, 1868, 1869, Vol. 12* (Tallahassee: Edward M. Cheney, State Printer, 1869), 12.

79. Ibid., 13.

80. Ibid., 15.

81. Ibid.

82. Ibid.

8

Grander in Her Daughters

Florida's Women during the Civil War

Tracy J. Revels

On February 2, 1861, the *Philadelphia Inquirer* reported, "The citizens of the Flowery are determined to maintain their just rights at all hazards; and the fair daughters of Florida are prompt to encourage and cheer their bold defenders."[1] The newspaper not only relayed the latest happenings in the secession movement but prophetically established the trend for the historical view of women's lives during the Civil War.

Florida has received only slight consideration in the vast historical refighting of the war, and if the female "citizens of the Flowery" are mentioned at all, they are portrayed in the traditional roles of motherly matrons and beautiful belles, sending their men off to the front, tending their wounds, and mourning their deaths. A reconsideration of this stereotype is long overdue, for the daughters of Florida were not merely handkerchief-waving supporters of "The Cause." They were Confederates, but they were also Unionists, collaborationists, and neutral observers. They were slave owners and slaves, refugees and rebels. While historians are increasingly examining women's contributions to the Civil War, they often focus only on Confederate women or those who managed large plantations, missing the vast diversity of female experiences on the home front. As a small state, but one that endured a wide range of wartime events, Florida lends itself to the study of women's roles in the conflict. Heroines, cowards, and those who merely wished to be left alone mingled in a state that witnessed virtually every aspect of war, including invasion, occupation, and deprivation.

Florida was a small state in terms of inhabitants. The 1860 census tallied 41,128 white men and 36,619 white women, with a slave population of 31,348 men and 30,397 women. The free black population was minuscule,

Figure 4.
Ellen Thompson, former slave of Martha Margaret Murry May,
courtesy of State Archives of Florida, Florida Memory

only 454 men and 478 women. Although these figures reflected remarkable growth during the prosperous years of the 1850s, the Northern press tagged Florida as "the smallest tadpole in the dirty pool of secession."[2] The population was clustered in the crescent known as Middle Florida. This region curved from the Panhandle to Ocala and represented the plantation belt of the state. Most Floridians resided on small farms, but the state's coastal towns were growing with diverse populations, including Yankee entrepreneurs and invalids. Women within the state lived in a variety of conditions, from frontier isolation to small town friendliness and even the pretension of cosmopolitan sophistication.[3]

The move toward secession drew female support. Many undoubtedly echoed the politics of their menfolk, but they gave their thoughts unique expression. Helen, Maria, Margaret, and Florida Broward, daughters of Colonel John Broward of Duval County, sent a states' rights manifesto to the *Jacksonville Standard* on November 6, 1860. After apologizing for daring to speak publicly on political issues, the women took the "Submissionists" to task, asking whether Floridians would "still remain in the Union and trust the tender mercies of the Yankees and protect us by smoky resolutions and compromise, or will they avail themselves of the means given them by God and nature and defend themselves?" Pledging to imitate the Revolutionary matrons if war came, the Broward women urged secession and threatened to send their crinolines to timid politicians.[4] Other women attended public assemblies on the subject and took to wearing palmetto cockades in their hats as a symbol of support for South Carolina. In Pensacola, the many raucous secession meetings led a naval officer to conclude that "men, women, and children seemed to have gone mad."[5]

When the secession convention assembled in Tallahassee on January 3, 1861, women packed the galleries and cheered the speakers. The vote for secession on January 10 met with feminine cheers. A day later, the first cannon salute to the new Republic of Florida was fired by Princess Achille Murat, widow of one of Napoleon's nephews and Tallahassee's most prominent socialite. Members of the convention entrusted the Ordinance of Secession to Elizabeth M. Eppes, a female descendant of Thomas Jefferson, who decorated the revered document with blue ribbon.[6] Women enjoyed the celebratory band concerts and fireworks displays held in Tampa and other cities. In the small town of Madison, Mrs. Enoch J. Vann hurrahed as fire-eaters with South Carolina pedigrees promised to drink all the blood spilled in the war.[7]

Not all Florida women, however, favored secession. Among those who attended the public meetings in Tampa was Catherine S. Hart, the wife of prominent judge and future governor Ossian Hart, who bemoaned the lack of a "Washington, Webster, or Clay" to cool tempers. In letters to relatives, she defended slavery but hoped disunion could be avoided. Octavia Stephens, a Boston native married to Florida planter Winston J. T. Stephens, shuddered to see militia troops drilling at the Duval County courthouse, declaring in a letter to her husband how grateful she was that he would never be in any military company. By the time her letter reached him, Winston had volunteered with the St. Johns Rangers and been elected first lieutenant. Ellen Call Long, prominent in Tallahassee society, as befitted the daughter of former governor Richard Keith Call, disapproved of the antics of the women attending the secession convention. A number of Tallahassee's Unionist women held a wake for their nation at Lake Jackson Church, learning of the vote for secession just as their meeting was being called to order. Some mothers vowed to prevent their sons from enlisting. Women of all political persuasions worried about their families' safety. The thoughts of slave women were not recorded, but certainly they watched and waited, knowing that the outcome of the unfolding events would change their lives forever.[8]

The first actions of Florida's women were mainly symbolic, fitting within the nineteenth-century ideals of chivalry and honor. Women served as reminders to the men that they were fighting for more than cotton and states' rights. On April 2, 1861, the Gadsden Young Guards were treated to a supper organized by the women of Quincy. Each soldier was served by a young woman "as if she were his sister." The troop's commander promised, "Every man who was at the supper will consider that it is his duty to *fight and die*, if necessary, in defense of our country's rights and the honor of the ladies of Quincy." Along with farewell suppers, Confederate women graced podiums and platforms, presenting battle flags with designs restrained only by their creativity. The Young Guards carried a blue silk flag embroidered with a globe and an eagle, and the state motto, "Let us alone."[9] The St. Augustine Independent Blues displayed a banner with a palmetto and an eagle, created by the ladies of the oldest city. The Franklin Rifles never carried their white flag into battle, perhaps because the seamstresses of Apalachicola had forgotten that white was the color of surrender. As soldiers departed, women surrounded them, often listening to or presenting maudlin speeches. They expressed, as young schoolmistress Sallie Partridge did in a speech to Captain Bradford's Madison volunteers, many "elegant, chaste and appropriate sentiments."[10]

With men marching away, women began to organize "thimble brigades," sewing circles that gave them both a patriotic and social outlet. Long after the war, a lady who identified herself only as Mrs. L. Thompson recalled the excitement among the women of Middleburg, who organized sewing, knitting, "and all other types of societies to relieve and lighten the burden of the brave men."[11] Women established soldiers' aid societies, spending evenings preparing bandages, lint, and flannel bags for cartridges. This work received official sanction and praise from the state government.

The legislature appropriated $10,000 in 1861 and $75,000 in 1863 for uniform materials, turning much of the cloth over to the ladies' military societies for manufacture into apparel. During 1862 and 1863 female societies produced 3,735 pairs of cotton drawers, 2,765 cotton shirts, 169 wool jackets, 809 pairs of wool pants, and 1,000 pairs of cotton socks. Governor John Milton expressed his thanks for the women's "generous, patriotic, and untiring efforts," but late in the war he called for a change in policy, leaving uniform distribution to the Confederate quartermaster. While Florida's Confederate women worked willingly, their products were not standardized, a common problem and concern in the ranks. Women continued to sew, especially for loved ones or local boys in the army.[12] Writing to Jesse Shaw Smith, his sister and personal tailor, Roderick Gospero Shaw of the Fourth Florida Infantry included patterns and descriptions of suits he desired, reflecting the Confederate propensity to design one's own uniform.[13]

Ladies' societies rarely coordinated their efforts, but Florida's women showed intriguing creativity in supporting "The Cause," especially when it came to fund-raising. Tallahassee's ladies opened a special fund that soon included cash, jewelry, napkin rings, forks, spoons, and silver tongs in its treasury. Unmarried women organized a "Misses' Fair and Festival" to sell flowers, handicrafts, and a dinner advertised as "sufficient to tempt the appetite of a king." The event, a "perfect success," raised $1,450.[14] "Bazaars, musical evenings, and amateur theatricals became common in Tallahassee and surrounding counties, providing an opportunity not only to raise money but also to boost morale on the home front. A troupe of lady thespians from Jefferson, Madison, and Leon Counties performed adaptations of *King Lear*, the burlesque *Bombastes Furiosos*, and the melodrama Tampa to large crowds in the capitol building. Youthful performers, such as a young Tallahassee woman who gave a recitation 'in cog' as Miss Nora Marshall, perhaps relished their moment on the stage. Children also contributed to musical evenings, which naturally drew rave reviews, no matter how talented the musicians. More importantly, every form of entertainment raised money for worthy causes: refugees, hospitals, and uniforms."[15]

Florida's Confederate women also responded immediately to the provisioning of hospitals. Newspapers in the first months of the war carried open letters of thanks to women like Mrs. Daniel Ladd, wife of a prominent Leon County businessman, who had donated articles for the Tallahassee Guards' hospital. Ladies' hospital societies were organized, drawing up lists that resembled the one made by the Marianna Society, calling for linens, towels, and even a precise number of dippers, spittoons, and bedpans. Sue M. Archer remembered the transformation of the Planter's Hotel in Tallahassee, how the "corps of ladies" under the direction of Mrs. Delceda Pearce turned an unoccupied structure into "a comfortable and cheery place for the soldiers." Women also established wayside hotels or homes near depots to provide food and homelike comforts to traveling soldiers.[16]

During the war, many women served as amateur nurses, though not always with distinction. Common anecdotes poked fun at unattractive spinsters who tried too hard to imitate Florence Nightingale, only to cause more suffering to their charges. Most women seemed content to deliver food and clothing to hospitals or nurse their own wounded at home. One woman, Mary Martha Reid, widow of territorial governor Robert R. Reid, won fame as the matron of the Florida hospital in Richmond. Since each state was responsible for its own facility, Reid worked tirelessly to make people aware of the hospital's needs. Known as "the mother of the Florida boys," Reid lost her own son, Raymond, in the Battle of the Wilderness near the end of the war.[17]

Support for the Confederacy centered in Middle Florida. Other regions, such as West Florida, Jacksonville, and St. Augustine, held large Unionist populations. These people were unfortunate in their neighbors, for during the war many atrocities occurred. In Walton County, a Union officer reported that one woman had been brutally assaulted by Confederates demanding to know where her husband was hiding. When she refused to reveal his whereabouts, her tormentors unleashed their dogs on her and killed her two children. Other Unionist families found themselves under fire as they tried to reach Federal gunboats. In August 1862, a Union commander rescued four families on the Blackwater River, reporting that the "people were delighted to escape the tyranny of their oppressors, and now, for the first time in months, felt safe."[18]

In an amazing incident late in the war, the Confederate government dispatched Lieutenant Colonel Henry D. Capers to capture a band of Confederate deserters and Unionists who were hiding out in the Taylor and Lafayette County swamps. Unable to locate the men, Capers rousted their wives and children from their homes, burned the dwellings, and then marched his prisoners back to Tallahassee. Held in hastily constructed stockades near Tallahassee, these unfortunate dependents quickly became a "nine days wonder" to local teenager Susan Bradford Eppes and other Confederate bystanders. After initial confrontations filled with threats of retribution, the women grew disheartened and accepted offers of food from concerned citizens. Outraged at Capers' action, Governor John Milton fired off notes protesting the idea of making war on women and children. The women also submitted a petition, arguing that they did not all agree with their husbands' choices, but as wives and daughters they were bound to obey the decisions of their men. On July 19, 1864, the families were transported to a Union blockading vessel off St. Marks.[19]

Many of Florida's important cities fell to Federal troops early in the war: St. Augustine, Key West, Pensacola, and Fernandina became Yankee strongholds and recreation areas during the conflict. For women of Unionist or collaborationist persuasion, the presence of Federal troops represented security and new opportunities. "There are about twenty five ladies in town, who have openly espoused the Union cause throughout the troubles," the Unionist St. Augustine *Examiner* reported on May 1, 1862, "and they deserve great credit for their courage and fidelity, sustained under the most perilous and trying circumstances." In the state's oldest city, Clarissa Anderson opened her plantation home, Markland, to Union officers. A Northerner by birth, the attractive widow established "a charming atmosphere of culture and refinement" while her black cook became known as a seller of orange pies. Elite women like Anderson were able to serve as mediators between the troops and townspeople, easing tensions during the occupation. Some young Minorcan women found romance with their guards, and less genteel relationships were established on a cash basis.[20] In occupied areas, the female population grew with the arrival of officers' wives, schoolteachers, and philanthropists, many of whom left observations—not always flattering—of the state and its natives.[21]

While the Confederate command did not fret about the taking of Florida's port cities, many of the female residents did, and they made their concerns known. The Federals who occupied St. Augustine encountered a constant barrage from the female fire-eaters, often led by Mrs. Frances Kirby Smith, the mother of Confederate general Edmund Kirby Smith. Working within social structures that permitted them to engage in activities for which men would have been arrested, Confederate dames chopped down flagpoles, enacted public mourning for Confederate memorials, and challenged Union officers directly. Shortly after receiving the surrender of the city from Mayor Cristobal Bravo, Commander C. R. P. Rodgers found himself under attack by a virago. Informing him that the men of the city had acted like cowards, the woman declared that there were stouter hearts in other bosoms, striking her own for dramatic effect. Although Union officers dismissed these actions as women's "theatrical desires to portray themselves as heroines," such activities annoyed the Union leaders. When coupled with the suspicion that women were passing messages and aid to Confederates beyond the lines, the pantomimes became intolerable. Confederate families in Key West were nearly deported, and a number of women and children were forcibly removed from St. Augustine in February 1863. Many of these dislocated families later fled to Lake City and Madison.[22]

The war came home for Florida's women by degrees, as prices inevitably rose and household management became a greater burden. During the conflict, "making do" became a theme of life. Florida's women encountered daily challenges to their flexibility and ingenuity. Women living in frontier conditions were probably better prepared for the rigors of deprivations than were their kinswomen who had become accustomed to stores and mills. Amanda Comerford's experience was typical. Her husband James E. Comerford enlisted in the 6th Florida Infantry in 1862, leaving Amanda on their Jackson County farm with a year's provisions, four small children, and a set of twins on the way. "It is difficult to describe my struggles to provide food and clothing for this large family," Comerford wrote. "I had to work on the farm during the day, go a long distance to milk, and a large part of the night was spent spinning and weaving to make cloth for wearing apparel. But somehow I managed to struggle through as did many other women during these trying times."[23] Some, like Mattie English Branch of Liberty County, helped look after "delicate" neighbors. Branch recalled making a circuit of her community, planting corn, potatoes, rice, peas, and pumpkins, because she "was young, healthy, and strong, and felt that [she] must do something for the general good."[24] But for every woman who set up a loom or managed a successful farm, there were others who lacked the education, skills, or aplomb to succeed.

Small luxuries and necessities long taken for granted were early casualties of the war. The price of calico cloth skyrocketed, and medicine became impossible to obtain. Women coped by repairing old dresses, "turning them out" until they resembled something different, if not exactly something new. Almost any food item could be substituted. When coffee grew scarce, Florida housewives brewed dried okra, acorns, or pumpkin seeds instead. Floridians were fortunate in the natural bounty of their land, so their diets were generally better than elsewhere in the Confederacy. Women in occupied areas were often forced to swallow their pride and trade with the

Yankees for provisions. Holidays grew more dismal, leading some women to tell their slaves and children that Santa Claus had been shot by the Yankees. Schools closed and churches lost ministers, disrupting the facets of life women considered sacred.[25]

A myriad of letters bear witness to the trauma of the war on the home front. Naturally, most surviving letters are from soldier husbands or fathers providing general advice or responding to what must have been direct questions. Edmund Lee, a Tampa chaplain in the CSA, sent dozens of messages home to his wife, Electra, who apparently had little business experience. Many of the letters concern the sale of roof tiles, and Lee urged his wife not to allow herself to be cheated.[26] Farm men wrote of feeding and plowing schedules and demanded to know what salt and pork were bringing on the market. Fathers prescribed for childhood ailments, one even telling his wife to inform their son that "he must not swallow any more tacks."[27] What have you done with my watch and your silver, don't buy a horse until you have to, talk to my sister who has "long experience" in making do—all were instructions from one absent husband in 1863.[28] Perhaps most perplexing to sheltered women were the complex financial arrangements, the seemingly endless lists of bonds, notes, and IOUs to be collected before the taxes could be paid.[29] Wives and dependents of soldiers turned to the state for relief but found little. Midway through the war, Governor Milton ordered county officials to compile lists of soldiers' families in need of aid, a figure that leapt from 11,673 individuals in 1863 to more than 13,000 by 1864. Efforts to secure corn, syrup, and other basic foodstuffs for these dependents were largely unsuccessful, and conditions worsened as the conflict progressed. Although the state spent $458,000 to aid families of men in the Confederate service—supporting approximately one noncombatant for every man it put in the field—letters and newspaper editorials constantly complained about the plight of the poor soldier's family. Other government efforts to provide assistance, such as distributing some $35,000 worth of cotton and wool cards, also met with criticism for the poor quality of the materials. By April 1864, Major C. C. Yonge, chief Confederate quartermaster for Florida, warned Governor Milton that many families in the state were "perilously near starvation."[30] The condition of soldiers' families and lower-class whites in general was shocking even to invaders. In February 1864, a reporter for the *New York Herald* found the women near Baldwin to be dirty, gaunt, "wolfish and unwomanly." Soldiers shared his evaluation. "The Whites who are living here still are wretchedly poor," Lieutenant Charles Duren of the

Fifty-Fourth Massachusetts Regiment wrote. "They are women and children—hardly enough clothing to cover their backs—and food I can not tell you what they live on. It is a pitiful sight."[31]

For many women, the greatest burden was simply the absence of a loved one. The dozens of letters between Julia and William Stockton of Quincy reveal a passion that was not dimmed by the war. "Dear Will, come home Darling," Julia urged in 1862, when it seemed likely that her husband, an officer in the First Florida Cavalry, would have a brief furlough. "Two or three weeks will be ages. I told you in my last letter how 'good' I would be."[32] As wives longed for physical contact, mothers worried about more than just their sons' health and survival. Sarah Ann Fletcher delivered numerous sermons to her two sons, Malcolm and John, noting in one letter, "Let me beg of you to watch and pray lest you fall into bad practices, let me urge you then to seek religion there is no safety without it." The men were not oblivious to their womenfolk's fears, and they likewise worried for the health and safety of those left at home. While serving in the Third Florida Infantry, Michael Raysor of Jefferson County pleaded with his wife, Sallie, to look after her health, "for it is you that I live for." Thomas Clark, a soldier in the Fifth Florida Infantry, shared a love of poetry with his wife, Martha, and they exchanged verses as well as letters. In one poem Clark empathized with his spouse's fears, taking the voice of a woman pleading with her husband not to become a soldier:

> An sentinel you'll be wounded
> In the Battlefield be slane
> My hart will Brake like thounder
> If I never see you a gain.

Exhausted from her labors on the farm, Sallie Raysor confessed plainly to her absent husband that "nothing but your presence could make me lively now."[33]

Bereavement stripped away the illusions of rapid, heroic triumphs. Learning that her fiancé had been killed, Susan Bradford's cousin locked herself away in a room, staring forlornly at her trousseau. When Lieutenant Joel C. Blake of the Florida Brigade met a violent end at Gettysburg, his widow was shocked that she could not bring his body home for burial. Unidentified remains and unknown graves tormented many grieving families. Mourning clothes were increasingly in short supply, and newspapers began to criticize the ritual attire as wasteful. Women comforted each other, urging widows and orphans to accept death as the will of God. "Think of your husband as a rejoicing angel," Sallie Raysor's sister-in-law wrote, reminding her that "you dear Sallie had the satisfaction of nursing him, and doing all you could to smoothe his dying pillow."[34]

Not all women lived up to the favorite Confederate image of the stoic matron. Men did not have a monopoly on cowardice, avarice, or unpatriotic behavior. While sojourning in Madison during her exile from St. Augustine, Frances Kirby Smith reported that the local women were pretentious snobs, interested only in comparing themselves to others and parading in finery purchased from blockade-runners. The *Tallahassee Floridian and Journal* scolded widows who were planting cotton rather than corn. "Let not widows think to shield themselves in the manner under the plea of their helplessness," the writer warned, "a rich widow is by no means helpless."

Another warning came from the Gainesville *Cotton States*, following a story of a deserter's execution. The man claimed he had been lured away from duty by his wife's pleading. "Soldiers' wives can not be too cautious in their letters to their husbands," the *Cotton States* argued. "They should not make them believe they are suffering when really they are not."[35]

The Civil War also had an immediate effect upon Florida's slave and free black populations. Approximately one-third of Florida's families owned slaves, and the majority of slaves were clustered in the "black arc" that extended from Gadsden eastward and southward to Alachua and Marion Counties. How a slave reacted to the war depended upon temperament, conditions of enslavement, and knowledge of events. Many owners worked to keep their bondsmen ignorant of the war or told them exaggerated stories to instill fear of "devilish" Yankees, but few if any slaves were fooled by these fables. The war placed new burdens and expectations on female slaves. However, it also gave them new opportunities for rebellion and retribution and, ultimately, freedom.[36]

Slave women retained valuable skills that plantation mistresses had forgotten, and Susan Bradford Eppes recalled black women instructing their mistresses in spinning and sewing, as well as sharing their herb lore for dyes and medicines. Like many Southerners, Eppes remembered the slave women on her father's plantation as faithful servants who dutifully performed their tasks, but it does not take much imagination to wonder if the smile a slave woman wore while stirring black dye for her mistress's mourning dress was not exactly a sweet expression of sympathy.[37] Many female slaves discovered they were disposable property, as families unwilling to sacrifice prime field hands often sold women and children to pay wartime debts. All females were expected to work harder than ever to support the cause that kept them enslaved, a fact noted sourly by a woman belonging to the Watkins family of Bartow. Loaned to another family to do laundry, on her return she commented to her young mistress, "Missis L. say your father he sending us to wash to help her husband fight to keep us slaves."[38]

With the war came new expressions of slave surliness and demonstrations of power. Flora and Jane, two teenage maids at Sylvania, Governor John Milton's Jackson County plantation, exasperated Sarah Jones, the English governess who had come to teach the large Milton brood. Flora would allow the baby to scatter his toys, while Jane purposefully failed at simple assignments. Encouraged by Mrs. Milton to cuff them for disobedience, the young teacher was foiled when Flora simply ignored the blows and Jane turned on her with a gruff, "underground" voice, frightening her almost to tears.[39] The female house servants at Rose Cottage, the Stephens's farm, objected when Octavia Stephens's mother-in-law took up residence during the war. They complained constantly about having "two bosses" and extra work. Octavia Stephens's threat to beat them drew a tart response: one slave replied that she would rather be beat to death than worked to death. Numerous letters filled with sage advice from absent husbands indicate that white mistresses faced new challenges in slave management within the plantation household as well as in the fields.[40]

Slave women further violated white codes of civility by refusing to show sympathy for the Confederate cause. Sarah Brown, a Tampa slave who had experienced much brutal treatment, had no patience with her dewy-eyed mistress. When she found her weeping in fear for her husband, Brown took the opportunity to remind her how many times she had been beaten for similar behavior and that crying "would not do her any good." Revenge was a common urge, even among the young, as Dr. Esther Hills Hawks, a Union physician with the troops during the 1864 occupation of Jacksonville, soon learned. Sarah, one of Dr. Hawks's contraband charges, openly fantasized about rebuking her former mistress, whom she claimed had never given her enough to eat. Begging to be taught to write, Sarah admitted her chief desire was to pen a letter to her owner, describing all the good food behind Yankee lines. Freed slaves could not resist the opportunity to mock their former masters. In Key West, one female slave enjoyed leaning on a fence, watching her onetime mistress labor in her garden and then asking "how she liked it."[41]

Free blacks, though a minuscule portion of the state's population, also lived under oppressive conditions. During the war, at least in Confederate areas, free blacks had to remain circumspect. An 1861 law required them to register with a probate judge, pay a fee, and maintain a white guardian.[42] Free blacks in areas such as Pensacola and St. Augustine fared better, often finding jobs as cooks and domestics for Union troops. They were also eligible to receive rations from Union commissaries. Aunt Eliza, a former slave and cook at Fort Jefferson, soon became a familiar figure, known as much for her odorous pipe, her missing teeth, and her much younger but terribly lazy lover as for her turtle soup.[43]

Wartime confusion made the ultimate resistance to slavery, escape, easier. Like their male counterparts, many female slaves took advantage of the crisis to make their bid for freedom, frequently as family units with young children in tow. They often disappeared from refugee convoys and were not missed for several days. Occasionally they slipped across rivers and inlets on boats, making their way to Union-occupied territories. Others were liberated by advancing Federal troops. Dr. Hawks interviewed contraband women in Jacksonville and came to the conclusion that they were "intelligent and active—many of them have picked up a little book learning. It is not uncommon to find a fair reader among those who have been slaves." An educated member of any escape party was an asset. The slave women who could read or forge passes were unsung heroines of Florida. Once free behind Union lines, women assumed domestic duties while the men were drafted for manual labor. Although some commanders sniffed at the squalor of contraband camps, others noted the determination, especially among the women, to see that their children received medical care and educational opportunities.[44]

Those who found freedom celebrated it vibrantly. In St. Augustine, black women marched with their children and spouses in the 1864 Emancipation Day parades. Mimicking white society, black matrons founded committees to oversee decorations and refreshments for various events. The *Peninsula* of Fernandina noted that two separate committees had been organized to plan the 1863 Independence Day celebration and that all members were married ladies known to be excellent cooks and caterers. "The affair," the paper predicted, "promises to be a complete success."[45]

While slaves struggled for freedom, white women were introduced to the grisly realities of war when the battles came home. Chivalry broke down as the war progressed, and while most Union officers would not tolerate the molestation of women and children, they sanctioned raids on henhouses, larders, and barns. On occasion, a woman's pleading or perhaps her efforts to shame an overzealous commander saved a family from becoming homeless.[46] Black troops were frequently accused of insulting or harassing white women. In 1864, Dr. Esther Hawks witnessed the execution of three black soldiers condemned for committing an "outrage" on a white woman. She later confided to her diary that similar conduct, quite common among white soldiers, went unnoted and unpunished.[47]

Women witnessed battles, skirmishes, and bombardments. Maria Louisa Daegenhard of Tampa, a child during the war, frequently fled with her family when the city was shelled, and from their refuge they watched the burning of the *Scottish Chief*, a famous blockade-runner. Women listened to the guns of Olustee and quickly mobilized to provide food and medical supplies for the survivors, both Confederate and Federal. Afterward, women wandered the battlefield, staring at the grim remains and questioning what purpose the conflict served. Natural Bridge, the concluding skirmish of the war in Florida, brought out morbid tourists, including women who asked to see the Federal bodies floating in the river.[48]

Whether the threat of death was real or imagined, many women fled from coastal areas, joining the mass exodus of humanity that created chaos for the Confederacy. Often these flights were rushed and desperate. Maria C. Murphy was caught in the frenzied Confederate retreat from Jacksonville in 1862, trying to calm three children, pack up her husband's medical library, and sell their furniture in a matter of hours. When she shifted her brood to a neighbor's home, she found the house filled with soldiers, and Murphy soon had the extra duty of baking biscuits for the departing troops. Equally heartrending was the evacuation of Unionist families when Federal troops departed Jacksonville later that year. "None of these [families] had more than ten hours to make preparations for leaving homes they had occupied for years," the *New York Herald* reported. "It was sad to see them hurrying down to the wharf, each carrying some article too precious to forsake."[49] Inland towns such as Madison were inundated with refugees, and relations were occasionally strained when coastal sophisticates, such as Frances Kirby Smith, found provincial accommodations somewhat less than adequate for their refined sensibilities. Military husbands advised wives to evacuate at the first sign of danger, warnings that were sometimes ignored. The extreme to which evacuation could be planned was evident in Major George W. Scott's 1864 letter to his wife, Rebekah, who lived near

Tallahassee. Fearful of a Federal raid on the coast in retribution for the Confederate victory at Olustee, Scott penned a 2,200-word commentary on "how to escape the Yankees," giving Rebekah directions for packing, travel, and slave management. He even included a sketch showing the proper construction of a tent.[50]

The spring of 1865 brought the Battle of Natural Bridge, which saved Tallahassee from Union occupation and took on heroic proportions in the minds of Confederate Floridians, but the Southern cause was already lost. In Tallahassee, Robert E. Lee's surrender coincided with yet another female-supported musical entertainment, a concert held in the house of representatives' chambers to raise money for soldiers' families. The news from Appomattox soon silenced the choruses of *Dixie* and *The Southern Marseillaise*.[51]

"To be a conquered people is a novel experience, and we have daily both amusing and mortifying incidents in our unadaptedness to the change," Ellen Call Long observed from her home in the state's occupied capitol soon after the surrender. "The women," Long reported, "are especially cantankerous, but General Vogdes . . . thinks a few fashionable bonnets will subdue them."[52] Many women feared for the safety of their sons, especially those who had worn the gray. Sarah Ann Fletcher took a decidedly dismal view, writing to her son, "If we are to be subjugated the negroes will be free and we will lose our land and everything else. . . . Do not tell that you killed a Yankee for they might want to kill you for it." Reprisals were surprisingly few, and most Floridians began the process of recovery and reconstruction. However, according to 1866 reports of the Freedmen's Bureau, Florida's women remained more hostile and bitter than the men, especially the "old women and silly girls."[53]

The end of the war meant freedom for the slaves and new opportunities for education and employment, as well as new perils from racism. Schools in Jacksonville and Fernandina continued to flourish, often under the leadership of Yankee women who would make Florida their new home. Most women, no matter their race or class, simply got on with the business of living, often taking up new burdens due to the loss of men or changes in family fortunes.[54]

As soon as the flags were furled, Florida's women began a new task, that of keeping the memory of the "gallant dead" alive and saving such treasures as Confederate banners and swords, to be handed down along with the embellished legends of J. J. Dickison as "Florida's Swamp Fox" and the Home Guard and seminary cadets' "Cradle and Grave" defense of Natural Bridge. As early as June 1865, a group of Tallahassee ladies organized a Memorial Association to perpetuate the memory of the Confederate dead.[55] They did their job well, but in the process of honoring their menfolk, they diminished their own roles as providers, supporters, and survivors.

Neglected for decades, the women of the Confederacy reemerged in the twentieth century. Numerous articles and books now examine the lives of famous women, and journals and diaries, such as those of Mary Chesnut and Sarah Morgan, have become familiar to the general public as well as to scholars. Recently, historians Catherine Clinton and Drew Faust have debated the role of Southern women in the war effort and its effect on them afterward. Unfortunately, Florida's women remain obscure and rarely considered in general historical works. They are beginning to receive consideration in state histories but are rarely incorporated into the overall fabric of the Confederacy. Much work remains to be done in this area, to find similarities and differences to the life experiences of women in other states. While Florida's women certainly had many common bonds with their Confederate sisters, the high proportion of Unionists, the frontier nature of the state, and the occupation of key cities demand special consideration.[56]

Mrs. Enoch Vann, a United Daughters of the Confederacy historian, lived through the Civil War in Florida. As the years passed, she often bemoaned the lack of women in its story. She urged readers of her UDC letters to remember their own experiences during the conflict. "As grand as the South was in her sons," Mrs. Vann declared, "she was grander in her daughters."[57]

Notes

1. *Philadelphia Inquirer*, February 2, 1861.

2. Joe M. Richardson, *The Negro in the Reconstruction of Florida, 1865–1877* (Tallahassee: Florida State University Press, 1965), 1.

3. Canter Brown Jr., "The Civil War, 1861–1865," in Michael Gannon, ed., *The New History of Florida* (Gainesville: University Press of Florida, 1996), 231–33.

4. Samuel Proctor, ed., "The Call To Arms: Secession From a Feminine Point of View," *Florida Historical Quarterly* 35 (January 1957): 266–70. Unfortunately, no copies of the *Jacksonville Standard* for this period exist, and it is not known whether this remarkable letter was ever published.

5. Karl H. Grismer, *Tampa: A History of the City of Tampa and the Tampa Bay Region of Florida* (St. Petersburg: St. Petersburg Print Company, 1950), 137; Caroline

Mays Brevard, *A History of Florida From the Treaty of 1763 to Our Own Times*, vol. 2 (DeLand: Florida Historical Society, 1925), 51; Brian R. Rucker, "Blackwater and Yellow Pine: The Development of Santa Rosa County, 1821–1865," vol. 2, (PhD diss., Florida State University, 1990), 631.

6. Ellen Call Long, *Florida Breezes: or, Florida, New and Old* (1883; facsimile, Gainesville: University of Florida Press, 1962), 306; Susan Bradford Eppes, *Through Some Eventful Years* (1926; facsimile, Gainesville: University of Florida Press, 1968), 142; "Notes on Secession in Tallahassee and Leon County," *Florida Historical Quarterly* 4 (October 1925): 63–64.

7. Jacksonville St. Johns Mirror, July 17, 1861; William H. Trimner in Florida Division, United Daughters of the Confederacy Scrapbooks, vol. 1, (hereafter UDC Scrapbooks) Florida State Archives, Tallahassee (hereafter FSA).

8. Catherine S. Hart to Charlotte Campbell, November 30, 1860, Dena E. Snodgrass Collection, P. K. Yonge Library of Florida History, University of Florida, Gainesville (hereafter PKY); Octavia Stephens to Winston Stephens, September 7, 1861, Stephens Family Collection, PKY; Long, *Florida Breezes*, 306.

9. *Qunicy Republic*, April 6, 1861.

10. Thomas Graham, *The Awakening of St. Augustine: The Anderson Family and the Oldest City, 1821–1924* (St. Augustine: St. Augustine Historical Society, 1978), 84; William H. Trimmer, untitled article, UDC Scrapbooks, vol. 1; T. C. Vann, "Captain Bradford's Company," UDC Scrapbooks, vol. 1.

11. L. Thompson, "Reminiscences of the War," UDC Scrapbooks, vol. 1.

12. John E. Johns, *Florida during the Civil War* (Gainesville: University of Florida Press, 1963), 171–72; Dorothy Dodd, "Florida in the War, 1861–1865," in Allen Morris, ed., *The Florida Handbook, 1961–62* (Tallahassee: Florida State University Press, 1961), 47–48; Bell Irvin Wiley, *The Life of Johnny Reb: The Common Soldier of the Confederacy* (Baton Rouge: Louisiana State University Press, 1943), 108–9.

13. Roderick Gospero Shaw to Jesse Shaw Smith, April 16, 1964, R. K. Shaw Papers, Special Collections, Robert Manning Strozier Library, Florida State University, Tallahassee (hereafter FSU).

14. Mary W. Keen, "Some Phases of Life in Leon County during the Civil War," *Tallahassee Historical Society Annual* 4 (1939): 26; *Tallahassee Sentinel*, April 28, 1863, May 6, 1863.

15. *Tallahassee Floridian and Journal*, May 26, 1863; June 9, 1863; Samuel Proctor, ed., *Florida A Hundred Years Ago* (Tallahassee: Florida State University Press, 1963), n.p.; *Qunicy Dispatch*, April 21, 1863.

16. Tallahassee Florida Sentinel, August 26, 1862; J. Randall Stanley, History of Jackson County (Marianna, 1950), 179–83; Sue M. Archer, "The Soldiers Hospital," UDC Scrapbooks, vol. 5; Tallahassee Florida Sentinel, November 17, 1862.

17. Johns, *Florida during the Civil War*, 172–73; Newspaper extracts, circa 1863, UDC Scrapbooks, vol. 6; Mary Martha Reid, "What I Know of the Travers Family"

(Florida Historical Records Survey, 1937), 14; C. W. Maxwell, "The 2nd Florida Regiment at Williamsburg and Seven Pines," UDC Scrapbooks, vol. 4.

18. Rucker, "Blackwater and Yellow Pine," vol. 2, 694–96.

19. Johns, *Florida during the Civil War*, 165–67; Eppes, *Through Some Eventful Years*, 223–24.

20. *St. Augustine Examiner*, May 1, 1862; Thomas Graham, "The Home Front: Civil War Times in St. Augustine," in Jacqueline Fretwell, ed., *Civil War Times in St. Augustine* (St. Augustine: St. Augustine Historical Society, 1986), 34–35; James M. Nichols, *Perry's Saints, or The Fighting Parson's Regiment in the War of the Rebellion* (Boston, 1886), 180; Diary of Elias A. Bryant, 56–57, Lewis Schmidt Collection, FSA.

21. See Gerald Schwartz, ed., *A Woman Doctor's Civil War: Esther Hill Hawks' Diary* (Columbia: University of South Carolina Press, 1984), and Frances Beecher Perkins, "Two Years With a Colored Regiment: A Woman's Experience," *New England Magazine*, September 1897–February 1898.

22. *Philadelphia Inquirer*, March 20, 1862; *St. Augustine Examiner*, May 1, 1862; Graham, "The Home Front," 26–34, Omega G. East, "St. Augustine during the Civil War," *Florida Historical Quarterly* 31 (October 1952): 82; Jefferson B. Browne, *Key West: The Old and the New* (St. Augustine: St. Augustine Historical Society, 1912), 92–95.

23. "Experiences of Mrs. Amanda Comerford," UDC Scrapbooks, vol. 1.

24. Mattie English Branch, "Story of Two Lovers," UDC Scrapbooks, vol. 1.

25. Mary Louise Ellis and William Warren Rogers, *Favored Land Tallahassee: A History of Tallahassee and Leon County* (Norfolk: Donning Company, 1988), 68; Graham, "The Homefront," 30; Eppes, *Through Some Eventful Years*, 253; Johns, *Florida during the Civil War*, 175–89.

26. Edmund C. Lee, *Civil War Letters* (Florida State Historical Records Survey, 1937), 13, 28–30.

27. Michael O. Raysor to Sallie Raysor, February 5, 1863, Michael O. Raysor Letters, PKY; Washington Waters to "Dear Wife," December 23, 1863, Washington Waters Papers, FSA; Samuel Augustus Palmer to Mary Rebecca Palmer, circa 1863, Palmer Family Letters, FSA.

28. Samuel Augustus Palmer to Mary Rebecca Palmer, circa 1863, Palmer Family Letters.

29. Hugh Black to Mary Ann Black, May 24, 1863, Captain Hugh Black Letters, Special Collections, FSU.

30. John F. Reiger, "Deprivation, Disaffection, and Desertion in Confederate Florida," *Florida Historical Quarterly* 48 (January 1970): 282–83; Dodd, "Florida in the Civil War," 48; Johns, *Florida during the Civil War*, 110–l1.

31. *New York Herald*, February 20, 1864; Charles M. Duren to "Mother," February 15, 1864, Charles M. Duren Letters, PKY.

32. Julia Stockton to William Stockton, February 12, 1862, Stockton Family Papers, FSA.

33. See Stockton Papers; S. A. Fletcher to "Dear Sons," May 6, 1861, Zabud Fletcher Family Papers, FSA; Thomas J. Clark to Martha Ann Law Clark, circa 1862, Thomas J. Clark Letters, FSA, Sallie Raysor to Michael O. Raysor, December 26, 1861, and Michael O. Raysor to Sallie Raysor, January 17, 1863, Raysor Family Papers.

34. Eppes, *Through Some Eventful Years*, 159–60, 168; J. Russell Reaver Jr., ed., "Letters of Joel C. Blake," *Apalachee* 5 (1957–1962): 8–9; Letter to Sallie Raysor, n.d., Raysor Family Papers.

35. Joseph Howard Parks, *General Edmund Kirby Smith, C.S.A.* (Baton Rouge: Louisiana State University Press, 1954), 329; *Tallahassee Floridian and Journal*, April 4, 1863; *Gainesville Cotton States*, April 16, 1864.

36. Kenneth M. Stampp, *The Peculiar Institution: Slavery in the Ante-Bellum South* (New York: Vintage, 1956), 30; Edwin L. Williams Jr., "Negro Slavery in Florida: Part II," *Florida Historical Quarterly* 28 (January 1950): 187; Joshua Hoyet Frier Memoirs, transcript, 13, Joshua Hoyet Frier Papers, FSA.

37. Susan Bradford Eppes, *The Negro of the Old South: A Bit of Period History* (Chicago: J. G. Branch, 1925), 109–11.

38. *Tallahassee Florida Sentinel*, December 9, 1862; March 2 and 13, 1863; *Pensacola Weekly Observer*, June 9, 1861; Margaret Watkins Gibbs, "Memory Diary of Mrs. George Gibbs," n.d., St. Augustine Historical Society Library, St. Augustine.

39. Catherine Cooper Hopley (pseud. Sarah E. Jones), *Life in the South*, vol. 2 (London, 1863), 279–85.

40. Ellen Hodges Patterson, "The Stephens Family in East Florida: A Profile of Plantation Life Along the St. Johns River, 1859–1864" (MA thesis, University of Florida, 1979), 51.

41. "One-Time Slave Sheds Light on Life in Tampa," *Tampa Tribune*, June 5, 1988; Schwartz, ed., *A Woman Doctor's Civil War*, 69–70; Emily Holder, "At the Dry Tortugas during the War: A Lady's Journal," *Californian Illustrated*, February 1892, 103.

42. Julia Floyd Smith, *Slavery and Plantation Development in Antebellum Florida, 1821–1860* (Gainesville: University of Florida Press, 1973), 111–12, 121.

43. *Fernandina Peninsula*, August 13, 1863; "At The Dry Tortugas," 87–89.

44. Mrs. L. Thompson, "Reminiscences of the War," UDC Scrapbooks, vol. 1; Brian E. Michaels, *The River Flows North: A History of Putnam County, Florida* (Palatka, FL: Taylor Publishing Company, 1976), 99; Schwartz, ed., *A Woman Doctor's Civil War*, 77, 82.

45. William Watson Davis, *The Civil War and Reconstruction in Florida* (1913; facsimile edition, Gainesville: University of Florida Press, 1964), 237; *Fernandina Peninsula*, July 2, 1863.

46. Lillie B. McDuffee, *The Lures of Manatee: A True Story of South Florida's Glamourous Past*, 2nd ed. (Atlanta: Manatee, 1961), 142–43; Mary Crary Weller, *Reminiscences of the Old South From 1834 to 1866* (Pensacola, 1984), 13–14.

47. Kyle S. VanLandingham, ed., "'My National Troubles': The Civil War Papers

of William McCullough," *The Sunland Tribune: Journal of the Tampa Historical Society* 20 (November 1994): 63–66; Schwartz, ed., *A Woman Doctor's Civil War*, 61.

48. Maria Louisa Dagenhardt, transcript, Snodgrass Collection; "Recollections of Service," unpublished manuscript, n.d., 88–89, Schmidt Collection, FSA; Mrs. Deliah Kelly, "My Experience," UDC Scrapbooks, vol. 1; Johns, *Florida during the Civil War*, 205.

49. *Philadelphia Inquirer*, April 22, 1862; Mary E. Baker, untitled article, UDC Scrapbooks, vol. 5; Maria C. Murphy, "The First Day of the Evacuation of Jacksonville," UDC Scrapbooks, vol. 4; *New York Herald*, April 22, 1862.

50. Parks, *General Edmund Kirby Smith, C.S.A.*, 346; Clifton Paisley, ed., "How to Escape The Yankees: Major Scott's Letter to His Wife at Tallahassee, March 1864," *Florida Historical Quarterly* 50 (July 1971): 53–59.

51. Proctor, *Florida A Hundred Years Ago*, n.p.; Eppes, *Through Some Eventful Years*, 265–67.

52. Long, *Florida Breezes*, 381.

53. S. A. Fletcher to "Dear Son," April 29, 1865, Zabud Fletcher Family Papers, FSA; Richardson, *The Negro in the Reconstruction of Florida*, 5–6.

54. Sarah Whitmore Foster and John T. Foster Jr., "Chloe Merrick Reed: Freedom's First Lady," *Florida Historical Quarterly* 71 (January 1993): 279–99.

55. Long, *Florida Breezes*, 385.

56. For general biographical studies of Southern women during the Civil War, see Francis Butler Simkins and James Welch Patton, *Women of the Confederacy* (Richmond: Literary Licensing, 1936), and Bell Irwin Wiley, *Confederate Women* (Westport, CT: Greenwood, 1975). Two of the most famous diaries of Southern women are C. Vann Woodward, ed., *Mary Chestnut's Civil War* (New Haven: Yale University Press, 1981), and Charles Frost, ed., *The Civil War Diary of Sarah Morgan* (Athens: University of Georgia Press, 1991). Recent works that consider women's roles and the war's impact on women include George C. Rable, *Civil Wars: Women and the Crisis of Southern Nationalism* (Urbana: University of Illinois Press, 1989), Catherine Clinton and Nina Silber, eds., *Divided Houses: Gender and the Civil War* (New York: Oxford University Press, 1992), and Drew Gilpin Faust, *Mothers of Invention: Women of the Slaveholding South and the American Civil War* (Chapel Hill: University of North Carolina Press, 1996). Florida's women receive attention in two book chapters: Canter Brown Jr., "The Civil War, 1861–1865," in Gannon, ed., *New History of Florida*, and Mary Ann Cleveland, "Florida Women during the Civil War," in *Florida Decades: A Sesquicentennial History, 1845–1995*, ed. James J. Horgan and Lewis N. Wynne (St. Leo, FL: St. Leo College Press, 1995).

57. Mrs. Enoch J. Vann, "Reminiscences of the Battle of Olustee," UDC Scrapbooks, vol. 1.

9

Florida Hispanics in the Civil War

Robert A. Taylor

In his classic Civil War study *The Life of Johnny Reb: The Common Soldier of the Confederacy*, Bell I. Wiley commented that while the majority of Confederates were Southern-born, a non-native group made up a significant number of gray-clad troops. While not as ethnically diverse as the Union armies, rebel ranks included Irish, German, British, Polish, Canadian, and Dutch soldiers. There was also a group Wiley referred to vaguely as "Mexicans." While offering relatively little information about these men, Wiley did state that "the South owes an incalculable debt of gratitude and honor" to these unique Confederate soldiers.[1]

While scholarship on the Confederate soldier experience has progressed since Wiley was writing in the 1940s, some aspects of that experience has not been fully explored by Civil War historians. One area of such semi-benign neglect is the Confederate state of Florida and its rebel troops. Florida's tradition of interaction with Hispanic culture goes back to the 1500s, so it should come as no surprise that Floridians of that ethnic background shouldered muskets in the third state to join the Confederacy. These ordinary men deserve the attention of Civil War historians, who often only refight major battles and rewrite general officer biographies. The war, as Lincoln described it, was a struggle between common people.

When secession and civil war came to Florida in 1861, men of military age flocked to enlist in the defense of their state and new country. Many of these men saw active service in both the Confederate Army of Northern Virginia and in the western Army of Tennessee. These new soldiers enjoyed the cheers and earnest prayers of family and friends left behind as they ventured far from home. One observer took note of a patriotic surge in the populace and recorded "what a glorious commentary is this on the spirit and character of our people, and what an augury for the future of our cause."[2] But out of the more than fifteen thousand Floridians to serve in the ranks of the Confederate Army, at least eighty citizens of Hispanic descent donned uniforms and shouldered rifles. These soldiers played a key, if unheralded, role in Florida's military participation in the Civil War.

It should come as no surprise that the peninsula state's Hispanic community was drawn into the struggle between North and South from the onset, as this community had deep roots in the region. Two long periods as a Spanish colony gave the future state a fluctuating Hispanic population in urban centers such as Saint Augustine and Pensacola that was augmented by immigrants from Cuba, known as "Floridanos," and from Mexico and Spain. Dr. Andrew Turnbull's ill-fated 1768 New Smyrna colony introduced hundreds of Minorcans to the region, and their descendants remained in the Saint Augustine area well into the 1860s.[3] Significant numbers of ethnic Minorcans from Saint Augustine signed on with volunteer companies like the Saint Augustine Blues, which in time became Company B of the Third Florida Infantry Regiment. Southward, in Tampa, others stepped forward to help defend Tampa Bay's long coastline from the Yankees by joining the newly formed Volunteer Coast Guard. A member of that unit recorded in his diary on February 23, 1862, that "this is a cosmopolitan company, it is composed of Yankees, Crackers, Conchs, Spaniards . . . but all are good southern men." At least eight men of Spanish origin served as Coast Guardsmen along the Gulf shore during the early days of the war.[4]

Soon every Florida military unit had at least one member with a Hispanic name on its muster roll, but two regiments had the highest concentration. The first was the Third Florida Infantry, organized in July 1861 and later reorganized, in May 1862, under the command of Colonel William S. Dilworth. After a stint in East Florida the Third was transferred to the Army of Tennessee, where it remained for the duration of the war. This veteran regiment's list of engagements included those at Perryville, Murfreesboro, Chickamauga, the Atlanta campaign, Franklin, and the final clash at Bentonville in 1865.[5]

The Third's eastern counterpart was the Eighth Florida Infantry Regiment, which contained considerable numbers of troops of Hispanic origin. Mustered into Confederate service in the summer of 1862 and eventually led by Colonel David Lang, it fought its way through most of the major battles alongside Lee's army in Virginia. Names like Second Bull Run, Fredericksburg, Gettysburg, and Petersburg were to be stitched on its battle flag, and it marched and fought to the end at Appomattox Court House.[6]

As these and other Florida regiments prepared to take the field, several Hispanic Florida soldiers were either elected officers in company voting or given direct commissions in the Confederate service. The Floridian of this group to achieve the highest field rank during the Civil War was William Baya of Saint Augustine. Beginning as an orderly sergeant in 1861, the twenty-seven-year-old accepted a lieutenancy in the Confederate States Marine Corps. He eventually raised his own Company D of the Eighth Florida and led it as a captain. Baya served with his men until he was wounded and taken prisoner by the Federals at Fredericksburg in December 1862. After a stay in the prison pen at Fort Monroe, Captain Baya was exchanged in time to rejoin his troops for the battles at Chancellorsville and Gettysburg. By the end of 1863, Baya, now a lieutenant colonel, was struck again during the clash at Bristoe Station and sidelined until his wound healed. The year 1864 found him back in action at the Weldon Railroad, where he suffered a third battlefield injury. The redoubtable Baya recovered sufficiently to serve with the Eighth Florida through the final Virginia campaign until his second and final capture after the April 6, 1865, debacle at Sailor's Creek.[7]

Baya was joined in service to the Confederacy beyond Florida's borders by Celestine Gonzales, who began in 1861 as a first lieutenant in the Gainesville Minutemen, later to become Company H of the First Florida Infantry Regiment. After proving himself a competent officer, Lieutenant Gonzales was detached from his unit in September 1862 and sent to Greenville, Alabama, to help enforce the Confederacy's new conscription laws. The unpopularity of this measure made this a difficult and at times a very dangerous assignment for Gonzales. By 1863 he had risen to captain and been transferred to the Quartermaster Department. Here his proficient work in acquiring vitally needed forage for army use caught the attention of his superiors. Major Alfred M. Barbour praised Gonzales that year as "the most efficient, energetic, active, and faithful man I have seen in this command" and urged his promotion. Gonzales's reputation as a rebel supply officer reached as high as theater commander General Joseph E. Johnston, who agreed with Barbour's recommendation.[8]

By the fateful year 1864 Captain Gonzales was commanding the important military post at West Point, Georgia. This critical rail center was where the railroad to Montgomery ended and the Atlanta and West Point Railroad began, making it a funnel through which supplies flowed to Confederate troops defending Atlanta. Warehouses and an extensive railroad yard made this a strategic location for both armies and a very tempting target for the Unionists. In 1865 this base came under the threat of a large

Federal cavalry force under General James H. Wilson, which was then cutting a swath through central Alabama. Gonzales was among a scratch force put together to attempt a defense of West Point from behind the walls of Fort Tyler on the Alabama side of the Chattahoochee River. After a sharp engagement the fort and the town fell to Yankee cavalrymen at the cost of eighteen dead Confederates. One of those killed at Fort Tyler was Captain Celestine Gonzales.[9]

Other Hispanic Floridians wore the insignia of a Confederate officer before the war's end. Alonzo A. Bravo served as a third lieutenant in Company D, Eighth Florida Infantry until he was relieved in 1862. John B. Oliveras was commissioned a first lieutenant in Company A of the Third Florida and in time moved up to the rank of captain. His war ended after he received a severe wound at the October 8, 1862, battle of Perryville, Kentucky, that by the following February had forced him to leave field service. Second Lieutenant Randolph Hernandez of Company A, First Florida Infantry, began as his company's first sergeant, but illness had rendered him temporarily unfit for duty by January 1863. Lieutenants Andreas B. Canova and Francis Baya led troops in the First Florida Cavalry and the Second Florida Infantry Regiments, respectively.[10]

Several Hispanic soldiers in Florida units served as noncommissioned officers or commissioned officers. The Eighth Florida had three sergeants and two corporals from this ethnic group. The First Florida boasted three Latin sergeants, while the Third Florida had three Hispanic corporals and the Second Florida Cavalry had two Hispanic noncommissioned officers on its muster roll. Clearly the opportunity to rise to leadership positions existed for Floridians of Hispanic descent in units with significant numbers of enlisted soldiers from the same group. At least one of these noncommissioned officers earned a battlefield commission and recognition for military competence and bravery.[11]

All Civil War soldiers faced the real possibility of combat and the very genuine chance of encountering the final, fatal bullet. Hispanic Floridians confronted such dangers and several paid the supreme price. Service records, while far from complete, tell a tale familiar to students of Civil War combat. Private Alonzo Lopez, age twenty-four, of Company B of the Third Florida was killed in action at Perryville in 1862. Gasper Carreas enlisted at Camp Finegan, Florida, as a private in Company I, Tenth Florida, in July 1863, but less than a year later died in the bloody clash at Cold Harbor. Company F of the same regiment lost Private Henry C. Sanchez a few months later in the muddy trenches of Petersburg, on November 8, 1864.[12]

Fear of death stood shoulder to shoulder with the chance of suffering a horrible wound and being thrown on the slender resources of Confederate military medicine for treatment. Edward A. Fernandez, only eighteen, signed up in Jacksonville with Company G of the Second Florida Infantry. With his comrades he was engaged on the Peninsula at the May 5, 1862, Battle of Williamsburg, where he suffered a serious leg wound that forced him to be left behind on the battlefield. Union troops quickly made the crippled Sergeant Fernandez a prisoner of war and admitted him to a Federal field hospital. Here a surgeon amputated a section of his right leg and ordered him to be moved to the Old Capitol Prison in Washington, DC. Fernandez was extremely fortunate to be exchanged and subsequently discharged from the rebel army by mid-August 1862. Another man, Emanuel M. Lopez of Company A, Third Florida, was unlucky enough to be wounded in battle at Murfreesboro that year and hit yet again near Dallas, Georgia, on May 4, 1864.[13]

The three bloody days of the Battle of Gettysburg in the summer of 1863 left no Florida troops unscathed, regardless of their heritage. Sergeant S. J. Sanchez of Company B, Second Florida, was wounded in action on July 2 and taken prisoner. Like thousands of others, he lost his leg to a Yankee doctor's saw that same day in hopes of saving his life. However, the Florida native was to die a lingering death some fifteen days later. Another luckless soldier was Private August Gonzales of Company D, Eighth Florida; he received a serious thigh wound that forced his comrades to leave him on the field. Gonzales spent the rest of the war as a Union prisoner until his release on May 10, 1865. Others no doubt suffered injuries during the titanic clash in Pennsylvania that in the rush of events they did not even bother to report.[14]

Hispanic soldiers in Confederate Army units ran the risk of being captured by the enemy, as has been seen. They too endured the hardest trial of the conflict: being held as prisoners of war. Private Joseph F. Baya of Company D, Eighth Florida, became a prisoner of the Union Army in the aftermath of Gettysburg and was held at Fort Lafayette, New York, at Fort Delaware, Delaware, and finally at Point Lookout, Maryland. It was from this prison camp that he was released to return home on February 18, 1865. Another enlistee, teamster Manuel Sanchez of Company H of the Second Florida Infantry, was likewise taken in Pennsylvania and incarcerated first at Fort McHenry and then at Point Lookout. Company A's Private A. J. Hernandez would follow Sanchez into the Union military prison system at roughly the same time.[15]

Florida soldiers fighting in the west found themselves as likely to become prisoners of war as their eastern-serving comrades. Twenty-two-year-old William Genovar enlisted in Company B of the Third Florida in 1861 and in time became the company's cook. Unfortunately, he was captured by elements of the Union Fourteenth Corps near Atlanta in 1864 and sent northward to prison at Camp Chase, Ohio. Here he continued his culinary trade until sent home in 1865. Another Company B man, Joseph B. Hernandez, was detached for duty in a military hospital in Chattanooga until he was called back into his regiment's ranks. During the disastrous battle of Nashville in late 1864 the thirty-seven-year-old Hernandez joined the hundreds of Confederates seized by the Federals on December 18. Corporal Emanuel B. Lopez, another luckless Company B trooper, also fell into Yankee hands in the wake of the rebel defeat.[16]

Some Hispanic soldiers were taken into custody in less than glorious circumstances. For example, Private Joseph Baya of Company B, Second Florida Cavalry, was captured near Picolata on the St. Johns River on April 22, 1864. While on his way home on a furlough, Private Baya ran into a detachment of United States Colored Troops stationed in the area and was quickly snared. Prisoner Baya then began a sorrowful journey that would take him north to the grim walls of Fort Delaware. Later his official service record would erroneously report that had he been captured at the February 1864 Battle of Olustee.[17]

For every Civil War soldier killed, wounded, or taken prisoner in battle many more died from disease. Floridians of Hispanic origins had no special immunity to the grimmest reaper of the war. Private Thomas Ponce of Company B, Third Florida, died of disease in a Mobile hospital on July 25, 1862, at the age of thirty. Also that year Privates John and Roman Sanchez of Company F, Tenth Florida Infantry, died of illness and an accidental gunshot wound, respectively. A third Sanchez in Company F, Private Francis A., died from a shooting accident while in camp. Company G lost Private Louis D. Cavedo on October 28, 1864, to typhoid fever. After his enlistment at Baldwin in 1862, he served as a clerk in a general hospital and by 1864 was working as a nurse in his brigade's infirmary. Chances are that he contracted his fatal malady from the infected patients he cared for in the field hospital.[18]

Disease cut down Florida soldiers regardless of age, rank, or ethnicity. Third Lieutenant Francis Baya of the Second Florida, age twenty-seven, was taken prisoner near Fredericksburg on May 5, 1863. From there he was moved to Old Capitol Prison and then on to the cold shores of Johnson's Island, Ohio. The island prison's frigid climate took its toll on the lieutenant's physical constitution, and he died there in February 1864. Almost a month later, nineteen-year-old David Castillo, a private in Company B, Eighth Florida, expired in his bed from pneumonia in Richmond's Winder Hospital Number Two on April 3, 1863.[19]

Desertion, like disease, was a problem that the armies of the Confederacy grappled with during the Civil War and never fully conquered. The causes of leaving without permission were many, and they multiplied as the rebel chances of victory waned. Hispanic soldiers were not exempt from temptations to flee the ranks and escape the hardships of army life. Gomocindo Salla, for example, joined the army in Sanderson on October 18, 1861, and by the end of the year had reached the rank of corporal. Then without warning he inexplicably deserted and was never seen by his unit, Company D of the First Florida Cavalry, again. Private Francis Sanchez of Company G, First Florida Cavalry, also left his company without leave in November 1862. Sanchez claimed that illness prevented him from serving and that returning home to Florida was his only option. Despite his assertion, however, Private Sanchez had been listed as a deserter by 1864. A fellow regimental absconder was Joseph Hernandez, a soldier in the Eighth Florida, who fled the ranks in May 1862. His service record ends with the terse line "gone [to] the Yankees."[20]

By 1864, desertions were on the rise throughout the Confederate Army, as the tide of war rolled against the South on many fronts. On August 23, Private Bartola Canova of Company I, Tenth Florida Infantry, joined dozens of other troops in going over to the Federals around Petersburg. He was briefly held at the large Union base at City Point before taking the oath of allegiance and being shipped northward to Philadelphia. Later in November, Private Predentes Oratogus of Company A, Third Florida, flagged down a US Navy gunboat from the shores of the St. Johns River near Mandarin and gave himself up. Oratogus had left the Third Florida three days after the Battle of Olustee was eager to take the oath of allegiance to the Union and give up the rebel cause. Private Oratogus also freely shared with the Yankee sailors what information he had about Confederate numbers and troop dispositions in the region.[21]

Death, disease, and desertion seemed part and parcel of the Hispanic soldier's Civil War experience, but the question remains as to how these men were treated by their fellow Floridians and by Confederates from other states. While data is sketchy at best, a partial pattern emerges of a less than perfect situation. For example, the Eighth Florida Infantry, with its considerable Hispanic members, left Florida with very mixed feelings. General Joseph Finegan of the Department of East and West Florida reported to the Confederate government on September 14, 1862, that the Eighth Florida troops had felt "some dissatisfaction . . . caused by misrepresentations of the captains, or some of them, while raising their companies, and by candidates before and after the election of field officers." Many of the Eighth's soldiers had volunteered in the mistaken belief that they would be retained for local defense on the Florida peninsula, and when orders for a move to Virginia came it was a bitter pill for all the Eighth Florida Infantry.[22]

This movement impaired morale in the regiment, which soon found itself facing the guns of the enemy as well as criticisms from its own army. The Eighth Florida was ordered to deploy by mid-December along the banks of the Rappahannock River below the town of Fredericksburg. Early on the morning of December 11, three companies of the regiment under the command of then-Captain William Baya were placed in an advanced picket position near the river. Their mission was to oppose the efforts of Federal engineers from the Army of the Potomac to construct pontoon bridges across the wide stream in prelude to a Union crossing. As pressure from blue-clad soldiers grew on Baya's small force, he protested to senior officers about the untenable spot his men were in by superior enemy numbers. The command for the Floridians to hold their ground was repeated and Captain Baya complied, no doubt smarting from the implied questioning of his men's courage.[23]

Events proved Baya's military judgment about the tactical situation correct, as his little command was forced to flee with casualties, and several of its members were taken prisoner during the retreat by the Seventh Michigan Infantry. However, complaints from other Confederate units about the Eighth Florida's performance soon arose. Officers from the neighboring Seventeenth Mississippi charged that Baya's troops had consistently refused to shoot at the enemy for fear of drawing Union artillery fire down on their positions. Others claimed the Floridians retreated without orders and in some confusion, creating a break in the rebel line that hurt efforts to stop the Yankee advance.[24]

In the aftermath of this action, even harsher words were aimed at Baya and both his Hispanic and non-Hispanic troops. Colonel John C. Fiser, commander of the Seventeenth Mississippi, charged in his report that any Floridian captured was taken "from inefficiency and fear of being killed in the retreat."[25] Perhaps Baya and his men were indeed placed at a difficult post from which escape was problematic at best. Could the negative comments about their conduct, echoed by modern historians such as Douglas Southall Freeman, be motivated at least in part by the ethnic origins of Baya and many of his fellow soldiers in the Eighth Florida? Were these men put in a dangerous situation and then damned for seeming to fail in the line of duty due to some covert form of racism on the part of other Confederates? The records, remaining all but silent, fail to provide an adequate answer either way.[26]

To find evidence of racial attitudes toward Hispanic Floridians in gray, one must return to Florida itself and look at the experience of one such person. Antonio A. Canova was a well-known citizen of northeast Florida in the antebellum years with political connections in Tallahassee. Although already thirty-six, he enlisted when hostilities began as a private in Company A of the Third Florida Infantry. Canova was not destined to shoulder a musket for long however, as he was soon commissioned a major in the Confederate Army's Commissary Department, on March 3, 1862, by a presidential order from Jefferson Davis. By December of that year he had been selected to become Florida's chief of subsistence and charged with collecting and forwarding the supplies needed to help feed rebel forces in and out of the state.[27]

Problems with supply often led to bitter grumbling among Confederate troops about the presumable incompetence of commissary and quartermaster officials, and such was the case in Florida. Major Canova soon had his share of detractors, but complaints against him took on a different tone. An officer in the Second Florida Cavalry angrily protested in a letter home in 1862 that his cavalrymen's hunger was caused by poor commissary work and that "Maj. Canova cant get any votes in this section." He went on in the same letter to charge that Canova was "like the rest of Manaucians [*sic*] when he gets power he feels he is of more importance than he should."[28] No doubt other soldiers would have readily supported these sentiments.

Canova would soon find himself involved in a legal dispute arising from his military duties that tested the government of the Confederacy's power to impress badly needed food and supplies for its survival. In July

1863, former US senator David Levy Yulee negotiated a business transaction wherein some fifty large hogsheads of valuable sugar would be sold to an agent representing the city of Savannah, Georgia. But before the kegs could be moved from their Waldo warehouse, Major Canova learned of their existence and the pending sale and moved to secure the sugar for the rebel government. Citing the authority given to him by an April 14 order from the Subsistence Department in Richmond, he seized it in the name of the Confederacy under the Impressment Act.

An outraged Yulee immediately brought suit in the Florida courts, claiming that Canova "had no authority whatsoever from the War Department or any other department to impress sugar, either upon an emergency or for collecting it to be stored in certain localities."[29] The state supreme court sitting in Tallahassee in time heard arguments in what would become *Yulee v. Canova* (1864). Plaintiff Yulee won his case to the regret of rebel authorities that had no Confederate supreme court to which to appeal the ruling. The legal proceedings themselves were followed with some interest throughout the Southern section of the Confederacy, making Antonio Canova probably the best known Floridian of Hispanic origin in the Civil War South, but far from the most popular.[30]

By the summer of 1865 the issues of impressment and states' rights had become academic, as Confederate armies surrendered one by one. With the end of hostilities, Florida's Hispanic community could look back with considerable pride at the conduct of its sons in the service of their state and the Southern cause. Their military experiences encapsulated that of all Civil War soldiers in many ways. They fought in epic battles far from home, from which some never returned. Some were wounded and held as prisoners of war for their country, while others suffered from various, and often fatal, illnesses. Some were gallant in action and some deserted to the Unionists. One veteran Confederate officer commented in 1864 that Florida troops in the rebel army were "a small but Spartan band."[31] There is more than ample evidence that Hispanic Floridians did indeed belong to that band and that their actions deserve to be studied and remembered.

Notes

1. Bell I. Wiley, *The Life of Johnny Reb: The Common Soldier of the Confederacy* (1943; Reprint, Baton Rouge: Louisiana State University Press, 1978), 322–24.

2. Charleston *Daily Courier*, June 4, 1862, September 16, 1863. For Florida's military experience during the Civil War, see William W. Davis, *The Civil War and*

Reconstruction in Florida (New York, 1913); John J. Dickison, "Florida," in *Confederate Military History* 11, ed. Clement A. Evans (Atlanta, 1899); and John E. Johns, *Florida during the Civil War* (Gainesville: University of Florida Press, 1963).

3. Patricia C. Griffin, *Mullet On the Beach: The Minorcans of Florida, 1768–1788* (Gainesville: University Press of Florida, 1991), preface, 195; David J. Weber, *The Spanish Frontier in North America* (New Haven: Yale University Press, 1992), 277–78; David J. Coles, "Ancient City Defenders: The St. Augustine Blues," *El Escribano: The Saint Augustine Journal of History* 23 (1986): 71–74. The Moreno family of Pensacola had thirteen male members in Confederate service. See William S. Coker, "The Moreno Family of the Gulf Coast," in *Spanish Pathways in Florida*, ed. Ann L. Henderson and Gary R. Mormino (Sarasota, FL: Pineapple, 1991), 234–36.

4. Ronald N. Pouty, ed., "War Comes To Tampa Bay: The Civil War Diary of Robert Watson," *Tampa Bay History* 10 (Fall/Winter 1988): 51. At least eight Hispanic men served in the various Florida Coast Guard units that existed early in the war. See Fred L. Robertson, comp., *Soldiers of Florida in the Seminole Indian, Civil, and Spanish-American Wars* (Live Oak, 1903; reprint, Macclenny, 1983), 49, 52, 57, 58 (hereinafter cited as *Soldiers of Florida*).

5. Stewart Sifakis, *Compendium of the Confederate Armies: Florida and Arkansas* (New York: Facts on File, 1992), 18 (hereinafter cited as *Compendium*).

6. *Compendium*, 24. For more on the Eighth Florida, see Bertram H. Groene, ed., "Civil War Letters of Colonel David Lang," *Florida Historical Quarterly* 54 (January 1976): 340–66.

7. For Baya's military career, see Compiled Service Records of Confederate Soldiers Who Served in Organizations from the State of Florida, Roll 81, National Archives, Washington, DC (hereinafter cited as Compiled Service Records); David W. Hartman and David Coles, comps., *Biographical Rosters of Florida's Confederate and Union Soldiers, 1861–1865*, 5 vols. (Wilmington, NC: Broadfoot, 1995), 2:808; *Soldiers of Florida*, 189; Dickison, "Florida," 221–22.

8. Compiled Service Records, Roll 27. General Johnston had spent considerable time in Florida during the Second Seminole War. See Craig L. Symond, *Joseph E. Johnston: A Civil War Biography* (New York: W. W. Norton, 1991), 30–43.

9. Hartman and Coles, *Biographical Rosters*, 1:122. For more on the clash at West Point, see US War Department, *The War of the Rebellion: A Compilation of the Official Records of the Union and Confederate Armies*, 128 vols. (Washington, DC, 1880–1901), Series 1, 49, Part II, 428–29 (hereinafter cited as O.R.); L. B. McFarland, "Battle of West Point," *Confederate Veteran* 23 (August 1915): 353; James P. Jones, *Yankee Blitzkrieg: Wilson's Raid Through Alabama and Georgia* (Athens: University of Georgia Press, 1976), 122; and Noah A. Trudeau, *Out of the Storm: The End of the Civil War, April–June 1865* (Baton Rouge: Louisiana State University Press, 1994), 253–54.

10. Compiled Service Records, Rolls 1, 27, 34; *Soldiers of Florida*, 59; Hartman and Coles, *Biographical Rosters*, 2:263, 808. Later Lieutenant Hernandez was cited for

gallantry at the September 1863 Battle of Chickamauga. See O.R., Series 1, 30, Part II, 537.

11. Compiled Service Records, Rolls 27, 37, 41, 46, 49, 50, 84, 85, 95; *Soldiers of Florida*, 59, 76, 90, 105, 195.

12. Compiled Service Records, Rolls 49, 93, 97: *Soldiers of Florida*, 105, 233. For more on Florida troops in Virginia in 1864, see Zack C. Waters, "'Tell Them I Died Like a Confederate Soldier': Finegan's Brigade at Cold Harbor," *Florida Historical Quarterly* 69 (October 1990): 156–77.

13. Francis P. Fleming, *Memoir of Capt. C. Seton Fleming, of the Second Florida Infantry, CSA, Illustrative of the Florida troops in Virginia During the War Between the States* (Jacksonville, 1884; facsimile ed., Alexandria, Va., 1985), 111; US War Department, Office of the Surgeon General, *The Medical and Surgical History of the War of the Rebellion*, 15 vols. (Washington, DC, 1875–1888; facsimile ed., Wilmington, NC: Broadfoot, 1990), 12:523 (hereinafter cited as *Medical History*); Compiled Service Records, Roll 37; *Soldiers of Florida*, 90, 105. See also Earl C. Hastings Jr. and David Hastings, *A Pitiless Rain: The Battle of Williamsburg, 1862* (Shippensburg, PA: White Mane, 1999).

14. Compiled Service Records, Rolls 41, 83; *Soldiers of Florida*, 82, 195; *Medical History*, 12:561.

15. Compiled Service Records, Rolls 38, 41, 81; *Soldiers of Florida*, 81, 92, 195. For more on the prisoner experience, see William B. Hesseltine, ed., *Civil War Prisons* (Kent: Kent State University Press, 1962), and Edwin B. Beitzell, *Point Lookout Prison Camp for Confederates* (Privately published, 1972).

16. Compiled Service Records, Roll 48; *Soldiers of Florida*, 104, 105. A good overview of these military actions can be found in James M. McPherson, *Battle Cry of Freedom: The Civil War Era* (New York: Oxford University Press, 1988), 743–50, 813–15.

17. Compiled Service Records, Roll 6; *Soldiers of Florida*, 262. See also Dickison, "Florida," 122–23.

18. Compiled Service Records, Rolls 50, 93, 97; *Soldiers of Florida*, 105, 229, 230. See also James I Robertson Jr., *Soldiers Blue and Gray* (Columbia: University of South Carolina Press, 1988), 145–69; and Bell I. Wiley, *The Life of Johnny Reb: The Common Soldier of the Confederacy* (Baton Rouge: Louisiana State University Press, reprint, 1978), 244–69.

19. Compiled Service Records, Rolls 34, 82; *Soldiers of Florida*, 91, 191.

20. Compiled Service Records, Rolls 83, 4; *Soldiers of Florida*, 203. Hernandez deserted from Camp Hunt. The latest study of wartime desertion can be found in James M. McPherson, *For Cause and Comrades: Why Men Fought in the Civil War* (New York: Oxford University Press, 1997), 137–38, 168–69.

21. Compiled Service Records, Rolls 50, 93; *Soldiers of Florida*, 103.

22. *O.R.*, Series 1, 52, Part 2, 351, 337. See also Richard S. Nichols, "Florida's Fighting Rebels: A Military History of Florida's Civil War Troops" (MA thesis, Florida State University, 1967), 77.

23. Captain David Lang, in command of the Eighth Florida at the Battle of Fredericksburg, wrote in his report of the action that Baya "regarded the position entrusted to him as so exposed and admitting of so little means of escape that he objected to occupying the same until the order was repeated." See *O.R.*, Series 1, 21, 619, 579, and Dickison, "Florida," 149.

24. *O.R.*, Series 1, 21, 603; Nichols, "Florida's Fighting Rebels," 88–89.

25. *O.R.*, Series 1, 21, 603. For more on the Eighth Florida's role at Fredericksburg, see *O.R.*, Series 1, 21, 283, 552, 558, 609; and Dickison, "Florida," 149.

26. Douglas S. Freeman, *Lee's Lieutenants: A Study in Command*, 3 vols. (New York, 1942–1944), 2:334–38. Also see Nichols, "Florida's Fighting Rebels," 88–89.

27. Compiled Service Records, Roll 46; *Soldiers of Florida*, 104; Hartman and Coles, *Biographical Rosters*, 1:265.

28. Ellen E. Hodges and Steven Kerber, eds., "'Rogues and Black Hearted Scamps': Civil War Letters of Winston and Octavia Stephens, 1862–1863," *Florida Historical Quarterly* 57 (July 1978): 67. These lines were omitted when the same letter was published in Arch F. Blakey, Ann S. Lainhart, and Winston B. Stephens Jr.'s edition, *Rose Cottage Chronicles: Civil War Letters of the Bryant-Stephens Families of North Florida* (Gainesville: University Press of Florida, 1998), 155.

29. *Reports of Cases Argued in the Supreme Court of Florida at Terms Held in 1864–1867*, (Tallahassee, 1867), 11:20. See also Robert A. Taylor, *Rebel Storehouse: Florida in the Confederate Economy* (Tuscaloosa: University of Alabama Press, 1995), 78–79.

30. See Charleston *Daily Courier*, May 20, 1864, for reaction to the Yulee case; and Taylor, *Rebel Storehouse*, 78.

31. Fleming, *Memoir of Capt. C. Seton Fleming*, 93.

10

Battles of Olustee

Civil War Memory in Florida

David Nelson

In February 2013, the Florida Park Service (FPS) "received a proposal from the Sons of Union Veterans of the Civil War to add a memorial specifically for the Union officers and soldiers" at the Olustee Battlefield Historic State Park.[1] The park was initially established as Florida's first historical memorial in 1909 (it became a state park only in 1949, when the Board of State Parks assumed responsibility of Florida's historical memorials) to commemorate Florida' s largest Civil War battle. More than eleven thousand soldiers fought for more than four hours on February 20, 1864, near Ocean Pond, located approximately fifty miles west of Jacksonville and fifteen miles east of Lake City. The Confederates ultimately won the battle, but they suffered 946 casualties (with 93 deaths). However, they killed more than 200 of the Union forces, more than one-third of which were African Americans, and an additional 1,100 were wounded, missing, or captured. As one news outlet reported, it was "proportionally, one of the bloodiest [battles] of the war."[2]

Because a Confederate memorial has been on the site for more than a century, in addition to two others dedicated to two Confederate generals,[3] a small Union memorial seemed a rather innocuous yet completely appropriate gesture for Florida Park Service officials to make during what would be the battle's 150th anniversary. It could also prove to be a token of historical reconciliation by balancing the park's representation. And with the involvement of the Colored Fifty-Fourth Regiment Massachusetts Voluntary Infantry in the battle, it gave the FPS a much-needed site to recognize the state's African American heritage, something sorely lacking in the park service's current roster of parks. Therefore, when a public meeting was scheduled at the Columbia County School District Auditorium in Lake City to decide the exact location for the proposed monument, the FPS was completely caught off guard when the meeting quickly took a negative turn.

Along with park supporters and staff, members of the Sons of Confederate Veterans (SCV) and other citizens concerned with the proposed memorial attended the meeting that evening. Attendance swelled to more than one hundred people. It soon became clear to FPS officials and attending media that this would not be a smooth decision-making process. As one speaker argued, "Putting a Union monument at Olustee would be like placing a memorial to Jane Fonda at the entrance to the Vietnam memorial."[4] Another attendee, H. K. Edgerton, African American president of *Southern Heritage 411*, who carried a huge Confederate battle flag while he spoke, announced that "there is no place in the South land of America to memorialize Yankee soldiers. This is an army that came here raping, robbing, killing and murdering our people. . . . [It was] total warfare against innocent men, women and children who could not defend themselves."[5] Mike Farrell, of the Sons of Union Veterans, counterargued for equal representation. "On every Civil War battlefield in the country . . . there is a Confederate and Union monument. . . . Our country is one united country." But going by the nationalist rhetoric on display at the meeting, and the hundreds of negative comments that the news accounts inspired once published online, any such consensus of unity seemed precarious indeed. By January 2014, the debate that started that evening had become national news.

What the FPS inadvertently came up against were not merely a few "unreconstructed rebels" but the power of historical memory. For the United States, there is nothing in its past that is as powerful, emotional, and contested as the Civil War. And for Florida, ground zero for that historical battle over memory, identity, and meaning is the site of its largest military battle, Olustee Battlefield.

The meeting was likely a lost cause from the start, thanks to the endurance of the Lost Cause ideology. As Eric Hobsbawm argued more than thirty years ago, the past legitimizes our identity and ideology, especially when we feel our legitimacy is under threat, as many white Southerners did (and some apparently continue to do) after defeat in the Civil War.[6] Proponents of the Lost Cause[7] maintain that the Civil War was fought not over slavery but rather over constitutional issues.[8] In addition, they argue that the South was never truly defeated, only outgunned and outnumbered by a misguided, immoral, and industrialized North. And while most Lost Cause proponents argue that Southern defeat was ultimately a positive occurrence, for it allowed the nation to remain together, the South was nevertheless correct in its right to both secede and to own slaves. Finally, while Southern leaders accepted emancipation, they argued that white superiority was both natural and Godly. Two common themes in Lost Cause discourse were the faithfulness of slaves and the moral superiority of the Old South compared to the chaos of modern life. While modern visitors to Florida, if they consider Florida's past at all, tend to focus on the state's more romantic and exotic historic features, Florida has nonetheless been an active participant in the construction of the South's public memory of the Old South and the Civil War since the 1880s.

Overwhelmingly, Florida's women, white and mostly from the elite classes, served as the prime agents in preserving what was essentially a male-dominated event, and not only of Olustee but for the entire war. Karen Cox, in her pioneering history of the United Daughters of the Confederacy (UDC), argues correctly that it was the "women [who] founded the Confederate tradition."[9] Much of this was as an emotional response. "To be a conquered people is a novel experience," wrote Ella Call Long of Tallahassee. "The humility of the South, her utterly crushed condition makes my heart ache."[10] The process of turning defeat into victory, converting their defeated leaders and soldiers, who Call once described as "chivalrous but hot-headed Southern people [with] their delusive struggle for independence,"[11] into heroes, and vindicating their political and racial ideals began through the efforts of women soon after Florida's May 10 surrender. In other words, in Florida, as elsewhere in the South, white and primarily elite women, usually with spousal or familial connections to the Confederacy, created the Lost Cause. And making their jobs easier, Florida's two main battles were both victories for the Confederate forces: Natural Bridge and Olustee.

In 1865, Tallahassee women founded the Memorial Commission, while twenty miles northwest, the women of Quincy founded the similar Ladies Confederate Memorial Association. Similar Ladies Memorial Association (LMA) organizations were springing up across the former Confederacy and throughout the state.[12] Their goals were to construct the narrative of Confederate righteousness and to control the message through writings, monuments, memorials, gravestones, statues, and education. Initially this was an emotional response, as many of these women personally witnessed and suffered the trauma and losses of war. But over time, this emotional construction became entrenched in the South's public narrative. Ironically, in the twenty-first century, working-class whites proved most active defending the once-elite narrative.

Although at the war's end Jefferson Davis was not universally liked or respected by most governors or military leaders, by the 1880s Davis had become a cult figure to many in the South, a Southern counterpoint to Abraham Lincoln.[13] In fact, ten Southern states began celebrating Davis's birthday, June 3, as a state holiday.[14] In addition, other states (North Carolina and South Carolina) celebrated Confederate Memorial Day on either May 10, which was the date of Davis's capture by Union forces, or April 26 (Georgia and Florida), when General Johnston surrendered in Durham.[15] But for the women engaged in memorial work in the late nineteenth century, no figure was as admired as Jefferson Davis's daughter, Winnie Davis, the "Daughter of the Confederacy," born in 1864 in the Confederate White House, who made her name working with war veterans.[16] In 1890, an LMA in St. Louis, Missouri, that at the time was creating a home for confederate veterans renamed themselves the Daughters of the Confederacy, because of Winnie's work with veterans.[17] Soon after that, LMAs, many of whom were likewise engaged in caring for CSA veterans, began renaming themselves Daughters of the Confederacy.

These Daughters of the Confederacy groups grew in such numbers that they decided to organize at the national level, and on September 10, 1894, in Nashville, Tennessee, the national United Daughters of the Confederacy (UDC) was born.[18] They had five objectives: to be benevolent, to create and/or fund memorials, to assist in Civil War education, to preserve history, and to organize social activities.[19] In 1897, there were 138 chapters, including one in New York. They counted more than thirty thousand members by 1904, with Texas alone contributing five thousand members. By 1910, chapters had been founded throughout the country, including in California, Illinois, Ohio, and Pennsylvania, as well as in all the former Confederate states. They reached their peak in 1918, with over one hundred thousand members.[20] Florida would join their ranks in 1896.

Two years later, in Virginia, a male counterpart to the UDC, the SCV, emerged with similar goals: to preserve history, including the battlefields and the records of all Southern soldiers, and to assist in the observance of Memorial Day.[21] According to their charge, "We will commit the vindication of the Cause for which we fought . . . defense of the Confederate soldier's good name, the guardianship of his history, the emulation of his virtues . . . and those ideals which made him glorious."[22] A Florida branch of the SCV formed in 1898 with two camps: Camp Charles Hemming (SCV Camp #80) in Ocala and Camp Stonewall Jackson (#85) in Jacksonville.[23]

But as UDC historian Karen Cox has noted, many women at the time were disappointed in the overall "apathy" displayed by young Southern men in promoting the Lost Cause and the heritage of the Confederacy.[24] The UDC across Florida would remain the driving force in Civil War memory and advocacy until well into the twentieth century.

To understand the impact of the UDC on public memory of the Civil War in Florida and in the nation, consider that the majority of Confederate-related parks, memorials, markers, statues, and educational outlets were created, funded, assisted, or initiated by members of the UDC. Historical geographer John J. Winberry estimates that 95 percent of all monuments were built after 1895, half between 1903 and 1912, the peak years for the UDC.[25] Even the United Confederate Veterans (UCV) would ask the UDC to raise funds for their projects, such as the Jefferson Davis Monument in Richmond.[26] In Florida, the state's UDC division was instrumental in commemorating and preserving nearly every Civil War–related site and monument in Florida, including the Battle of Natural Bridge, the Battle of Marianna, the Judah P. Benjamin Memorial at Gamble Plantation, Hemmings Park and Yellow Bluff, in Jacksonville, and, of course, Olustee Battlefield.

Florida's initial involvement with the UDC sprung out of efforts to create a Florida Confederates Home, as veteran benevolence had been a major focus for Florida's various LMAs and veteran groups. Along with Louisiana, Florida was one of the first states to offer Confederate pensions. On May 8, 1892, at the Board of Trade building in Jacksonville, a joint meeting between the Robert E. Lee Camp, Florida Division (UCV), and a local Sons of Confederate Veteran organization met to plan for a Confederates Veteran home in Jacksonville.[27] At the meeting, they drew up a request for "a group of Jacksonville ladies to form an auxiliary to assist them in the interest of the Veterans and to provide a banquet which was to be held in the Sub-Tropical [Exhibition] Building."[28] In response, several "wives, widows and daughters of Confederate veterans" met on May 23, 1892, in Jacksonville's old library building and agreed to take charge of the Confederates Home.[29] Several of the women present at that meeting donated $500 each for the home.[30] By December 1895, at its Second Annual Convention, in Atlanta, the UDC approved the Jacksonville group as the nineteenth UDC chapter, renamed the Martha Reid Chapter in January 1897, after "the Florence Nightingale of Florida,"[31] who famously "nursed Florida soldiers in Virginia hospitals during the Civil War."[32] Over the next year, four more Florida chapters were formed: Stonewall Jackson Chapter in Lake City (#47), J. J. Dickison Chapter in Ocala (#56), and the Brooksville (#75), and Palatka (#76) chapters. In July 1896, they gathered to form the Florida Division of the UDC and held their first full meeting, in Ocala, in 1897.[33] Initially they had 239 registered members.[34] By 1899, the Florida UDC had eleven chapters, adding chapters in Tampa, Tallahassee, Sanford, Orlando, Gainesville, Madison, and Pensacola, with a total of five hundred members.[35] By 1905, they had 963 members and 19 chapters (now including West Palm Beach, Deland, Quincy, Apalachicola, Bartow, New Smyrna Beach, Leesburg, and Miami).[36] Similar to the national UDC, the Florida UDC's peak years were the 1910s, with more than fifty chapters and nine Children of the Confederacy chapters.[37] Their peak membership was in 1914, with 2,003 members.[38]

In the early years, the main goal of the Florida UDC was the maintenance of the Confederates Home and commemoration of the deceased. As UDC president Julia Foster Weed stressed in 1899, "The care of the living and the preservation of the memory of our dead Confederate soldiers is all that remains for a grateful people to do."[39] Marking Confederate graves was a common service. Typical of the time was the Madison chapter, which in 1898 held a "Holly Tea" to raise funds for grave markers.[40] In its first twenty-five years, hundreds of grave markers and thousands of wreaths were placed in Florida. Often these services were completed on Confederate Memorial Day, which Florida celebrated on April 26. With public schools and most businesses closed, communities with UDC chapters followed a similar pattern. In addition to band concerts and speeches by local dignitaries, the highlight of these celebrations was the parade of surviving Confederate veterans and UDC ladies to the local cemetery, followed by schoolchildren bearing flowers for the Confederate graves.[41] The message was clear across the generations: these men were heroes, and what they fought for was honorable. Messy issues such as secession, slavery, emancipation, or racial equality were not part of the program.

One of the most historically significant impacts of the UDC in Florida was its role in the preservation of manuscripts and other archival materials. This was particularly valuable, as Florida was without a state records repository until a century after the Civil War. From its start, the UDC actively collected diaries, letters, memoirs, newspapers, photographs, and memories of anyone connected with the war in Florida. While these collections were from the Confederate viewpoint, they were invaluable to our present understanding of the war, especially from the perspective of woman and their families. The UDC scrapbooks in the Florida State Archives are some of the most used records for the Civil War era.

Once history was preserved, it needed to be disseminated to the next generation, and that led to the next concern of the UDC: education. As Florida UDC president Weed said in her opening remarks in 1900, "To the young Southerner we look to preserve the memories that have been handed down to them. . . . It is to the young Southerner we must leave our land and its memories. We must teach them what a glorious thing it is to be a representative Southerner and no one can be such who not bear in his heart love and reverence for the great deeds of our Confederacy."[42] At the same meeting, the chair of the history committee, Mrs. Horatio Davis, explained, "The boys and girls of the South must be taught the true history of the South. As now taught in many of our schools . . . these children have heard nothing but the shout of the victors, and it is our duty to see that they are taught the facts as they are." For the Daughters, there was only one correct view of history, and that was theirs.[43]

Throughout the early twentieth century, the UDC would pressure school boards to remove or censor books, publish their own textbooks, and donate "unbiased" history texts to any that needed them. Their most public campaign, though, was their role in the forced resignation of Enoch Marvin Banks from the University of Florida in 1911.[44] In 1907, the school hired the Georgia-born, Columbia University–trained Banks as a professor of history and economics. But when he published an article in the New York magazine the *Independen*t in which he proclaimed, "the North was relatively right" while the "South was relatively in the wrong" regarding secession and slavery, Banks's days were numbered.[45] After a *Florida Times Union* editorial, the outcry was swift and virulent. The UDC, among others, demanded his removal for the attack on the South, and the university complied.

The most visible accomplishment of the Florida UDC, as well as the most lasting in regard to shaping public dialogue about the Civil War, was the monuments, memorials, and parks it created. By 1920, the Florida Division of the UDC had initiated, sponsored, and/or funded eighteen Confederate monuments in Florida and contributed to an additional fifteen monuments in other states.[46] They donated $1,500 each to the Shiloh and Arlington cemetery monuments, unveiled in 1914 and 1917, respectively.[47] Confederate monuments in Florida included those in Jacksonville (1899), Lake City (1904), Gainesville (1904), Monticello (1904), Ocala (1908),

Madison (1909), Lakeland (1910), Tampa (1911), Orlando (1911), and Brooksville (1916).[48]

During Reconstruction, state and local officials saw Confederate monuments as politically dangerous and therefore refused to allow them on public lands, though the first Confederate monument was erected in 1871 in Walton County on the grounds of the Euchee Valley Presbyterian Church.[49] After Reconstruction, though, locals relocated it to a more prominent location: the DeFuniak Springs courthouse lawn.[50] A similar pattern could be found in St. Augustine, where the local LMA[51] was not able to secure permission from the local government to place it in the town's plaza.[52] Eventually, they unveiled it in 1872 on property of the local Catholic Church.[53] In 1879, soon after the end of Reconstruction, city officials enlarged and relocated the monument to the town plaza. We can see this pattern with the conception, erection, and dedication of the Confederate monument in downtown Pensacola on Robert E. Lee Square (renamed in 1899 from its original name, Florida Square). Future Florida governor Edward Perry, a Civil War veteran, pushed for a state Confederate monument in 1881 on the grounds of the state capitol.[54] Despite citizens (mostly from Perry's hometown of Pensacola) raising more than $3,000, the project was not yet realized when he died in 1890. Colonel William Chipley revived the plans, suggesting it be relocated to Pensacola, and several politically connected women formed an LMA.[55] They completed the fund-raising (through bake sales, dances, plays, and speeches), hired a sculptor, and purchased two old cannons and eight hundred cannonballs.[56] The dedication for the monument, a thirty-foot-tall granite shaft topped with an eight-foot statue of a Confederate soldier, was scheduled for Jefferson Davis's birthday.[57] Reconstruction goals and Union victories were clearly fading from the public consciousness, replaced by a vibrant Lost Cause view of the past.

While Confederate-focused monuments far outnumbered Union edifices by the twentieth century, it was ironically the Union viewpoint that first emerged in Florida, erected by the Army and Navy Club in downtown Key West in 1866.[58] It was dedicated to the "officers, sailors and soldiers of the Army, Navy and Marine Corps of the United States who lost their lives."[59] However, in a reversal of the Reconstruction-era governments' refusal to allow Confederate monuments, only a handful of Union monuments would be erected in post-Reconstruction and twentieth-century Florida, all by the Grand Army of the Republic (GAR) and almost all on private lands. The first GAR monument, and the second Union monument in Florida, was in Jacksonville's Evergreen Cemetery, completed in 1891. Most of the few other Union monuments were likewise located in cemeteries, including in St. Cloud, Orlando, Miami, Tampa (cosponsored by the Women's Relief Corps), and Lynne Haven.[60]

By contrast, there were more than thirty Confederate memorials in Florida by 1940, mostly on public lands. These included ten on county courthouse lawns, nine in city parks, six on historic sites (now state parks), two along highways, and one on the grounds of the state capitol.[61] But the most important monuments, culturally and historically, were the state legislative–approved State Historic Memorials for the Battle of Natural Bridge (1921), Judah P. Benjamin at Gamble Plantation (1925), and the Battle of Marianna (1929). All were initiated and, until 1949, cared for by the UDC. But none were more significant, or contested, than the Battle of Olustee Historical Memorial.

On January 27, 1897, at their second annual meeting in Ocala, the Florida Division of the UDC passed a resolution that stated that the "UDC pledge themselves to raise a fund for the proper erection of a shaft to mark the Battle of Olustee, Florida's most famous battle."[62] Two years later, the Olustee Committee chair Mrs. Joseph Whitner (whose husband fought at Olustee) prepared a legislative bill for the creation and funding of a monument.[63] It passed the Senate "with no dissent for $1500" and moved to the House.[64] She urged local chapters to honor their "patriotic duty" by contributing funds. "The battle scars of that blood consecrate spot, so dear to every true Floridian, are fast fading from view. So likewise the survivors, through whose personal acquaintances with the grounds, the place of special interest may yet be designated, are too rapidly passing away. Let us not falter but push rapidly to finish this work."[65] While the bill passed the House as well, the UDC would not be thrilled with the result.

In Chapter 4815, the Florida Legislature stated that it agreed with the "laudable efforts" of the UDC for an Olustee monument. It "was [the] greatest in magnitude most important in results, of all battles fought on Florida soil. . . . It is eminently fitting that a suitable monument should be erected to mark the ground . . . to commemorate the valor and patriotism of those who participated."[66] The Legislature authorized the creation of a five-member commission to create the monument and funded it at $2,500. According to the bill's final wording, the resultant monument would be for "the Federal and Confederate officers and soldiers who participated in said battle."[67]

It was only three words, but they set off a firestorm: "the Federal and . . ." The Lake City UDC chapter was the first to respond with "a formal protest against the erection of a monument at Olustee." The group's defiant stance was immediate and nonnegotiable as they "positively refuse[d] to couple the record of our fallen dead with that of aliens to the Confederate states."[68] Likewise, the Palatka chapter had been actively fund-raising for the memorial, "but learning of the Bill as presented in the Legislature, the Chapter was unwilling to do anything further."[69] Finally, the Pensacola chapter also "unanimously rejected" the measure.[70] Olustee chair Mrs. Whitner felt because the bill "was so changed" that they should "defer action" until a revised bill was passed that was "harmonious" with UDC goals.[71] At the next legislative session, they got exactly what they demanded. Chapter 5053 was the identical bill but with all references to Federal troops and the United States removed.[72] Political peace was restored.

It would be more than a decade before anyone saw an Olustee monument erected. The gubernatorial commission remained unfulfilled for years, and the funding languished. In 1905, state UDC Chair Helen Parramore expressed "the belief that the time has arrived when the work of erection of the Olustee monument . . . should begin" instead of waiting for the State to act."[73] Chapters resumed their fund-raising efforts through dances, cake sales, and donations, although money only trickled in over the next few years. In 1908, the UDC lamented that so far, the state committee had not responded to their inquiries, and there were no discernible funds, lands, or completion dates. After a heated and futile debate to move the monument to Lake City, the UDC resolved to yet again attempt "to expedite the work of creating this monument as soon as possible."[74]

Everything changed in 1909 when two landowners donated property to the state for the memorial. On August 6, 1909, Austin Fletcher of Lake City donated two acres for "its only proper use and behoof forever."[75] Then a month later, Eliza and John Brown sold for one dollar an adjacent acre for the same purpose. Finally, after many construction and funding delays, the Memorial shaft was unveiled to the public on October 23, 1912, with much fanfare. UDC presidents Esther Carlotta and Helen Parramore were the matrons of honor, and Mrs. J. N. Whitner officially presented the monument to Governor Albert Gilchrist.[76] Surviving veterans and their families attended the daylong festivities.[77] But once the celebrations were over, and the political rewards achieved, the reality set in that the physical and financial maintenance was another matter altogether.

For the next eight years, it was left to the UDC to care for the State Historic Memorial, despite their pleadings for the state to assume responsibility. In 1913 the UDC president reported that while the State Senate had passed a bill "for the care and preservation of Olustee Monument," the bill had failed in the House, "thus leaving the monument without any provision for its care except what we can give it."[78] In 1913, Olustee Committee chair Sister Esther Carlotta "at her own expense decorated the Monument" with a Confederate battle flag and personally "cleared away the weeds and trash around it."[79] At their 1914 meeting, the Florida UDC resolved to present another bill to the legislature for the funding and care for the monument, which it badly needed, as "the concrete paving around it is already badly broken and shows how faulty the work of laying it was."[80] That failed as well. In 1921, the legislature approved a onetime sum of only $400 for Olustee, and finally in 1925, the legislature approved two payments of $1,800 to construct a caretakers' home.[81] Seeing the potential to attract tourists, the legislature partially funded the site's maintenance until 1949, when it finally assumed full control of the site. But these funds were more subsidies than true operating budgets, as the UDC remained the site's main caretaker. Its Olustee Committee hired the caretaker, arranged for the construction of his house, and planned the design and maintenance of the evolving park's landscaping. They also convinced US Representative R. A. Green to secure two twelve-pound cannons from a New York arsenal.[82] Throughout this period, the UDC was likewise taking care of sites at Natural Bridge, Marianna, and the Judah P. Benjamin Memorial at Gamble Mansion in Manatee County. The UDC constantly pushed for more funding and state control but later would come to regret the resultant loss of control once their goals were realized.

World War II resulted in a richer, stronger, and more unified America, but it also left the world a much more dangerous place. Atomic bombs and an emerging Cold War left little room for memorials to national divisions and Confederate rebels; consensus and unity were the buzz words in the late 1940s and the 1950s. And because World War II was as much a war against racial intolerance as anything else, it spurred on a modern civil rights movement that focused on expanding opportunities for African Americans. Such a movement prompted a reevaluation of Southern history, one that celebrated the Emancipation Proclamation, the Thirteenth Amendment, and the goals of Reconstruction while abhorring slavery and its elite planter class. This shift forced groups such as the UDC and other custodians of state memorials, such as the one at Olustee, to carefully negotiate this new reality to merely survive.

This link between the modern civil rights movement and the Civil War and Reconstruction was first made obvious in 1948, with the upstart and short-lived Dixiecrat or States' Rights Democratic Party. Led by South Carolinian Strom Thurmond, this group of breakaway Southern Democrats formed as a result of President Harry Truman's integration of the US armed forces, itself a reaction against the intolerance of the Germans and the treatment of black veterans by segregated communities. Throughout the 1950s and 1960s, Southern politicians appropriated Confederate symbols and phrases to reject gains by the civil rights movement. Both sides saw the movement as a Second Civil War, and groups such as the UDC and SCV again found themselves on the wrong side of history. Lastly, complicating the new post–World War II political and racial climate was the transference of who now "kept" Florida's Civil War past. The decades after World War II saw an expansion of the state government and universities. Agencies such as the Florida Park Service, the State Library, and the new Florida Library and Historic Commission, often advised and assisted by professional historians, assumed many of the civic and historical activities and responsibilities previously carried out by volunteer groups such as the UDC. By the 1970s, there would be a functioning State Archives, a Bureau of Florida Folklife, and a Florida State Museum, all located within a Division of History, Archives and Records Management. While the UDC would continue to advise and assert their viewpoint, they would find that their influence had rapidly diminished by the 1960s and 1970s, allowing other voices, including black and Union, to emerge.

The first sign of this change in historical power came when the FPS assumed control of all State Historic Memorials in 1949, including those that the UDC had been the caretakers for.[83] Soon they began hiring academically trained scholars to interpret their parks. In addition to the first state archaeologist, the FPS also hired a state historian, Mark F. Boyd. In 1951, the FPS published and sold (for 15 cents each) three Civil War–related booklets written by Boyd, which were also published in the *Florida Historical Quarterly*: *The Battle of Olustee*, *The Battle of Natural Bridge*, and *The Battle of Marianna*.[84] Unlike earlier popular accounts of the war in Florida, these were well researched, balanced, and devoid of any Lost Cause verbiage.

While researching the Olustee battle, Boyd learned of the possibility of Union troops buried at the site. Thanks to the UDC, cooperating government officials, and prevailing attitudes of the time, the Union side of the Olustee story had been virtually ignored since the 1860s. Boyd, hoping to rectify that historical void, wrote several letters for information on Union burials, including to the US National Cemetery.[85] He found that either there were no surviving records or those with possible knowledge were now gone. After the first edition of the Olustee booklet was published, Boyd received a letter from retired Brigadier General R. C. Langdon, whose father, Loomis Langdon, had fought as a US Army captain in the Battle of Olustee.[86] After describing Boyd's account of Olustee as "the best that I have seen," he then discussed the matter of Union burials at the battlefield.

"Two facts seem to me," Langdon wrote, "that in all probability there are still some remains of the federal dead under the ground of the Olustee Battlefield." One fact was the report by Lieutenant Grossman of the Seventh Infantry, who describes returning under orders to the battlefield in May 1866 to locate Union dead.[87] As Grossman described it, the Union soldiers' remains "were buried by the Confederates in such a careless manner that the remains were disturbed by the hogs within weeks of the battle." He described bones and skulls "scattered broadcast over the ground" as his men approached the site. His men then found "portion of bones [that] protruded" that "were removed from the earth and disinterred all the bones that had not been destroyed by the hogs." Grossman "collected two wagon loads and half of bones." They dug an eighteen-foot-by-twelve-foot grave, into which they buried, among other human remains, 123 human skulls. They then enclosed the grave with a twenty-seven-foot-by-eighteen-foot whitewashed fence and then a ditch. Finally, under orders of Colonel J. T. Sprague, Grossman erected a twelve-foot-high wooden marker, painted white with black lettering. Inscribed on its south face: "To the memory of the officers and soldiers of the US Army who fell in the Battle of Olustee, Feb 20, 1864."

Another contributing and convincing factor for Langdon was that in 1873, his father "passed by the place where the bones of the Federal dead had been reburied in a pit." From the railroad, "all that could be seen were parts of two sides of a weather stained and broken down fence, and even this would have been passed unnoticed except for the conductor having pointed it out to" him.[88] Over the next few months, Boyd and Langdon worked on locating the site. Their goal, as Langdon described it, was a Federal monument "over the large grave in which Lt. Grossman deposited the skulls and bones."[89] Despite the "great pains" of the FPS to locate the burial, they proved ultimately unsuccessful.[90] Few in the area in the 1950s cared to tell or preserve that part of the story, but such feelings were not universal. Langdon describes a visit to the site in May 1954, where he "was touched by seeing a tiny wreath of artificial flowers, only about five inches in diameter, fastened to the Confederate monument. Attached to it was a card giving the name of a man who put the wreath there in memory of a friend who was killed in the battle while serving in the 155th New York Volunteers." To date, it is the last Union monument erected on the state park property.[91]

The Civil War centennial would prove to be both a final victory for the UDC's influence and the turning point for who controlled Florida's historical memory of the Civil War. In 1957, the nation began gearing up for what everyone hoped would be a lucrative and exciting national celebration of the American Civil War. Toys, books, and brochures were planned as state and local chambers of commerce hoped for increased visitation and tourism.[92] That year, Congress authorized a Civil War Centennial Commission to coordinate the various state commissions. In Florida in September 1959, UDC's Florida Division president Mrs. Herbert Vance convinced Florida governor Leroy Collins to create a Florida Civil War Centennial Commission, to consist of the governor, the superintendent for public instruction, and the secretary of state. At their inaugural meeting, the commission nominated an eleven-member planning committee (four of whom were UDC members),[93] which essentially ran the centennial celebrations in Florida.[94] In 1963 the gubernatorial Commission was abolished, with its duties and assets transferred to the newly created Florida Library and Historic Commission, chaired by Secretary of State Adam Adams of Miami, who promptly retained the same planning committee.[95] Also at that session, the state Legislature funded the commission to the tune of $12,000.[96]

Since most of the Civil War was fought far away from Florida's soil, the commission had little to coordinate, and because of the involvement of the UDC and of elected officials, they followed a generally safe, conservative path. State dignitaries attended some of the national celebrations. For instance, Chair and Secretary of State Adams represented Florida at the national Gettysburg centennial,[97] Judge Ben Wills represented Florida at the Chickamauga commemoration, and Jacksonville-based historian Dena Snodgrass spoke at Florida Day at Valley Forge.[98] Adams also headed up the Gettysburg Florida Memorial Committee, which negotiated $10,000 from the state Legislature to create and install the memorial at the National Park Service site, while US Senators Spessard Holland and George Smathers negotiated federal approval for its design.[99]

After hiring University of Florida history professor Dr. Samuel Proctor in July 1961 as their historic consultant, the Florida Civil War Centennial Commission focused primarily on publishing, with Proctor writing a forty-page manual for local governments arranging local commemorations.[100] The commission also underwrote the publishing by the University Press of Florida (UPF) of what are now considered two essential works in Florida Civil War historiography. The deal worked out with the UPF allowed the commission to get 75 percent of the net returns until they recouped their outlay. They then would continue to receive 50 percent of the proceeds.[101] The first was a reprint of the long out of print 1913 work by William W. Davis, *Florida in the Civil War and Reconstruction*. Originally published by Columbia University Press, it was a Lost Cause tome from the infamous William Dunning School of History. The other was a new study by Stetson University professor John E. Johns, based on his doctoral dissertation at the University of North Carolina.[102] The most well-known publications were the monthly newspaper pieces compiled by Dr. Proctor titled *Florida: A Hundred Years Ago*, based on an initial idea by University of Miami professor Charlton Tebeau. Also published as leaflets, these monthly entries traced Florida's role in the war from December 1860 through June 1865.[103] Once completed, the entries were compiled into a book of the same name.[104] All the commission's publications were distributed to schools, colleges, television and radio stations, and newspapers. Proctor's monthly leaflets were also available to individual subscribers, which included people in Great Britain, Canada, New Zealand, Australia, and Japan.

Despite its conservative approach, the commission was not without controversy. Because the centennial coincided with increased momentum in the civil rights movement, any discussion of slavery and emancipation was both muted and disputed. In his *Florida: A 100 Hundred Years Ago*, Proctor generally sidestepped slavery and race. His one entry on the matter, in December 1860, was vague on details. "No part of the country was isolated from the slavery and states' rights controversies which were raging. The people of Florida, although they were living in the newest of the slaveholding territories, were caught up in this maelstrom."[105] But the commission's involvement with the National Centennial Commission forced it to confront the racial issues at hand.

In January 1962, Adams attended the National Commission meeting in Washington, DC. He was also attending the simultaneous Confederate States Centennial Commission, its existence the result of a dispute between the Southern states and the federal government over segregation in Charleston in 1961 during the Fort Sumter planning meetings.[106] As a result, many centennial celebrations consisted of two events: a national celebration and a Confederate celebration. As he wrote after the meeting, Adams had the "feeling . . . that the Negro question was going to be inserted into the commission."[107] The New York Commission had submitted its "boiler plate" language for news releases regarding the Emancipation Proclamation, which, according to Adams, was described as "The Greatest Document Ever Penned by Mortal Man."[108] He mentioned that the New York commission included historians Bruce Catton, a biographer of Ulysses S. Grant, and John Hope Franklin, "a negro."[109] He also noted in passing that the director of the New Jersey Commission was with a "colored woman" and that the Illinois Commission had raised $1.5 million "and had turned the money over to an organization of Negroes in Chicago."[110] For Adams, these observations "substantiate the ideas which this writer had formerly, that the National Commission and certain states are beginning to take steps to make the Commission a political tool." According to Adams, many delegates from the South shared the "feeling that the pressure on the National Commission on the Director of some states commissions for political ends is severe."[111] Adams agreed with the resolution passed by the Confederate Commission, which he attached to his letter. It stated that the "real purpose" of the centennial was to "commemorate the bravery and gallantry of the fighting men . . . on both sides" and to educate people about "how our men on both sides fought to death for what they believed was just and right." Furthermore, they believed "it would be a mistake for the National Civil War Commission to engage in any activity or to promote in anyway any proposal . . . that would tend to offend the people of any section of our nation . . . and reopen the wounds of war."[112] The Lost Cause was in danger of being lost.

Aside from publishing, the largest and most anticipated event for the Florida Centennial Commission was the 100th anniversary of the Battle of Olustee. As early as March 1963, Adams began soliciting concepts for the event: "PLEASE let me have your ideas . . . [I] trust that each of you will not only lend his advice but help in making this commemoration successful." Thanks to a legislative appropriation of $5,000 from "general revenue funds" to the commission for "observing the anniversary of the Battle of Olustee," the ceremony would be one to remember.[113] However, there was some skepticism over costs. As one journalist noted, "It now appears that the centennial celebration may . . . cost more money than the original battle did."[114]

The resultant celebration was a three-day affair comprising two memorial services that bookended a dramatized reenactment of the battle. The first memorial service was held on February 20, 1964, by the eleven local chapters of the UDC at the Old City Cemetery in Jacksonville in honor of Confederate General Joseph Finnegan. The other was held on February 23 at Olustee Park in downtown Lake City for Confederate General Alfred Colquitt, arranged by the UDC chapter from Smyrna, Georgia.[115] While there were no memorial services for the Union soldiers, the organizers struck a strong patriotic tone typical of Cold War America. From the commemorative program: "We pay tribute to the valor of our forefathers, both Confederate and Union, who fought at Olustee . . . and glorify the heroism, devotion to duty, spirit of sacrifice, and willingness to fight and die for the cause in they believed, exhibited by the Americans on both sides. . . . When we Americans, now united as a nation, no longer admire and pay tribute to such qualities, when we are no longer willing to fight and die, if need be for our country, no longer will we remain a free nation or a free people."[116] What those "causes" that they were so willing to die for were, of course, remained unspoken. As was common throughout the centennial in Florida, organizers attempted to balance their Confederate past with a patriotic, nationalistic present.

The main event was Florida's first Civil War reenactment, held in Jacksonville's football stadium, the Gator Bowl. Following a parade, a barbecue lunch, and a welcome speech by Jacksonville mayor and future governor Haydon Burns, reenactors took to the field for a narrated battle. Reenactors hailed from all over the country, including Michigan, Pennsylvania, Ohio, Tennessee, Arkansas, Maryland, South Carolina, and Georgia, with the Confederate units far outnumbering the Union ones. Any gaps were filled by youth from the Jacksonville Recreation Department and students from Nathan B. Forrest, Robert E. Lee, and Andrew Jackson high schools. Finally, that evening, a grand costume ball was held at the five-star Hotel George Washington, complete with a Grand March and Miss Olustee contest.[117] Unfortunately, stormy weather kept many away, but more than five thousand people still attended the reenactment.[118]

In the post–civil rights 1970s and early 1980s, the Old South celebrated by the UDC and Confederate memorials had transformed into the modern, popular, and urban New South. Governors such as Florida's Reuben Askew led the South into the modern era with political, education, and integration reforms. Floridian Burt Reynolds became one of the top box office stars during this era and epitomized this new, urban chic South. Southern-based shows such as the *The Waltons*, *Carter's Country*, and *The Dukes of Hazzard*, with its Dixie-blaring sports car the General Lee, ruled the airwaves. Southern rebels in popular culture were more likely to be young moonshiners, truckers, or rock-and-roll stars rather than secessionists fighting over slavery. Confederate symbols were appropriated by Hollywood and the music industry as both badges of regional authenticity and symbols of individuality and the working class. Florida-based bands such as Lynyrd Skynyrd, Allman Brothers, and .38 Special, along with other Southern acts such as Charles Daniels, Hank Williams Jr., and Alabama, proudly displayed the Confederate flag without the troublesome historical or overt racial connotations.

Reflecting both changing public attitudes and new historical trends, with greater emphasis on social, racial, and gendered forces, Florida's museums and park officials changed how the state presented its Confederate past. Although the interpretation at most parks, museums, and historical sites did not completely shy away from the troublesome aspects of the Civil War, mentions of slavery and emancipation were de rigueur now, they nonetheless strove to avoid controversy. Neutrality seemed to be the guiding force. For instance, in 1983, when the Museum of Florida History in Tallahassee was installing its new Florida in the Civil War exhibit, its curator made sure to point out that it was not taking sides. "We're not romanticizing what happened. More soldiers died of diseases than on the battlefield and Florida paid the price."[119]

But for many, the same forces that ushered in Southern modernity also rendered the Confederate past a relic that should be shed. For them, images of the Confederacy were painful reminders of a dark past that should neither be forgotten nor civically celebrated. Tensions grew from the 1970s over how to remember the past and its symbols. In 1968, the newspaper in Gettysburg, Pennsylvania, complained that Southern states such as Florida refused to recognize Abraham Lincoln's birthday, as many others did. But in the following decades, Florida had diversified its observances. Today, while Florida still statutorily celebrates both Confederate Memorial Day (April 26) and Robert E. Lee's Birthday (January 3), since 1991, it has also observed Juneteenth Day on June 19, which in the past had been celebrated as Jefferson Davis's birthday.[120] But diversity also brought tensions. An example of tensions boiling over into violence occurred in 1973 at several Florida high schools. At Pensacola High School, African American students rioted over "the use of Confederate symbols. Although school officials there have refused to ban Dixie as the school song, a federal judge ordered a temporary injunction to halt display of the Confederate Flag and the use of the nickname 'Rebels.'"[121] Fifty armed guards were called out, and they employed tear gas to break up fighting between more than two hundred students.[122] Similar protests were held at Chipley, Delray Beach, and West Palm Beach High Schools. Ultimately, Pensacola civil rights activist Reverend H. K. Matthews led a successful protest to end Pensacola High School's use of Confederate symbols.[123]

Because of his role in the development of the original Ku Klux Klan and his treatment of black Union soldiers during the Civil War, Jacksonville's Nathan B. Forrest High School was perhaps the most notorious high school name in Florida.[124] In 1959, a new high school opened in the city, temporarily named New School 207. Students rejected the original proposal of Westconnett, in favor of Valhalla High School, with the Vikings as their team name. But partly in response to the board's inability to agree on a name and partly owing to the efforts of local UDC member Mrs. John E. Walker, who wanted it named for "a distinguished southern leader," the school board voted to instead name the all-white school Nathan B. Forrest, on a last-minute suggestion by a board member.[125] In July 2013, Jacksonville resident Ty Richmond, formerly of Long Island, generated an online petition to change the name, receiving over 162,000 signatures.[126] As he noted, "Jacksonville is too much of a beautiful city to have that ugly blemish." In December 2013, the Duval County School Board voted unanimously to change the name to Westside High School. At the time, the school superintendent Nikolai Vitti said that in 1959 "politics reigned and as a response to desegregation and the civil rights movement, the school was named for" Forrest.[127] Other news accounts of the name change gave the same anti-integration rationale. But history is rarely so clear-cut. A journalists' survey of Jacksonville newspapers from the period, including the African American–owned *Jacksonville Star* revealed that segregation was not mentioned at all, nor did anyone protest.[128] Beyond student disappointment at losing the Viking-inspired name, local opposition to the new name and its Rebels mascot occurred only in the 1970s, once the school became integrated.

While not everyone approved the 2013 renaming (about one-third of the students and faculty rejected the change), it was generally popular in the city that once organized the state's first SCV and UDC, conducted the state's first Olustee reenactment, and was home to Confederate Park.

The Confederate flag, however, has been the biggest lightning rod for disputes over Civil War memory in Florida. Once flown at state functions and pledged to by schoolchildren, by the 1980s, it had virtually disappeared from civic life, and in February 2001, even the state capitol complex in Tallahassee stopped flying it, on the orders of Governor Jeb Bush, who "decided it was time."[129] At the time, the flag had been flying at the old historic capitol since 1978, when the new twenty-two-story capitol opened. This action by Bush followed an attempt five years earlier, when black legislators and the Southern Christian Leadership Conference attempted to have it removed.[130] In 2009, the Florida government rejected the SCV design for a Confederate flag license plate. But Floridians' changing attitudes over the flag is perhaps best illustrated in the controversies that erupted over the world's largest Confederate flag, erected in Tampa in 2008.

Hillsborough County had been distancing itself from its Confederate past for more than a decade by 2008 and in 1994 had removed the Confederate flag from its county seal.[131] In 2007, it stopped proclaiming April as Southern Heritage Month and dropped its Robert E. Lee birthday observances.[132] Marion Lambert, a welder and a member of the Jubal A. Early Camp 556 of the SCV, purchased a small plot of land on US 92 near Interstate 75. His plan was to continue the work of the Confederate Flags Flying Across Florida, a group started in 2000 by Floridians wanting to raise awareness of Florida's Confederate heritage. The group had already successfully (and controversially) placed large flags on private property in White Springs, Florida, visible from US 75 and Havana, Florida, alongside US 27. What made this one different, as reported by several national outlets, was that Lambert's flag, at thirty feet high and fifty feet long, would be the world's largest Confederate flag.

While they had no legal recourse, county commissioners pleaded with Lambert not to fly the flag. They worried about the effects it would have on tourism and business investments, as the NAACP and the Anti-Defamation League had already asked the county to stop it.[133] One commissioner argued, "I don't think [Robert E.] Lee would do it."[134] Another said, "It's not that you honor it, it's how you honor it," referring to the flag's racially divisive nature.[135] Lambert countered, echoing the stance of many over the decades, that the flag "honors our ancestors and [is] about celebrating our heritage."[136] On the same day that presidential candidate Barack Obama secured the Democratic nomination, which also coincided with President Jefferson Davis's birthday, Lambert unfurled his flag atop a 139-foot pole.

Reactions to the flag were mixed and often fell along racial and political lines. One black resident said, "It's a symbol of hate. Even Caucasian people would say that."[137] But many of the white residents in the poor, working-class area did not find fault. "I think it is greatest thing in the world," said one white resident. "It's honoring the people of the South. . . . It's only a race thing if you want it to be."[138] One local columnist argued that he felt there was a connection between the flag and the political rise of black America, as personified by Barack Obama.[139] He quoted Lambert: "We've been marginalized and put off and ostracized for the last twenty years. . . . We're using the ultimate weapon we have been given by a society who ostracized it." Flag owner Lambert remarked, "We've been marginalized, put off the table, now they want to talk to us."[140] In many ways, Florida supporters of a pro-Confederate view of the past had returned to their rebellious origins.

Before 2013, Olustee had avoided such controversies.[141] Battlefields were always popular with the American public. Also, Olustee's history remained little known outside of North Florida, so it carried little historical baggage in the public's mind. Plus, the site gave off an air of inclusiveness thanks to the role of the Fifty-Fourth Massachusetts, offering a role for African Americans that for once did not involve slavery or segregation. The biggest reason for Olustee's good reputation with the public, however, was that since 1977, the park had been the site of the Southeast's largest Civil War reenactment. While quite accurate in its depiction of events, Olustee's battle re-creation focused more on spectacle and entertainment than on messy historical controversies. In fact, from the outset, the reenactors fight two battles, one, an authentic and faithful rendition of the battle, and the other, a longer, more exciting (i.e., more cannons and explosions) bonus skirmish that ends with a Union victory. Everyone wins, in other words.

When FPS Chief Naturalist Jim Stevenson wrote the reenactment group, the First Regiment, Florida Volunteers, in January 1976 to re-create the battle, it had been more than a decade since the last (and only) Olustee reenactment had taken place. But by then, thanks in large part to the activities of the Civil War centennial, reenactments had become a major endeavor for parks, museums, local governments, and history buffs. By the early 1970s, as the UDC and other heritage groups were fading in influence, several reenactment groups were springing up throughout the state, especially in South Florida. Chapters of the North-South Skirmish Association (NSSA) were organizing in towns such as Lake Worth, Sarasota, and Tampa.[142] Many of the participants, often transplants from the North and the West, were more interested in re-creating the material culture of the war than in keeping the "Spirit of the '60s" alive.

Stevenson's plan was that the Olustee reenactment would be part of the FPS's contribution to the nation's bicentennial. Ray Giron, a Philadelphia transplant who ran the group, was skeptical.[143] With only a few weeks to prepare, the logistics proved insurmountable, so the first official reenactment at Olustee Battlefield Historic State Park took place on February 20, 1977. More than two hundred costumed "civil war buffs" met on the park's trail loop.[144] Visibility was poor, so the event was later moved to a clear-cut field a few hundred yards to the north on adjacent land belonging to Osceola National Forest. By the 130th anniversary of the battle in 1994, the popular program had grown to more than two thousand participants each year, plus twenty-eight artillery, fifty mounted cavalry members, and more than one hundred preplanned charges.[145] In addition, the public could visit a hundred sutlers and a military encampment. After Olustee's reenactment started, in 1977, reenactments of other, smaller skirmishes began, including the Battle of Natural Bridge, the Brooksville Raid, the Battle of Ocklawaha, Battle of Ballast Point, and Battle of Fort Myers. Most of the historic events these reenactments were based on were in reality small affairs of no more than a few dozen soldiers. In many cases, the reenactments dwarfed their historical counterparts. Strangest of all may have been a 1979 reenactment of several battles by the newly organized Florida Brigade at the Six Gun Territory roadside attraction in Ocala, which was a mock Western town. Held on February 16, 1979, with a military encampment in the attraction's parking lot, reenactors attacked visitors on the park's train and re-created both the Olustee and Natural Bridge battles.[146]

Because it is a state-funded FPS event, education and inclusion are the goals of the Olustee experience. In 1978, the Blue-Gray Army was incorporated for assisting in the event, and they worked hard to offer balance to the affair, bringing new voices to the conversation. Although journalist Julie Barrett asserted, "I am a Yankee and no Civil War buff," she found the Olustee battle "irresistible."[147] Both Lincoln and General Grant are represented in the event, and for years, African American reenactors have helped to re-create the Fifty-Fourth Massachusetts. The event's reputation was such that in 1989, portions of the Hollywood film *Glory* were filmed at the battle.[148] *Gainesville Sun* columnist Bill Maxwell, an African American, described visiting the reenactment in 1993: "I felt I was inside the very soul in America." He admitted to a love-hate relationship to the war, yet "as an African-American, the great War Between the States and its battles held special place in my heart."[149] The Olustee festivities about the divisive past seemed to reflect Florida's diverse, multicultural present.

Therefore, when the FPS agreed to entertain the notion of a Union memorial at the Olustee Battlefield Historic State Park, it was in the same inclusive, balanced vein as its reenactment. FPS officials were perhaps unaware that Olustee is situated along a historical and cultural fault line. Not only was it the original and most sacred symbol of Florida's Lost Cause, one that was preserved and championed by the UDC and the SCV, but Olustee was also a symbol of the entire Civil War for all Floridians. From debates over national historical standards in education and arguments over public commemorations, place names, and state flags to discussions of racial inequality and slave reparations, the memory of the Civil War is a living, evolving entity in this nation. Like other Americans, Floridians are constantly searching for a useful past; but the problem remains: for whose use, and for what?

A few weeks after the contentious public meeting in December 2013, the FPS released a statement that they would "continue to review comments [as] a decision has not been made" regarding the proposed Union monument. In March 2014, Representative Bill Baxley (R-Ocala), who attended the December meeting, introduced House Bill 493,[150] which added the requirement for legislative approval to any marker placed on any state lands.[151] It failed to pass in the Senate. In June 2014, the FPS released another statement that it was still deciding on the monument. When introducing the bill, Baxley argued that the UDC gave the land with the expectation that it would honor their ancestors, which is something Florida should respect. Their descendants fought "to avoid the strafing and burning of their state," Baxley said. "They were defending Florida."[152] As of early 2015, a decision had yet to be made, and so the battle continues.

Notes

1. Margie Menzel, "Fight Over Civil War Monument Breaks Out," *Orlando Sentinel*, December 3, 2013, http://articles.orlandosentinel.com/2013–12-03/news/os-civil-war-memorial-battle-florida-20131203_1_union-veterans-olustee-monument.

2. Eric Lach, "Confederates Look to Win 'Second Battle of Olustee' in Florida," *Talking Points Memo*, accessed March 5, 2014, http://talkingpointsmemo.com/muckraker/confederates-look-to-win-second-battle-of-olustee-in-florida.

3. For Joseph Finnegan and Albert Colquitt.

4. Margie Menzel, "Fight Over Civil War Monument Breaks Out."

5. Trevor Sikkema, "New Civil War Monument Triggers Debate in Lake City," *WUFT News*, December 3, 2013, http://www.wuft.org/news/2013/12/03/new-civil-war-monument-triggers-debate-in-lake-city/.

6. Eric Hobsbawm, "The New Threat to History," *New York Review of Books*, December 16, 1993, 62.

7. The term "Lost Cause" was probably first used by *Richmond Examiner* publisher Edward Pollard in his 1867 book, *The Lost Cause: The Standard Southern History of the War of the Confederates*.

8. The Lost Cause is well-trodden ground for Southern histories. Essential works include C. Vann Woodward, *The Origins of the New South: 1877–1913* (Baton Rouge: Louisiana University Press, 1971); Charles Reagan Wilson, *Baptized in Blood: The Religion of the Lost Cause: 1865–1920* (Athens: University of Georgia Press, 1980); Gaines Foster, *Ghosts of the Confederacy: Defeat, the Lost Cause, and the Emergence of the New South* (New York: New York University Press, 1987); David Blight, *Race and Reunion: Civil War in American Memory* (Cambridge, MA: Harvard University Press, 2001); and James C. Cobb, *Away Down South: A History of Southern Identity* (Oxford: Oxford University Press, 2005).

9. Karen Cox, *Dixie's Daughters: The United Daughters of the Confederacy and the Preservation of Confederate Culture* (Gainesville: University Press of Florida, 2003), 2.

10. Call quoted in Tracy J. Revels, *Grander in Her Daughters: Florida's Women during the Civil War* (Columbia: University of South Carolina Press, 2004), 235.

11. Call quoted in Revels, *Grander in Her Daughters*, 136.

12. Revels, *Grander in Her Daughters*, 136.

13. The term "cult figure" comes from Cox, *Dixie's Daughters*, 14.

14. Charles Reagan Wilson, "Confederate Memorial Day," in Wilson, ed., *The New Encyclopedia of the South, Volume 4: Myth, Manners and Memory* (Chapel Hill: University of North Carolina Press, 2006), 217.

15. Ibid.

16. On April 30, 1886, in West Point, Georgia, Governor (and former CSA general and US senator) John Gordon introduced Winnie as the "Daughter of the Confederacy," and the title stuck. At the time, Gordon was organizing the United

Confederate Veterans (UCV), a national organization of various local veteran reunion groups (organized as "camps") that would emulate the Grand Army of the Republic, a Union veterans groups founded in 1866. Their first national meeting was held in 1889, with Gordon as their commander in chief. In 1890, a Ladies Memorial Association (LMA) in St. Louis, Missouri, that at the time was creating a home for confederate veterans renamed themselves the "Daughters of the Confederacy," because of Winnie's work with veterans. Cox, *Dixie's Daughters*, 15.

17. Ibid.

18. Ibid., 16–17.

19. Ibid., 19.

20. Ibid., 28.

21. Sons of Confederate Veterans website, accessed December 23, 2014: www.florida-scv.org.

22. Ibid.

23. Ibid.

24. Cox, *Dixie's Daughters*, 47.

25. J. J. Winberry, "'Lest We Forget': The Confederate Monument and Southern Townscape," *Southeastern Geographer* 23, no. 2 (November 1983).

26. Cox, *Dixie's Daughters*, 53.

27. *Proceedings of the Annual State Convention of the Florida Division, UDC, Tampa Florida 25 January 1899* (Jacksonville: Vance Printing Company, 1899), 3; Nell Murfree, *History of the Martha Reid Chapter No. 19, UDC* (Jacksonville, FL: Self-published, 1971), 3.

28. Nell Murfree, *History of the Martha Reid Chapter No. 19, UDC*, 3.

29. Murfree, *History of the Martha Reid Chapter No. 19, UDC*, 3–4; UDC Proceedings (1899), 12–13.

30. Murfree, *History of the Martha Reid Chapter No. 19, UDC*, 13.

31. See, for instance, "Professor Commemorates Efforts of Mary Martha Reid in Civil War," *Palm Beach Post*, October 1, 1962, 5.

32. Cathryn Lancaster, *Early Years of the Florida Division of the UDC, 1896–1921*; UDC Proceeding (1899), 13.

33. UDC Proceedings (1899), 4.

34. Lancaster, *Early Years of the Florida Division of the UDC, 1896–1921*, 74.

35. UDC Proceeding (1899), 13.

36. *Proceedings of the Annual State Convention of the Florida Division, UDC, Pensacola Florida 3–5 May 1905* (Jacksonville: Vance Printing Company, 1905), 14–15.

37. Chapters included two more in Jacksonville, an additional one in Gainesville, and new chapters in Starke, Muscogee, Fort Myers, Live Oak, Kissimmee, Inverness, Green Cove Springs, Tarpon Springs, Oviedo, Little River, Monticello, Dade City, St. Petersburg, Jasper, Defuniak Springs, Dunellon, White Springs, and Marianna.

38. Lancaster, *Early Years of the Florida Division of the UDC, 1896–1921*, 74.

39. UDC Proceeding (1899), 4.

40. UDC Proceeding (1899), 20.

41. Lancaster, *Early Years of the Florida Division of the UDC, 1896–1921*, 63.

42. *Proceedings of the Annual State Convention of the Florida Division, UDC, Jacksonville, Florida 17 January 1900* (Jacksonville: Vance Printing Company, 1900), 3.

43. *UDC Proceedings* (1900), 9.

44. The best account is Fred Arthur Bailey, "Free Speech at the University of Florida: The Enoch Marvin Banks Case," *Florida Historical Quarterly* 71, no. 1 (July 1992): 1–17. Banks's papers and materials relating his resignation can be found at the Manuscripts Collection at Emory University.

45. Literally, as he died in November 1911 at the age of thirty-four. The article was "A Semi-Centennial View of Secession," *Independent* 70 (1911): 299–303.

46. Lancaster, *Early Years of the Florida Division of the UDC, 1896–1921*, 67.

47. Lancaster, *Early Years of the Florida Division of the UDC, 1896–1921*, 65–66.

48. Lancaster, *Early Years of the Florida Division of the UDC, 1896–1921*, 62–63; William B. Lees, "Memory in Stone and Blood: Civil War Monuments in Florida," paper presented at the 2011 Annual Conference of the Florida Historical Society, Jacksonville, Florida, pp. 9–10.

49. W. Stuart Towns, "Honoring the Confederacy in Northwest Florida: The Confederate Monument Ritual," *Florida Historical Quarterly*, Vol. LVII, no. 2 (October 1978), p. 210; Lees, 6.

50. Lees, 6.

51. Founded in September 1866 by Miss Anne Dummett to fulfill her idea of a monument to the forty-six local Confederates who died in the war.

52. Herbert Greenleaf, "History of the Confederate Monument, St. Augustine, Florida," (St. Augustine: Camp William Loring Camp, Sons of Confederate Veterans, n.d.), 3; Lees, 7.

53. Greenleaf, "History of the Confederate Monument, St. Augustine, Florida," 4.

54. Ibid.

55. Including Mrs. Stephen Mallory (president), Mrs. William Chipley (vice-president), Mrs. Annie McGuire (secretary), and Mrs. Laura Thornton (treasurer). They ended up dedicating the memorial to Horne, Chipley, Perry, and the Confederate soldiers who died. Towns, 206.

56. Towns, 206–8.

57. But it was delayed until June 17. Towns, 208.

58. Lees, 5.

59. Lees, 5.

60. Lees, 8.

61. Ibid.

62. Quoted in Murfree, 9.

63. *UDC Proceedings* (1899), 27.

64. Ibid.

65. *UDC Proceedings (1899)* 27–28.

66. *1899 Laws of Florida*, 213.

67. Ibid.

68. *Proceedings of the Annual State Convention of the Florida Division, UDC, Jacksonville, Florida 17 January 1900*, 13–14.

69. *UDC Proceedings (1900)*, 16.

70. *UDC Proceedings (1900)*, 21.

71. *UDC Proceedings (1900)*, 26.

72. *1901 Laws of Florida.*

73. *Proceedings of the Annual State Convention of the Florida Division, UDC, Pensacola, Florida 3–5 May 1905*, 65.

74. *Proceedings of the Annual State Convention of the Florida Division, UDC, Tallahassee, Florida 6–9 May 1908*, 35–37.

75. Copy of the deeds can be found in the Olustee Management Criteria Statement file in S 1955 Management Criteria Statements, Box 2, folder: Olustee State Battlefield Site, FSA. The originals can be found in Baker County Deed Book K, 199 and 201.

76. Barrett Codieck, "Keepers of History, Shapers of Memory: The Florida Division of the United Daughters of the Confederacy, 1895–1930," (Florida State University, MA thesis, 2012), 50.

77. Mark F. Boyd, *The East Florida Campaign of 1864* (Tallahassee: State of Florida, 1956), 1.

78. *Proceedings of the Annual State Convention of the Florida Division, UDC, Live Oak, Florida 7–9 May 1913*, 6.

79. *Proceedings of the Annual State Convention of the Florida Division, UDC, Kissimmee, Florida 4–6 November 1914*, 69–70.

80. Ibid.

81. For more on the caretakers and the park maintenance, see M96–198 UDC Scrapbooks, FSA.

82. The cannons were twelve-pound muzzle loading #122s and twelve-pound #105s. M96–198. Unfortunately, they were destroyed as scrap metal during World War II.

83. Ch 25353, *1949 Laws of Florida*. The FPS would institute citizen advisory boards, through which the UDC maintained some influence, however.

84. Published in the *Florida Historical Quarterly* 19, nos. 1 (July 1950), 2 (October 1950), and 4 (April 1951), respectively.

85. See, for instance, Boyd to CC Codrington, June 5, 1950, Boyd to Williams Goats (Supt. of National Cemetery), July 5, 1950; JT Geisey to Boyd, June 3, 1950, found in M86–40 Mark F. Boyd Papers, Box 1, folder: History—Civil War, Battle of Olustee, FSA.

86. First Artillery, Company M. Langdon to Boyd, September 3, 1956, in M86–40 Mark F. Boyd Papers, Box 1, folder: History—Correspondence—Brig Gen RC Langdon Re: Olustee, Seminal War, etc., FSA. Loomis Langford's report on the Battle of Olustee can be found at the Olustee Battlefield's website: www.battleofolustee.org/reports/langdon.htm.

87. A copy of Grossman's May 25, 1866, report can be found at www.battleofolustee.org/reports/grossman.htm.

88. Langdon to Boyd, September 3, 1956, in M86–40 Mark F. Boyd Papers, Box 1, folder: History—Correspondence—Brig Gen RC Langdon Re: Olustee, Seminal War, etc., FSA.

89. Langdon to Boyd, December 2, 1956, in M86–40 Mark F. Boyd Papers, Box 1, folder: History—Correspondence—Brig Gen RC Langdon Re: Olustee, Seminal War, etc., FSA.

90. "Great pains" from Langdon to Boyd, December 11, 1956; "as a boy" from FPS director C. H. Schaefer to Langdon, January 18, 1957, in M86–40 Mark F. Boyd Papers, Box 1, folder: History—Correspondence—Brig Gen RC Langdon Re: Olustee, Seminal War, etc., FSA.

91. A small replica of Grossman's marker was located off property in 1991.

92. The only full-length study of the American Civil War Centennial is Robert J. Cook, *Troubled Commemoration: The American Civil War Centennial, 1961–1965* (Baton Rouge: LSU Press, 2007).

93. Report of the Centennial Commission by Mrs. Herbert Vance, *Proceedings of the Annual State Convention of the Florida Division, UDC, Orlando, Florida 3–6 October 1960*, 28.

94. Report of the Florida Library and Historic Division, 1/1/1963–12/31/1965 Tallahassee; State of Florida, 4, 7; report found in S 1508 State Librarian Dorothy Dodd Correspondence files 1961–1968, Box 7, FSA.

95. Ch63–99 (House Bill 382), *1963 Laws of Florida*, 79–80.

96. Ch61–404 (House bill 1440).

97. Governor Bryant to Adams, July 10, 1863, S 756 Governor Farris Bryant correspondence files, Box 22, folder 3: "Civil War Centennial Commission, 1962," FSA.

98. Report of the Florida Library and Historic Division, 1/1/1963–12/31/1965 Tallahassee; State of Florida, 4, 7; report found in S 1508 State Librarian Dorothy Dodd Correspondence files 1961–1968, Box 7, FSA.

99. The monument was designed by JB Hill Architects of Tate, Georgia, and erected by Burns Monument Co. of Columbia, South Carolina. Adams to Bryant, July 8, 1963, S 756 Governor Farris Bryant correspondence files, Box 22, folder 3: "Civil War Centennial Commission, 1962," FSA.

100. Published as *Florida Commemorates the Civil War: A Manuel for the Observation of the Civil War by the Counties and Cities of the State of Florida*.

101. Adams to John Evans (AA to Governor Bryant), June 29, 1962, S 756

Governor Farris Bryant correspondence files, Box 22, folder 3: "Civil War Centennial Commission, 1962," FSA.

102. The publishing of which cost roughly $5,000. Adams to Evans, March 16, 1962, and September 11, 1962. S 756 Governor Farris Bryant correspondence files, Box 22, folder 3: "Civil War Centennial Commission, 1962," FSA.

103. Report of the Florida Library and Historic Division, 1/1/1963–12/31/1965 Tallahassee; State of Florida, 4; report found in S 1508 State Librarian Dorothy Dodd Correspondence files 1961–1968, Box 7, FSA.

104. Samuel Proctor, *Florida: A 100 Years Ago, 1860–65* (Tallahassee: Florida Centennial Civil War Commission, Florida Library and Historic Division, 1963). The book is a compilation of unpaginated pamphlets arranged in monthly chronological order.

105. Proctor, *Florida: A 100 Years Ago, 1860–65*, December 1860 entry.

106. For more on this, see Allen Kevin, "The Second Battle of Fort Sumter: The Debate Over the Politics of Race and Historical Memory at the Opening of America's Civil War Centennial, 1961," *Public Historian* 33, no. 2 (2011): 94–109.

107. Adams to Planning Commission, February 8, 1962. S 756 Governor Farris Bryant correspondence files, Box 22, folder 3: "Civil War Centennial Commission, 1962," FSA.

108. Ibid.

109. Ibid.

110. Ibid.

111. Ibid.

112. Ibid.

113. Chaps. 63–571 (House bill 2538), pg. 1576, 1963 Laws of Florida; "Senate Clears Nill for Battle of Olustee," *St. Petersburg Times*, June 18, 1963, 54. The bill was initiated by Rep. John Crews.

114. Ann Waldron, "The Battle Over the Marking of the 1864 Battle of Olustee," *St. Petersburg Times*, October 27, 1963, 14.

115. *Program for the Battle of Olustee: Centennial Observance: Feb 1864–1964* (Jacksonville: Battle of Olustee Centennial Observance Inc., 1964), 11.

116. *Program for the Battle of Olustee: Centennial Observance: Feb 1864–1964* (Jacksonville: Battle of Olustee Centennial Observance Inc., 1964), 1.

117. Ibid.

118. Dean Boggs (President of the Battle of Olustee Centennial Observance Inc.) to Adams, April 8, 1964, S 756 Governor Farris Bryant correspondence files, Box 22, folder 4: "Civil War Centennial Commission, 1964," FSA.

119. Sharon Robinson, "Museum to Depict Civil War Camps," *Gainesville Sun*, June 14, 1983, 5B.

120. Chapters 683.1 and 683.21, *Florida Statutes*. Juneteenth Day was created with chaps. 91–251.

121. February 9, 1973, *Gadsden Times* (AL), 11; the riot is summarized in

J. Michael Butler, "Pensacola Riot of 1976," in *Encyclopedia of Race Riots*, ed. Edward Rucker and James Upton (Westport, CT: Greenwood, 2007), 505.

122. Ibid.

123. Melissa Nelson, "Pensacola Reverend Who Fought for Civil Rights Honored Years Later," October 30, 2006, *Ocala Star Banner*, www.ocala.com/article/20061030/news/210300337, accessed September 10, 2014. For more on Matthews and Pensacola, see the work of Flagler historian J. Michael Butler, including Matthew and Butler, *Victory After the Fall* (Montgomery: NewSouth, Inc., 2007).

124. There have been numerous attempts throughout the South in recent years to rename landmarks and memorials honoring Forrest.

125. Mark Woods, "54 Years Later and Continuing for the Longest meeting," *Florida Times Union*, September 18, 2013, http://jacksonville.com/opinion/premium/blog/401820/mark-woods/2013–09–28/mark-woods-54-years-and-counting-jacksonvilles-longest.

126. Michael Pearson, "Florida School Will Drop Confederate Nathan B. Forrest's Name," CNN, December 17, 2013, www.cnn.com/2013/12/17/us/florida-school-name-change/; Valerie Strauss, "School Named After KKK Grand Wizard To Be Renamed . . . Finally," *Washington Post*, December 16, 2013, www.washingtonpost.com/blogs/answer-sheet/wp/2013/12/16/school-named-after-kkk-grand-wizar-to-be-renamed-finally/. As of December 30, 2014, the petition could still be accessed at www.change.org/p/duval-public-school-no-more-kkk-high-school/. An earlier petition to change the name in 2007 had failed in a 5–2 school board vote.

127. Strauss, "School Named After KKK Grand Wizard To Be Renamed . . . Finally."

128. Woods, "54 Years and Counting."

129. Shelley Opel, "Confederate Flag Quietly Removed," *St. Petersburg Times*, February 10, 2001, www.sptimes.com/news/021001/confderate_flag.htm.

130. Led by Rep. Meek of Miami and Rev. R. N. Gooden of Tallahassee. Diane Hirth, "Black Legislators: Down With the Confederate Flag," *Sun Sentinel*, April 11, 1996, www.articles.sun-sentinel.com/1996–04–11/news/960900570_1_confderate-flag-rev-rn-gooden-black-legislators.

131. Jessica Velde, "Confederate Group Plans Giant Flag in Hillsborough County," *Tampa Bay Times*, May 30, 2008, www.tampabay.com/news/humaninterest/confederate-group-plans-giant-flag-in-hillsborough-county/551722.

132. Bill Varian, "Hard Feelings Unfurl with Huge Confederate Flag," *Tampa Bay Times*, June 4, 2008, www.tampabay.com/news/humaninteres-feelings-unfurl-with-huge-confederate-flag/607830.

133. Jessica Velde, "Confederate Group Plans Giant Flag in Hillsborough County."

134. Bill Varian, "Hard Feelings Unfurl with Huge Confederate Flag."

135. Ibid.

136. Shelley Opel, "Confederate Flag Quietly Removed," *St. Petersburg Times*,

February 10, 2001, www.sptimes.com/news/021001/confderate_flag.htm.

137. Thomas Becnel, "Beneath an Infamous Rebel Flag in East Tampa," *Herald Tribune*, October 27, 2010, A1.

138. Ibid.

139. Eric Deggans, "On Day When History Is Made, Ugly Past Rears Its Head," *Tampa Bay Times*, June 4, 2008, www.tampabay.com/news/politics/on-day-when-history-is-made-ugly-past-rears-its-head/607819.

140. Bill Varian, "Hard Feelings Unfurl with Huge Confederate Flag."

141. The closest Olustee came to modern controversy was when the local NAACP protested the Olustee parade because the city of Lake City still used a Confederate flag as its logo. Some picket signs read, "Follow Jeb's Leadership," referring to Governor Bush's removal of the flag from the Historic State Capitol that month. "NAACP Protest Confederate Flag in Lake City Logo," *Lakeland Ledger*, February 16, 2001, B5.

142. See, for instance, *Sarasota Herald Tribune*, February 23, 1973, 1a; and *Palm Beach Post*, August 21, 1973, C2.

143. Giron was a consultant to several Civil War–related Hollywood productions. He died in 2011 in Virginia. http://www.imdb.com/name/nm0320958/.

144. "Crucial Battlefield Set for Reenactment," *Palm Beach Post*, January 30, 1977, B12; *Olustee Battle Festival Program* (Lake City: North Central Florida Advertising, Inc., 2014), 54.

145. *Olustee Battle Festival Program*, 54.

146. "Civil War Re-enactment Set for Stat at Six Gun" *Ocala Star Banner*, February 13, 1979, 3A.

147. Julie Barrett, "historymaking," *Gainesville Sun*, February 17, 2005, http://www.gainesville.com/article/20050217/SCENE/202170307?Title=Historymaking.

148. Ibid.

149. Bill Maxwell, "A Deep Love-Hate," *Lakeland Ledger*, July 20, 1993, 7A.

150. See http://www.myfloridahouse.gov/Sections/Documents/loaddoc.aspx?FileName=_h0493__.docx&DocumentType=Bill&BillNumber=0493&Session=2014.

151. Michael Van Sickler, "Baxley's Bill Protects Confederate Heritage by Adding Layer of Government," *Tampa Bay Times*, March 24, 2014, http://www.tampabay.com/blogs/the-buzz-florida-politics/baxleys-bill-protects-confederate-heritage-by-adding-layer-of-government/2171751.

152. Ibid.

Bibliography

Primary Sources

Census

Eighth Census of the United States—1860—Florida

Government Documents

Calba Sumpter v. The State of Florida (1866). 11 Fla. 247, 1866 WL 1106 (Fla.)

Cato, a slave, Plaintiff in Error, v. The State (1860). 9 Fla. 163, 1860 WL 2051 (Fla.)

Charles K. Miller, Appellant, v. James M. Gaskins, Appellee (1864). 11 Fla. 73, 1864 WL 1117 (Fla.)

Daniel R. June v. Thomas J. Myers (1867). 12 Fla. 310, 1867, Florida Reports

David S. Walker, Appellant, v. James H. Gatlin, Appellee (1867). 12 Fla. 9, 1867 Florida Reports

Emily L. Donaldson, Appellant, v. The State (1861). 9 Fla. 402, 1861 WL 1288 (Fla.)

Frances, a slave, Appellant, v. The State (February Term 1855). 6 Fla. 306, 1855 WL 1389 (Fla.)

Franklin Branch and Edward A. Clark, Appellants, v. William R. Wilson, Appellee (1868). 12 Fla. 543, 1868 WL 1400 (Fla.)

Henry Slaback, Appellant, v. Leoma L. Cushman, Appellee (1868). 12 Fla. 472, 1868 WL 1394 (Fla.)

Jason Gregory, Plaintiff in Error, v. Adam McNealy, Defendant in Error (1869). 12 Fla. 579, 1869 Florida Reports

John Holland, Appellant, v. The State of Florida, Appellee (1867). 12 Fla. 117, 1867 WL 1453 (Fla.)

Josiah T. Budd, Administrator of Jackson Kemp, Deceased, Appellant, v. William Ryal Long, Appellee (1869). 13 Fla. 288, 1869 WL 1547 (Fla.)

Thomas J. Linton, Appellant, v. Hamilton K., and Mary H. and Minor W. Walker, Appellees (1858). 8 Fla. 144, 1858 WL 1644 (Fla.)

William Judge, Appellant, v. Forsyth's Executors, Appellee (1867). 11 Fla. 257, 1867 Florida Reports

Winder H. Harrison, Plaintiff in Error, v. The State (1860). 9 Fla. 156, 1860 WL 2049 (Fla.)

Record Group 102 Governors (1929–1971)

S 131 Governors Haydon Burns correspondence files

S 756 Governor Farris Bryant correspondence files

Record Group 197 Library and Historical Commission
S 1508 State Librarian Dorothy Dodd correspondence files 1961–1968
Record Group 510 Division of Recreation and Parks
S 1943 Director Emmett Hill administrative files
S 1955 Florida Park Service Management Criteria Statements

Record Group 900000 Manuscripts
M76–131 Anna Jackson Chapter, UDC
M86–40 Mark F. Boyd Papers
M96–198 UDC Scrapbooks

State of Florida. 1899 Laws of Florida.
———. 1901 Laws of Florida.
———. 1949 Laws of Florida.
———. 1961 Laws of Florida.
———. 1963 Laws of Florida.
———. 1991 Laws of Florida.
———. Florida Commemorates the Civil War: A Manuel for the Observation of the Civil War by the Counties and Cities of the State of Florida.

Legal Cases and Government Documents

Archer, James T. Reports of Cases Argued and Adjudged in the Supreme Court of Florida, at January Term, 1848, Vol. 2. Tallahassee: Southern Journal Office William Bartlett, printer, 1848.

Branch, Joseph. Reports of Cases Argued and Determined in the Supreme Court of Florida: January Terms, 1846–1847, Vol. 1. Tampa: Tribune Publishing Company, 1914.

Bush, Allen H. A Digest of the Statute Law of Florida of a General and Public Character, in Force Up to the First Day of January 1872. Tallahassee: Charles H. Walton, State Printer, 1872.

Cocke, William Archer. Reports of Cases Argued and Adjudged in the Supreme Court of Florida at Terms Held in 1871, 1872, 1873, 1874, Vol. 14. Tallahassee: Floridian, 1874.

Compiled Service Records of Confederate Soldiers in Organizations from the State of Florida. Roll 81. National Archives, Washington, DC.

Cooper, Charles M. Cases Argued and Adjudged in the Supreme Court of Florida, During the Year 1886, Vol. 22. Tallahassee: Floridian Book and Job Office, 1887.

Davis, J. C. Bancroft. Cases Argued and Adjudged in the Supreme Court of the United States, October Term, 1883. New York: Banks & Brothers, Law Publishers, 1884.

———. Cases Adjudged in the Supreme Court at October Term, 1895. New York: Banks & Brothers, Law Publishers, 1896.

Drew, James B. C. Reports of Cases Argued and Adjudged in the Supreme Court of Florida During the Years 1869, 1870, 1871, Vol. 13. Tallahassee: Charles H. Walton, State Printer, 1871.

DuVal, John P. Compilation of the Public Acts of the Legislative Council of the Territory of Florida Passed Prior to 1840. Tallahassee: Samuel S. Sibley, Printer, 1839.

Federal Writers' Project of the Works Progress Administration for the State of Florida. Slave Narratives: A History of Slavery in the United States from Interviews with Former Slaves, Vol. 3: Florida Narratives. Washington, DC: N.p., 1941.

Florida. Journal of the Constitutional Convention of 1865 at Tallahassee, Florida. Microfilm, Florida State University Library.

Florida. Journal of the Proceedings of the Senate of the General Assembly of the State of Florida at the 2nd Session of the 14th General Assembly. Office of the Floridian: Printed by Dyke and Sparhawk, 1866.

Florida. Journal of the Proceedings of the House of Representatives of the General Assembly of the State of Florida at the 2nd Session of the 14th General Assembly. Office of the Floridian: Printed by Dyke and Sparhawk, 1866.

Florida. Acts and Resolutions adopted by the 14th General Assembly of Florida, at its 2nd Session, Dec. 18, 1865. Tallahassee: Dyke and Sparhawk, 1866.

Florida. Acts and Resolutions adopted by the 14th General Assembly of Florida, at its 2nd Session, Nov. 14, 1866. Tallahassee: Dyke and Sparhawk, 1867.

Florida. Journal of the Proceedings of the Constitutional Convention, 1868 of the State of Florida Begun and Held at the Capitol, at Tallahassee, on Monday, January 20, 1868. Tallahassee: Edward M. Cheney, Printer, 1868.

Florida. A Journal of the Proceedings of the Assembly of the State of Florida at its First Session begun on Monday, June 8th, 1868. Tallahassee: Tallahassee Sentinel, 1868.

Florida. The Acts and Resolutions adopted by the Legislature of Florida at its 1st Session (1868) under the Constitution of A.D. 1868. Tallahassee: Tallahassee Sentinel, 1868.

Florida. A Journal of the Proceedings of the Joint Convention of the Florida Legislature Held in the Capitol, Nov. 3, 1868, and of the Senate and Assembly of the State of Florida at an extraordinary session of the Legislature Convened Nov. 3, 1868. Tallahassee: Office of the Tallahassee Sentinel, Hiram Potter Jr., State Printer, 1868.

Florida. A Journal of the Proceedings of the Assembly of the State of Florida at its Extra Session held on June 8th, 1869. Tallahassee: Edward M. Cheney, State Printer, 1869.

Frances v. State of Florida (1855). Florida State Archives. Record Group 1100, Series 49, Box 773.

Galbraith, John B. Reports of Cases Argued and Adjudged in the Supreme Court of Florida, at Terms Held in 1860–1861, Vol. 9. Tallahassee: Office of Floridian & Journal, Dyke & Carlisle, 1861.

———. Reports of Cases Argued and Adjudged in the Supreme Court of Florida, at Terms Held in 1864, 1865, 1866, & 1867, Vol. 11. Tallahassee: Dyke & Sparhawk, 1867.

Galbraith, John B., and A. R. Meek. Reports of Cases Argued and Adjudged in the Supreme Court of Florida, at Terms Held in 1867, 1868, 1869, Vol. 12. Tallahassee: Edward M. Cheney, State Printer, 1869.

Gardenhire, Jasper B. Reports of Cases Argued and Decided in the Supreme Court of the State of Missouri, Vol. 15. Jefferson City: James Lusk, Public Printer, 1852.

Hogue, David P. Reports of Cases Argued and Determined in the Supreme Court of Florida: January Terms 1849. Tallahassee: Office of the Florida Sentinel, Joseph Clisby, 1849.

———. Reports of Cases Argued and Determined in the Supreme Court of Florida in 1851–1852, Vol. 4. Tallahassee: Office of the Floridian & Journal, Dyke, 1852.

Holland v. State of Florida (1867). Florida State Archives. Record Group 1100, Series 49, Box 779.

Howard, Benjamin C. Report of the Decision of the Supreme Court of the United States and the Opinions of the Judges Thereof, in the Case of Dred Scott Versus John F. A. Sandford: December Term, 1856. Washington: Cornelius Wendell, Printer, 1857.

Journal of the Proceedings of the House of Representatives of the General Assembly of the State of Florida, 1848.

Journal of the Proceedings of the House of Representatives of the General Assembly of the State of Florida, 1860.

Journal of the Proceedings of the House of Representatives of the General Assembly of the State of Florida, 1861.

Judge v. Forsyth (1867). Florida State Archives. Record Group 1100, Series 49, Box 779.

June v. Myers (1867). Florida State Archives. Record Group 1100, Series 49, Box 834.

Kelly v. Wallace (1856). Florida State Archives. Record Group 1100, Series 49, Box 773.

Luke, a slave, v. State of Florida (1853). Florida State Archives, Record Group 1100, Series 49, Box 440, Wallet 773.

Miller v. Gaskins (1864). Florida State Archives. Record Group 1100, Series 49, Box 780.

Official Records of the Union and Confederate Navies in the War of the Rebellion, 30 vols. Washington, DC: Government Printing Office, 1894–1922.

Papy, Mariano D. Reports of Cases Argued and Adjudged in the Supreme Court of Florida, at Term Held in 1853, Vol. 5, No. 1. Tallahassee: Office of Floridian & Journal, Charles E. Dyke, 1853.

Provost Marshal Records, Florida Report, No. 14356, 1–4–1865, Florida report (G. W. Long).

———. Reports of Cases Argued and Adjudged in the Supreme Court of Florida, at Terms Held in 1855–1856, Vol. 6, No. 1. Tallahassee: Office of Floridian & Journal, James S. Jones, 1856.

———. Reports of Cases Argued and Adjudged in the Supreme Court of Florida, at Terms Held in 1857, Vol. 7. Tallahassee: Office of Floridian & Journal, James S Jones, 1857.

———. Reports of Cases Argued and Adjudged in the Supreme Court of Florida, at Terms Held in 1858–1859, Vol. 8. Tallahassee: Office of Floridian & Journal, Jones & Dyke, 1859.

Raney, George, P. Cases Argued and Adjudged in the Supreme Court of Florida, During the Years 1878, 1879, 1880, Vol. 17. Tallahassee: Floridian Book and Job Office, 1880.

Reports of Cases in the Supreme of Florida Held in 1864–1867. Tallahassee, 1867.

US War Department. Office of the Surgeon General. The Medical and Surgical History of the War of the Rebellion. 15 vols. Washington DC: 1878–1888, facsimile ed., Wilmington, NC, Broadfoot, 1990.

———. *War of the Rebellion: A Compilation of the Official Records of the Union and Confederate Armies.* 128 vols. Washington, DC, 1880–1901.

Slaback v. Cushman (1868). Florida State Archives, Record Group 1100, Series 49, Box 835.

Sumpter v. State of Florida (1866). Florida State Archives, Record Group 1100, Series 49, Box 779.

Thompson, Leslie A:, Esq. Manual or Digest of the Statute Law of the State of Florida, of a General and Public Character, in force at the end of the Second Session of the General Assembly of the State, on the sixth day of January 1847.

Boston: Charles C. Little and James Brown, 1857.

United States. Congress. House of Representatives. *The War of the Rebellion: A Compilation of the Official Records of the Union and Confederate Armies.* Washington, DC: Government Printing Office, 1880–1901, Series 1, Vol. 49 (Part 2).

United States Congress. House. Index to the Reports of Committees of the House of Representatives for the First Session of the Forty-Seventh Congress, 1881–1882. Washington, DC: Government Printing Office, 1882.

———. Senate. Instructions Given to Commanding Generals under Act of Congress August 6, 1861. 37th Congress, 2nd Sess., Senate Executive Document 67.

———. House. Message of the President. 37th Congress, 2nd Sess., House Executive Document 69.

———. House. Report of Major General Wool. 37th Congress, 2nd Sess., House Executive Document 85.

———. House. Emancipation of Slaves of Rebels. 37th Congress, 2nd Sess., House of Representatives Report 120.

———. Memorial of the Emancipation League. 37th Congress, 3rd Sess., Misc. Document 10.

———. Report of the Freedmen's Inquiry Commission. 38th Congress, 1st Sess., Executive Document 53.

———. Senate. Treatment of Colored Refugees. 38th Congress, 2nd Sess., Senate Executive Document 28.

———. House. Report of the Joint Select Committee on the Condition of the Insurrectionary State. 42nd Congress, 2nd Sess., House Report #22, pt. 13.

———. House. Proceedings of the Florida Convention. 40th Congress, 2nd Sess., Misc. Doc. #114.

———. Senate. Report of Committees of the Senate of the United States for the Second Session of the Forty-Fourth Congress, 1876–77, Vol. 2 (Washington, DC: Government Printing Office, 1877).

———. House. Index to the Miscellaneous Documents of the House of Representatives for the First Session of the Forty-Seventh Congress, 1881–82 (Washington, DC: Government Printing Office, 1882).

US Senate. *A statement showing the amount of revenue collected annually, in each collection district, from June 30, 1854, to June 30, 1859, together with the amount expended and number of persons employed in each district*, 36th Congress, 1st Session. Washington, DC: George W. Bowman, 1860.

US War Dept. *Official Records of the Union and Confederate Armies in the War of the Rebellion*, 128 vols. Washington, DC: Government Printing Office, 1880–1901.

———. *Official Records of the Union and Confederate Navies in the War of the Rebellion*, 31 vols. Washington, DC: Government Printing Office, 1894–1927.

Walker v. Gatlin (1867). Florida State Archives. Record Group 1100, Series 49, Box 779. US Congress. *Report on the internal commerce of the United States*, 49th Congress, 2nd Session. Washington, DC: Government Printing Office, 1886.

Wallace, John William. Cases Argued and Adjudged in the Supreme Court of the United States, December Term, 1872, Vol. 16. New York: Banks & Brothers, Law Publishers, 1889.

War of the Rebellion, The: A Compilation of the Official Records of the Union and Confederate Armies, 70 vols. Washington, DC: Government Printing Office, 1880–1901.

Manuscript Collection

Benjamin Waring Partridge Papers, 1824–1945. Manuscript Department, William R. Perkins Library, Duke University, Durham, NC.

Newspapers

Atlanta Southern Confederacy

Augusta Chronicle

Augusta Daily Constitutionalist

Boston Herald

Charleston Daily Courier

Cleveland Plain-Dealer

Fort Lauderdale Sun-Sentinel

Gainesville Sun

Harper's Weekly

Herald Tribune

Jacksonville, Florida-Republican

Jacksonville Florida Times-Union

Lake City Florida Index

Lakeland Ledger

Macon Daily-Telegraph

Marianna Florida Whig

Monticello The Family Friend

New Orleans Times-Picayune

New York Evening Post

Ocala Star Banner

Orlando Sentinel

Palm Beach Post

Pensacola, Gazette
Philadelphia Inquirer
Richmond Daily Dispatch
Richmond Enquirer
Richmond Examiner
Sacramento Daily Union
Sarasota Herald Tribune
St. Augustine, Ancient City
St Petersburg Times
Tallahassee Florida Sentinel
Tallahassee Floridian and Journal
Tampa Bay Times
The New York Times
Washington Evening Star
Washington National Tribune

Published Primary Sources

Bethlehem Baptist Association (GA). Minutes of the Annual Session of the Bethlehem Baptist Association, 1861. N.p.: 1861.

Bethlehem Baptist Association (GA). Minutes of the Bethlehem Baptist Association, Held with the Belleville Church, Conecuh County, Ala., on the 26th, 27th, and 28th of September 1863. Montgomery, AL: Memphis Appeal Book and Job Printing Office, 1864.

"Cabell to Governor Brown," February 12, 1850, published in Jacksonville, *Florida Republican*, March 7, 1850.

Call, Richard Keith. Union.—Slavery.—Secession: Letter from Governor R. K. Call, of Florida, to John S. Littell, of Germantown, Pennsylvania. Philadelphia: C. Sherman & Son, Printers, 1861.

Dickison, Mary Elizabeth. Dickison and His Men: Reminiscences of the War in Florida. Facsimile reproduction—Jacksonville, FL: San Marco, 1962.

Doty, Franklin A. "The Civil War Letters of Augustus Henry Mathers, Assistant Surgeon, Fourth Florida Regiment, C.S.A." *Florida Historical Quarterly* 36 (October 1957): 94–124

DuBose, John E. [Sermon to] Capt. Parkhill's Company, "The Howell Guards," on the Eve of Their Departure for the Seat of War, August 26, 1861. Tallahassee, FL: Office of the Floridian and Journal, 1861.

"Governor Brown to Yulee, Morton, and Cabell," February 22, 1850, published in *Jacksonville, Florida Republican*, March 7, 1850

Greeley, Mellen C. "Musings of Mellen Clark Greeley, Written in His Anec-Dotage." P. K. Yonge Library of Florida History, University of Florida, Gainesville, FL.

Groene, Bertram H., ed. "Civil War Letters of Colonel David Lang." *Florida Historical Quarterly* 54 (January 1976): 349–66.

Hodges, Ellen E., and Steven Kerber, eds. "'Rogues and Black Hearted Scamps': Civil War Letters of Winston and Octavia Stephens, 1862–1863." *Florida Historical Quarterly* 57 (July 1978): 54–82.

Lees, William B. "Memory in Stone and Blood: Civil War Monuments in Florida," paper presented at the 2011 Annual Conference of the Florida Historical Society, Jacksonville, Florida.

"Morton to Governor Brown." March 10, 1850, published in Jacksonville, *Florida Republican*, April 4, 1850.

Mrs. Herbert Vance, Proceedings of the Annual State Convention of the Florida Division, UDC, Orlando, Florida, October 3–6, 1960.

Pouty, Ronald N., ed. "War Comes to Tampa Bay: The Civil War Diary of Robert Watson." *Tampa Bay History* 10 (Fall/Winter 1988): 50–54.

United Daughters of the Confederacy. Florida Chapter. Proceedings of the Annual State Convention of the Florida Division, UDC, Tampa, January 25, 1899.

———. Proceedings of the Annual State Convention of the Florida Division, UDC, Jacksonville, Florida, January 17, 1900.

———. Proceedings of the Annual State Convention of the Florida Division, UDC, Pensacola, Florida, May 3–5, 1905.

———. Proceedings of the Annual State Convention of the Florida Division, UDC, Tallahassee, Florida, May 6–9, 1908.

———. Proceedings of the Annual State Convention of the Florida Division, UDC, Live Oak, Florida, May 7–9, 1913.

———. Proceedings of the Annual State Convention of the Florida Division, UDC, Kissimmee, Florida, November 4–6, 1914.

Verrot, Augustin. *A Tract for the Times: Slavery & Abolition, Being the Substance of a Sermon*, Preached in the Church of St. Augustine, Florida, on the 4th Day of January 1861, Day of Public Humiliation, Fasting and Prayer. New Orleans: Catholic Propagator Office, 1861.

"Yulee, Morton, Cabell to Governor Brown," February 6, 1850, published in Jacksonville, *Florida Republican*, March 7, 1850.

Secondary Sources

Books

Akerman, Joe A., and J. Mark, *Jacob Summerlin: King of the Crackers*. Cocoa: Florida Historical Society Press, 2004.

Aldridge, Daniel W. *Becoming American: The African American Quest for Civil Rights, 1861–1976*. Wheeling, IL: Harlan Davidson, Inc., 2011.

Aptheker, Hebert, ed. *A Documentary History of the Negro People in the United States, Volume I: From the Colonial Times Through the Civil War*. New York: Citadel Press Book, 1951.

Baptist, Edward E. *Creating an Old South: Middle Florida's Plantation Frontier before the Civil War*. Chapel Hill: University of North Carolina Press, 2002.

Barney, William L. *The Secessionist Impulse, Alabama and Mississippi in 1860*. Princeton: Princeton University Press, 1974.

Battle of Olustee Centennial Observance Inc. *Program for the Battle of Olustee: Centennial Observance: Feb 1864–1964*. Jacksonville: Battle of Olustee Centennial Observance, Inc., 1964.

Beitzell, Edwin B. *Point Lookout Prison Camp for Confederates*. Privately published, 1972.

Bender, Shelby Jean Roberson, and Elizabeth Laramie Dunham. *Tampa's HistoriCemeteries*. Charleston: Arcadia Publishing, 2013.

Bentley, George. *A History of the Freedman's Bureau*. New York: Oxford University Press, 1955.

Berg, Manfred. *"Ticket to Freedom": The NAACP and the Struggle for Black Political Integration*. Gainesville: University Press of Florida, 2005.

Beringer, Richard E., et al. *The Elements of Confederate Defeat: Nationalism, War Aims, and Religion*. Athens: University of Georgia Press, 1988.

Berlin, Ira, ed. *The Destruction of Slavery*. New York: Cambridge University Press, 1985

Berry, Mary Frances. *Black Resistance/White Law: A History of Constitutional Racism in America*. New York: Appleton-Century-Crofts, 1971.

Blakey, Arch Fredric, Ann Smith Lainhart, and Winston Bryant Stephens Jr., eds. *Rose Cottage Chronicles: Civil War Letters of the Bryant-Stephens Families of North Florida*. Gainesville: University of Florida Press, 1998.

Blight, David. *Race and Reunion: Civil War in American Memory*. Cambridge, MA: Harvard University Press, 2001.

Bodenhamer, David J., and James W. Ely Jr., eds. *Ambivalent Legacy: A Legal History of the South*. Jackson: University Press of Mississippi, 1984.

Boyd, Mark F. *The East Florida Campaign of 1864*. Tallahassee: State of Florida, 1956.

Boykin, Samuel. *History of the Baptist Denomination in Georgia*. 1881; reprint, Paris, AR: Baptist Standard Bearer, 2000.

Brown, Canter, Jr. *Florida's Black Public Officials, 1867–1924*. Tuscaloosa: University of Alabama Press, 1998.

Brown, David, and Clive Webb. *Race in the American South: From Slavery to Civil Rights*. Gainesville: University Press of Florida, 2007.

Browning, Robert M., Jr. *Success Is All That Was Expected: The South Atlantic Blockading Squadron during the Civil War*. Washington, DC: Brassey's, 2002.

Buker, George. *Blockade, Refugees, and Contrabands: Civil War of Florida's Gulf Coast, 1861–1865*. Tuscaloosa: University of Alabama Press, 1993.

Butler, J. Michael. "Pensacola Riot of 1976." In *Encyclopedia of Race Riots, ed.* Edward Rucker and James Upton. Westport, CT: Greenwood, 2007.

Carpenter, John A. *Sword and Olive Branch*. Pittsburgh: University of Pittsburgh Press, 1964.

Carswell, E. W. *Holmesteading: The History of Holmes County, Florida*. Tallahassee, FL: Rose Printing Company, 1986.

Cassanello, Robert. *To Render Invisible: Jim Crow and Public Life in New South Jacksonville*. Gainesville: University of Florida Press, 2013.

Cassanello, Robert, and Melanie Shell-Weiss, eds. *Florida's Working-Class Past: Current Perspectives on Labor, Race, and Gender from Spanish Florida to the New Immigration*. Gainesville: University Press of Florida, 2009.

Catterall, Helen T. *Judicial Cases Concerning American Slavery and the Negro*. New York: Octagon Books, 1968.

Cheshire, Joseph Blount. *The Church in the Confederate States: A History of the Protestant Episcopal Church in the Confederate States*. New York: Longmans, Green and Co., 1911.

Cobb, James C. *Away Down South: A History of Southern Identity*. Oxford: Oxford University Press, 2005.

Cohen, William. *At Freedom's Edge: Black Mobility and the Southern White Quest for Racial Control, 1861–1915*. Baton Rouge: Louisiana State University Press, 1991.

Coker, William S. "The Moreno Family of the Gulf Coast." In *Spanish Pathways in Florida*, ed. Ann L. Henderson and Gary R. Mormino. Sarasota, FL: Pineapple, 1991.

Colburn, David R., and Jane L. Landers. *The African American Heritage of Florida*. Gainesville: University of Florida Press, 1995.

Cook, Robert J. Cook. *Troubled Commemoration: The American Civil War Centennial, 1961–1965*. Baton Rouge: Louisiana State University Press, 2007.

Cox, Dale. *The Battle of Natural Bridge, Florida: The Confederate Defense of Tallahassee*. Fort Smith: Dale Cox, 2001.

Cox, Karen. *Dixie's Daughters: The United Daughters of the Confederacy and the Preservation of Confederate Culture*. Gainesville: University Press of Florida, 2003.

Crowley, John G. *Primitive Baptists of the Wiregrass South: 1815 to the Present*. Gainesville: University Press of Florida, 1998.

Current, Richard Nelson. *Lincoln's Loyalists: Union Soldiers from the Confederacy*. Boston, MA: Northeastern University Press, 1992.

Dale, Elizabeth. *Criminal Justice in the United States, 1789–1939*. Cambridge: Cambridge University Press, 2011.

David, William Watson. *The Civil War and Reconstruction in Florida*. 1913; reprint, Gainesville: University of Florida Press, 1964.

Davis, Frederick T. *History of Jacksonville, Florida and Vicinity, 1513 to 1924*. Gainesville: University of Florida Press, 1964.

Davis, Thomas Frederick. *History of Early Jacksonville, Florida: Being an Authentic Record of Events from the Earliest Times to and Including the Civil War*. Jacksonville: The H. & W. B. Drew Company, 1911.

Davis, William C. *Jefferson Davis: The Man and His Hour*. New York: Harper Collins, 1991.

Denham, James M. *A Rogue's Paradise: Crime and Punishment in Antebellum Florida, 1821–1861*. Tuscaloosa: University of Alabama Press, 1997.

Denham, James M., and Canter Brown Jr., eds. *Cracker Times and Pioneer Lives: The Florida Reminiscences of George Gillett Keen and Sarah Pamela Williams*. Columbia: University of South Carolina Press, 2000.

Dickison, John J. "Florida." In *Confederate Military History*, ed. Clement A. Evans. 13 vols. Atlanta: Blue and Grey Press, 1899.

Dodd, Dorothy. *Florida Becomes a State*. Tallahassee: Florida Centennial Commission, 1945.

Doherty, Herbert J. *Richard Keith Call, Southern Unionist*. Gainesville: University of Florida Press, 1961.

Donald, David. *Charles Sumner*. New York: De Capo Press, 1996.

———, ed. *Why the North Won the Civil War*. 1960. Reprint. New York: Touchstone, 1996.

Dowd, Clifford, and Louis H. Manarin, eds. *The Wartime Papers of R. E. Lee*. New York: Bramhall House, 1961.

Eicher, John H., and David J. Eicher. *Civil War High Commands*. Stanford: Stanford University Press, 2001.

Eppes, Susan Bradford. *Through Some Eventful Years*. Macon, GA: J. W. Burke Company, 1926.

Favorite, Merab-Michal. *Bradenton*. Charleston: Arcadia Publishing, 2013.

Finkleman, Paul, ed. *Rebellions, Resistance, and Runaways within the Slave South*. New York: Garland, 1989.

Fleming, Francis P. *Memoirs of Capt. C. Seton Fleming, of the Second Florida Infantry, CSA, Illustrative of the Florida Troops in Virginia during the War between the States*. Jacksonville, FL: 1888, facsimile ed., Alexandria, VA, 1985.

Foster, Gaines. *Ghosts of the Confederacy: Defeat, the Lost Cause, and the Emergence of the New South*. New York: New York University Press, 1987.

Foster, George A., Mrs. Roy F. Thomas, and Jennie C. Weaver. *The First United Methodist Church of Ocala, Florida, 1844–2000*. Ocala, FL: First Impressions Printing, n.d.

Fowler, William M. *Under Two Flags: The American Navy in the Civil War*. 1990. Reprint. Annapolis: Naval Institute Press, 2001.

Franklin, John Hope, and Loren Schweniger. *Runaway Slaves: Rebels on the Plantation*. New York: Oxford University Press, 1999.

Freeman, Douglas Southall. *R. E. Lee: A Biography*. Vol. 1. 1964. Reprint. New York: Charles Scribner's Sons, 1932.

———. *Lee's Lieutenants: A Study in Command*. 3 vols. New York: Scribner's, 1942–1944.

Friedman, Lawrence. *A History of American Law*. New York: Simon & Schuster, 1973.

Gannon, Michael. *Florida: A Short History*. Gainesville: University Press of Florida, 1993.

———. *Rebel Bishop: The Life and Era of Augustin Verot*. Milwaukee: Bruce Publishing Company, 1964.

Gerteis, Louis. *From Contraband to Freedmen: Federal Policy toward Southern Blacks, 1861–1865*. Westport, CT: Greenwood, 1973.

Gleeson, David T. "'No Disruption of Union': The Catholic Church in the South and Reconstruction." In *Vale of Tears: New Essays on Religion and Reconstruction*, ed. Edward J. Blum and W. Scott Poole, 164–86. Macon, GA: Mercer University Press, 2015.

Goen, C. C. *Broken Churches, Broken Nation: Denominational Schisms and the Coming of the American Civil War*. Macon, GA: Mercer University Press, 1985.

Greenleaf, Herbert. "History of the Confederate Monument, St. Augustine, Florida," St. Augustine: Camp William Loring Camp, Sons of Confederate Veterans, n.d.

Griffin, Patricia C. *Mullet on the Beach: The Minorcans of Florida, 1768–1788*. Jacksonville: University of North Florida Press, 1991.

Hahn, Steven. *The Political Worlds of Slavery and Freedom*. Cambridge, MA: Harvard University Press, 2009.

Hall, Kermit, ed. *The Oxford Companion to the Supreme Court of the United States.* New York: Oxford University Press, 1992.

Harding, Vincent. *There Is a River: The Black Struggle for Freedom in America.* New York: Harcourt Brace Jovanovich, 1981.

Hartman, David W., and David Coles, comps. *Biographical Roster of Florida's Confederate and Union Soldiers, 1861–1865.* 5 vols. Wilmington, NC: Broadfoot, 1995.

Hesseltine, William B. *Civil War Prisons.* New York: Ungar, 1962.

Hill, Samuel S. "Florida." In *Religion in the Southern States: A Historical Study,* edited by Samuel S. Hill, 57–76. Macon, GA: Mercer University Press, 1983.

Hillhouse, Don. *Heavy Artillery and Light Infantry: A History of the 1st Florida Special Battalion and 10th Florida Infantry.* Jacksonville: Privately published, 1992.

Horwitz, Morton J. *The Transformation of American Law, 1870–1960: The Crisis of Legal Orthodoxy.* New York: Oxford University Press, 1992.

Johns, John E. *Florida during the Civil War.* Gainesville: University of Florida Press, 1963.

Jones, James P. *Yankee Blitzkrieg: Wilson's Raid through Alabama and Georgia.* Athens: University of Georgia Press, 1976.

Jordan, Winthrop D. *White Over Black: American Attitudes toward the Negro, 1550–1812.* Chapel Hill: University of North Carolina Press, 1968.

Koblas, John J. *John J. Dickison: Swamp Fox of the Confederacy.* St. Cloud, MN: North Star Press, 2000.

Lake City Advertiser. *Olustee Battle Festival Program.* Lake City: North Central Florida Advertising, Inc.

Lancaster, Cathryn. *Early Years of the Florida Division of the UDC, 1896–1921.* United Daughters of the Confederacy. Florida Division. Winter Park, FL, 1984.

Ley, John C. *Fifty-Two Years in Florida.* Nashville: Publishing House of the M. E. Church, South, 1899.

Litwack, Leon. *Been in the Storm So Long: The Aftermath of Slavery.* New York: Vintage Books, 1979.

———. North of Slavery: *The Negro in the Free States, 1790–1860.* Chicago: University of Chicago Press, 1961.

Magdol, Edward. *A Right to the Land: Essays on the Freedmen's Community.* Westport, CT: Greenwood, 1977.

Mahon, John K. *History of the Second Seminole War, 1835–1842.* Gainesville: University Press of Florida, 1985.

Manley II, Walter W., ed., E. Cantor Brown, and Eric W. Rise. *The Supreme Court of Florida and Its Predecessor Courts, 1821–1917.* Gainesville: University Press of Florida, 1997.

McPherson, James M. *Battle Cry of Freedom: The Civil War Era*. New York: Ballantine, 1988.

———. *For Cause and Comrade: Why Men Fought in the Civil War*. New York: Oxford University Press, 1997.

Merrill, James M. *The Rebel Shore: The Story of Union Sea Power in the Civil War*. Boston: Little, Brown and Company, 1957.

Michaels, Brian E. *The River Flows North: A History of Putnam County, Florida*. Palatka, FL: Putnam County Archives and History Commission, 1976.

Morris, Thomas D. *Southern Slavery and the Law, 1619–1860*. Chapel Hill: University of North Carolina Press, 1996.

Murfree, Nell. *History of the Martha Reid Chapter No. 19, UDC*. Jacksonville, FL: Self-published, 1971.

Murray, Pauli, ed. *States' Laws on Race and Color and Appendices: Containing International Documents, Federal Laws and Regulations, Local Ordinances and Charts*. Cincinnati: Methodist Church Literature Division, 1951.

Murray, Vince. *Dixie's Land Ocala: Florida*. Focus Publications, 1992.

Napolitano, Andrew P. *Dred Scott's Revenge: A Legal History of Race and Freedom in America*. Nashville: Thomas Nelson, 2009.

Nevins, Allan. *Ordeal of the Union*, Volume 1. New York: Scribner, 1947.

Nulty, William H. *Confederate Florida*. Tuscaloosa: University of Alabama Press, 1990.

Oakes, James. *Slavery and Freedom: An Interpretation of the Old South*. New York: W. W. Norton, 1998.

O'Brien, Sean Michael. *Mountain Partisans: Guerrilla Warfare in the Southern Appalachians, 1861–1865*. Westport, CT: Praeger, 1991.

Ortiz, Paul. *Emancipation Betrayed: The Hidden History of Black Organizing and White Violence in Florida from Reconstruction to the Bloody Election of 1920*. Berkley: University of California Press, 2005.

Ott, Eloise Robinson, and Louis Hickman Chazal. *Ocala Country, Kingdom of the Sun: A History of Marion County, Florida*. Ocala, FL: Perry Printing Company, 1966.

Paisley, Clifton. *Red Hills of Florida, 1528–1865*. Tuscaloosa: University of Alabama, 1989.

Palmer, Beverly, ed. *The Selected Letters of Charles Sumner*, Volume 2. Boston: Northeastern University Press, 1990.

Proctor, Samuel. *Florida: A 100 Years Ago, 1860–65*. Tallahassee: Florida Centennial Civil War Commission, Florida Library and Historic Division, 1963.

Ramage, James A. *Rebel Raiders: The Life of General John Hunt Morgan*. Lexington: University of Kentucky, 1986.

Revels, Tracy J. *Grander in Her Daughters: Florida's Women during the Civil War.* Columbia: University of South Carolina Press, 2004.

Richardson, Joe M. *Christian Reconstruction: The American Missionary Association and Southern Blacks, 1861–1890.* Athens: University of Georgia Press, 1986.

———. *The Negro in the Reconstruction of Florida.* Tallahassee: Florida State University Press, 1965.

———. *Trial and Imprisonment of Jonathan Walker, at Pensacola, Florida, for Aiding Slaves to Escape from Bondage: A Facsimile Reproduction of the 1845 Edition with an Introduction and Index.* Gainesville: University Presses of Florida, 1974.

Richardson, Simon Peter. *The Lights and Shadows of Itinerant Life: An Autobiography.* Nashville: Publishing House Methodist Episcopal Church, South, 1900.

Ripley, C. Peter, ed. *The Black Abolitionist Papers, Volume III: The United States, 1830–1846.* Chapel Hill: University of North Carolina Press, 1991.

———. *The Black Abolitionist Papers, Volume IV: The United States, 1847–1858.* Chapel Hill: University of North Carolina Press, 1991.

Rivers, Larry Eugene. *Rebels and Runaways: Slave Resistance in Nineteenth-Century Florida.* Urbana: University of Illinois Press, 2012.

———. *Slavery in Florida: Territorial Days to Emancipation.* Gainesville: University Press of Florida, 2000.

Rivers, Larry Eugene, and Canter Brown Jr. *Laborers in the Vineyard of the Lord: The Beginnings of the AME Church in Florida, 1865–1895.* Gainesville: University of Florida Press, 2001.

Roberts, William H. *Now for the Contest: Coastal and Oceanic Operations in the Civil War.* Lincoln: University of Nebraska Press, 2004.

Robertson, Fred L., comp. *Soldiers of Florida in the Seminole Indian, Civil, and Spanish-American Wars.* Live Oak, 1903, reprint ed. Macclenny, 1983.

Robertson, James I., Jr. *Soldiers Blue and Gray.* Columbia: University of South Carolina Press, 1988.

Rogers, William Warren, and Erica R. Clark. *The Croom Family and Goodwood Plantation: Land, Litigation, and Southern Lives.* Athens: University of Georgia Press, 1999.

Rosser, John Leonidas. *A History of Florida Baptists.* Nashville, TN: Broadman, 1949.

Rothman, Adam. *Slave Country: American Expansion and the Origins of the Deep South.* Cambridge, MA: Harvard University Press, 2005.

Saint Mark's Church (Palatka, Fla.). *History of St. Mark's Church, Palatka, Florida.* St. Augustine, FL: Record Company, 1920.

Schafer, Daniel L. *Thunder on the River: The Civil War in Northeast Florida.* Gainesville: University Press of Florida, 2009.

Schmidt, James D. *Free to Work: Labor Law, Emancipation, and Reconstruction, 1815–1880*. Athens: University of Georgia Press, 1998.

Schmidt, Lewis G. *The Civil War in Florida: Florida's East Coast; A Military History*. Allentown, PA: n.p., 1991.

Shofner, Jerrell H. *Jackson County, Florida: A History*. Greenwood: Penkevill, 1985.

———. *The History of Brevard County*, Volume 1. Stuart, FL: Southeastern Printing Company, 1995.

———. *History of Jefferson County, Florida*. Tallahassee, FL: Sentry, 1976.

———. *Nor Is It over Yet: Florida in the Era of Reconstruction, 1863–1877*. Gainesville: University of Florida Press, 1974.

Sifakis, Stewart. *Compendium of the Confederate Armies: Florida and Arkansas*. New York: Heritage Books, 1992.

Silver, James W. *Confederate Morale and Church Propaganda*. New York: W. W. Norton, 1957.

Sins, Elizabeth H. *A History of Madison County, Florida*. Madison, FL: Madison County Historical Society, 1986.

Smith, Geo. G. [George Gilman], Jr. *The History of Methodism in Georgia and Florida, from 1785 to 1865*. Macon, GA: Jno. W. Burke & Co., 1877.

Smith, Julia Floyd. *Slavery and Plantation Growth in Antebellum Florida, 1821–1860*. Gainesville: University Press of Florida, 1973.

Stoker, Donald. *The Grand Design: Strategy and the U.S. Civil War*. New York: Oxford, 2010.

Sugrue, Thomas J. *Sweet Land of Liberty: The Forgotten Struggle for Civil Rights in the North*. New York: Random House, 2008.

Sutherland, Daniel E. *A Savage Conflict: The Decisive Role of Guerrillas in the American Civil War*. Chapel Hill: University of North Carolina Press, 2009.

Sweett, Zelia Wilson. *New Smyrna, Florida, in the Civil War*. New Smyrna Beach, FL: Volusia County Historical Commission, 1963.

Swint, Henry L., ed. *Dear Ones at Home: Letters from Contraband Camps*. Nashville: Vanderbilt, 1990.

Symonds, Craig L. *Lincoln and His Admirals: Abraham Lincoln, the U.S. Navy, and the Civil War*. Oxford: Oxford University Press, 2008.

Tanner, Robert G. *Retreat to Victory? Confederate Strategy Reconsidered*. Wilmington, DE: A Scholarly Resource, 2001.

Taylor, Robert A. *Rebel Storehouse: Florida's Contribution to the Confederacy*. Tuscaloosa: University of Alabama Press, 2003.

Tebeau, Charlton W. *A History of Florida*. Coral Gables: University of Miami Press, 1971.

Thomas, Emory. *The Confederate Nation, 1861–1865*. New York: Harper Torchbooks, 1979.

Thompson, Ernest Trice. *Presbyterians in the South*, Volume 1: *1607–1861*. Richmond, VA: John Knox, 1963.

Trudeau, Noah A. *Out of the Storm: The End of the Civil War, April–June 1865*. Boston: Little, Brown, 1994.

Tsesis, Alexander. *We Shall Overcome: A History of Civil Rights and the Law*. New Haven, CT: Yale University Press, 2008.

Tushnet, Mark V. *The American Law of Slavery, 1810–1860: Considerations of Humanity and Interest*. Princeton: Princeton University Press, 1981.

———. *Making Civil Rights Law: Thurgood Marshall and the Supreme Court, 1936–1961*. New York: Oxford University Press, 1994.

VanderVelde, Lea. *Mrs. Dred Scott: A Life on Slavery's Frontier*. New York: Oxford University Press, 2009.

Vorenberg, Michael. *Final Freedom: The Civil War, the Abolition of Slavery, and the Thirteenth Amendment*. Cambridge: Cambridge University Press, 2001.

Walker, David. *Walker's Appeal to the Coloured Citizens of the World*. University Park: Pennsylvania State University Press, 2000.

Wallenstein, Peter, ed. *Higher Education and the Civil Rights Movement: White Supremacy, Black Southerners, and College Campuses*. Gainesville: University Press of Florida, 2008.

Walther, Eric. *The Fire Eaters*. Baton Rouge: Louisiana State University Press, 1992.

Warner, Ezra J., and W. Buck Yearns. *Biographical Register of the Confederate Congress*. Baton Rouge: Louisiana State University Press, 1975.

Waters, Zack C., and James C. Edmonds. *A Small but Spartan Band: The Florida Brigade in Lee's Army of Northern Virginia*. Tuscaloosa: University of Alabama Press, 2010.

Weber, David J. *The Spanish Frontier in North America*. New Haven, CT: Yale University Press, 1992.

Weinfeld, Daniel R. *The Jackson County War: Reconstruction and Resistance in Post-Civil War Florida*. Tuscaloosa: University of Alabama Press, 2012.

Welke, Barbara Young. *Recasting American Liberty: Gender, Race, Law, and the Railroad Revolution, 1865–1920*. Cambridge: Cambridge University Press, 2001.

Wiley, Bell I. *The Life of Johnny Reb: The Common Soldier of the Confederacy*. Baton Rouge: Louisiana University Press, 1943, 1978 edition.

Willis, Lee. *Southern Prohibition: Race, Reform, and Public Life in Middle Florida, 1821–1920*. Athens: University of Georgia Press, 2011.

Wilson, Charles Reagan. *Baptized in Blood: The Religion of the Lost Cause, 1865–1920.* Athens: University of Georgia Press, 1980.

———, ed. *The New Encyclopedia of the South,* Volume 4: *Myth, Manners and Memory.* Chapel Hill: University of North Carolina Press, 2006.

———. "Confederate Memorial Day." In *The New Encyclopedia of the South, Volume 4: Myth, Manners and Memory, ed.* Wilson, 217. Chapel Hill: University of North Carolina Press, 2006.

Winsboro, Irvin D. S., ed. *Old South, New South, or Down South: Florida and the Modern Civil Rights Movement.* Morgantown: West Virginia University Press, 2009.

Wise, Stephen R. *Lifeline of the Confederacy: Blockade Running during the Civil War.* Columbia: University of South Carolina Press, 1988.

Wong, Edlie L. *Neither Fugitive nor Free: Atlantic Slavery, Freedom Suits, and the Legal Culture of Travel.* New York: New York University Press, 2009.

Woodward, C. Vann. *Mary Chestnut's Civil War.* New Haven, CT: Yale University Press, 1981.

———. *The Origins of the New South: 1877–1913.* Baton Rouge: Louisiana University Press, 1971.

Zanca, Kenneth J., ed. *American Catholics and Slavery, 1789–1866: An Anthology of Primary Documents.* Lanham, MD: University Press of America, 1994.

Articles

"Address of John C. McGehee Before the Southern Rights Association of Madison County, June 7, 1851." *Florida Historical Quarterly* 5, no 2.

Andrews, Dee E. "Reconsidering the First Emancipation: Evidence from the Pennsylvania Abolition Society Correspondence, 1785–1810." *Pennsylvania History* 64 (Summer 1997): 230–49.

Bailey, Fred Arthur. "Free Speech at the University of Florida: The Enoch Marvin Banks Case." *Florida Historical Quarterly* 71, no. 1 (July 1992): 1–17.

Banks, Enoch. "A Semi-Centennial View of Secession." *Independent* 70 (1911): 299–303.

Barr, Ruth B., and Modeste Hargis. "The Voluntary Exile of Free Negroes of Pensacola." *Florida Historical Quarterly* 17, no. 1 (July 1938): 3–14.

Bates, Thelma. "The Legal Status of the Negro in Florida." *Florida Historical Quarterly* 6, no. 3 (January 1928): 159–81.

Berlin, Ira. "The Structure of the Free Negro Caste in the Antebellum United States." *Journal of Social History* 9, no. 3 (Spring 1976): 297–318.

Boman, Dennis K. "The Dred Scott Case Reconsidered: The Legal and Political Context in Missouri." *American Journal of Legal History* 44, no. 4 (October 2000): 405–28.

Boyd, Joseph A., Justice, and Randall O. Reder. "A History of the Supreme Court of Florida." *University of Miami Law Review* 35, no. 5 (September 1981); 1019–66.

Boyd, Mark F. "The Apalachicola or Chattahoochee Arsenal of the United States." *Apalachee* 4 (1956): 29–43.

Buettinger, Craig. "Did Slaves Have Free Will? Luke, a Slave, v. Florida and Crime at the Command of the Master." *Florida Historical Quarterly* 83, no. 3 (Winter 2005), 241–57.

———. "Masters on Trial: The Enforcement of Laws against Self-Hire by Slaves in Jacksonville and Palatka, Florida." *Civil War History* 46, no. 2 (June 2000): 91–106.

Cash, William T. "Taylor County History and Civil War Deserters." *Florida Historical Quarterly* 27 (1948): 28–58.

Cha-Jua, Sundiata Keita, and Clarence Lang. "The 'Long Movement' as Vampire: Temporal and Spatial Fallacies in Recent Black Freedom Studies." *Journal of African American History* 92, no. 2 (Spring 2007): 265–88.

Coles, David J. "Ancient City Defenders: The St. Augustine Blues," edited by Jacqueline K. Fretwell, *Civil War Times in St. Augustine* (Port Salerno: Florida Classic Library, 1988) 65–89.

Cushman, Joseph D., Jr. "The Episcopal Church in Florida during the Civil War." *Florida Historical Quarterly* 38, no. 4 (April 1960): 294–301.

Denham, James M. "From a Territorial to a State Judiciary: Florida's Antebellum Courts and Judges." *Florida Historical Quarterly* 73, no. 4 (April 1995): 443–55.

Dillon, Rodney E., Jr. "A Gang of Pirates: Confederate Lighthouse Raids in Southeast Florida, 1861." *Florida Historical Quarterly* 67 (1989): 441–57.

———. "The Battle of Fort Myers." *Tampa Bay History* 5 (1983): 27–36.

Dodd, Dorothy. "The Secession Movement in Florida, 1850–1861, Part I." *Florida Historical Quarterly* XII, no. 1 (1933): 45–66.

Doherty, Herbert J. "Florida and the Crisis of 1850." *Journal of Southern History* 19, no.1 (February 1953): 447–67.

Doyle, Christopher. "Judge St. George Tucker and the Case of Tom V. Roberts: Blunting the Revolution's Radicalism from Virginia's District Courts." *Virginia Magazine of History and Biography* 106, no. 42 (Autumn 1998): 419–42.

East, Omega G. "St. Augustine during the Civil War." *Florida Historical Quarterly* 31 (1952): 75–91.

Ernst, Daniel R. "The Critical Tradition in the Writing of American Legal History." *Yale Law Journal* 102, no. 4 (January 1993): 1019–76.

Fairclough, Adam. "Historians and the Civil Rights Movement." *Journal of American Studies* 24, no. 3 (December 1990): 387–98.

Finkelman, Paul. "Slaves as Fellow Servants: Ideology, Law, and Industrialization." *American Journal of Legal History* 31, no. 4 (October 1987): 269–305.

Gardner, Eric. "'You Have No Business to Whip Me': The Freedom Suits of Polly Wash and Lucy Ann Delany." *African American Review* 41, no. 1 (Spring 2007): 33–50.

Garvin, Russell. "The Free Negro in Florida before the Civil War." *Florida Historical Quarterly* 46, no. 1 (July 1967): 1–17.

Gordon, Robert W. "J. Willard Hurst and the Common Law Tradition in American Legal Historiography." *Law and Society Review* 10, no. 1 (Autumn 1975): 9–55.

Grossberg, Michael. "Legal History and Social Science: Friedman's 'History of American Law,' the Second Time Around." *Law & Social Inquiry* 13, no. 2 (Spring 1988): 359–83.

Hall, Jacquelyn Dowd. "The Long Civil Rights Movement and the Political Uses of the Past." *Journal of American History* 91 (2005): 1233–63.

Hall, Robert L. "Tallahassee's Black Churches, 1865–1885." *Florida Historical Quarterly* 58, no. 2 (October 1979): 185–96.

———. "'Yonder Come Day': Religious Dimensions of the Transition from Slavery to Freedom in Florida." *Florida Historical Quarterly* 65, no. 4 (April 1987): 411–32.

Hunt, James L. "Who Pays for Progress? Accident Law in Florida, 1845–1886." *Florida Historical Quarterly* 82, no. 2 (Fall 2003): 129–54.

Jones, Allen W. "Military Events in Florida during the Civil War, 1861–1865." *Florida Historical Quarterly* 39 (1960): 42–45.

Kearney, Kevin E., and William Marvin. "Autobiography of William Marvin." *Florida Historical Quarterly* 36, no. 3 (January 1958): 179–222.

Kharif, Wali R. "Black Reaction to Segregation and Discrimination in Post- Reconstruction Florida." *Florida Historical Quarterly* 64, no. 2 (October 1985): 161–73.

Klein, Allen. "The Second Battle of Fort Sumter: The Debate Over the Politics of Race and Historical Memory at the Opening of America's Civil War Centennial, 1961." *Public Historian* 33, no. 2 (2011): 94–109.

Knetsch, Dr. Joe. "Armed Boats off Crystal River." *At Home: Citrus County Historical Society* 18 (2001): 1, 6–7.

———. "Forging the Florida Frontier: The Life and Career of Captain Samuel E. Hope." *Sunland Tribune* 20 (1994): 31–40.

Krueger, Thomas A. "American Labor Historiography, Old and New." *Journal of Social History* 4, no. 3 (Spring 1971): 277–85.

Lawson, Steven F. "Freedom Then, Freedom Now: The Historiography of the Civil Rights Movement." *American Historical Review* 96, no. 2 (April 1991): 456–71.

McArdle, Andrea. "The Confluence of Law and Antebellum Black Literature: Lawyerly Discourse as a Rhetoric of Empowerment." *Law and Literature* 17, no. 2 (Summer 2005): 183–223.

McFarland, L. B. "Battle of West Point." *Confederate Veteran* 23 (August 1915): 351–53.

Moore, Wilbert E. "Slave Law and the Social Structure." *Journal of Negro History* 26, no. 2 (April 1941): 171–202.

Newman, Richard S. "The Age of Emancipating Proclamations: Early Civil War Abolitionism and its Discontents." *Pennsylvania Magazine of History and Biography* 137, no. 1 (January 2013): 33–55.

Nicholls, Michael L. "The Squint of Freedom': African-American Freedom Suits in Post-Revolutionary Virginia." *Slavery & Abolition: A Journal of Slave and Post-Slave Studies* 20, no. 2 (1999): 47–62.

Painter, Nell Irvin. "The New Labor History and the Historical Moment." *International Journal of Politics, Culture, and Society* 2, no. 3 (Spring 1989): 367–70.

Price, Marcus W. "Ships That Tested the Blockade of the Georgia and East Florida Ports, 1861–1865." *American Neptune* XV (1955): 97–132.

Reiger, John E. "Florida After Secession: Abandonment by the Confederacy and its Consequences," *Florida Historical Quarterly* 50 (1971): 128–42.

Richardson, Joe M. "The Freedmen's Bureau and Negro Labor in Florida." *Florida Historical Quarterly* 39 (October 1960): 168–86.

———, ed. "A Northerner Reports on Florida: 1866." *Florida Historical Quarterly* 40 (April 1962): 382–91.

———. "An Evaluation of the Freedmen's Bureau in Florida." *Florida Historical Quarterly* 41 (January 1963): 224–39.

———. "Florida Black Codes." *Florida Historical Quarterly* 47 (April 1969): 366–80.

———. "We Are Truly Doing Missionary Work: Letters from American Missionary Association Teachers in Florida, 1864–1874." *Florida Historical Quarterly* 54 (October 1975): 179–96.

Schafer, Daniel L. "A Class of People Neither Freemen Nor Slaves: From Spanish to American Race Relations in Florida, 1821–1861." *Journal of Social History* 26, no. 3 (Spring 1993): 587–609.

Scheiber, Harry N. "American Constitutional History and the New Legal History:

Complementary Themes in Two Modes." *Journal of American History* 68, no. 2 (September 1981): 337–50.

Sharfstein, Daniel J. "The Secret History of Race." *Yale Law Journal* 112, no. 6 (April 2003): 1472–1509.

Shofner, Jerrell H. "Custom, Law, and History: The Enduring Influence of Florida's 'Black Code.'" *Florida Historical Quarterly* 55, no. 3 (January 1977): 277–98.

———. "Judge Herbert Rider and the Lynching at LaBelle." *Florida Historical Quarterly* 59, no. 3 (January 1981): 292–306.

Soifer, Avaim. "Willard Hurst, Consensus History, and the Growth of American Law." *Reviews in American History* 20, no. 1 (March 1992): 124–44.

Solomon, Irvin D. "Southern Extremities: The Significance of Fort Myers in the Civil War." *Florida Historical Quarterly* 72 (1993): 129–52.

Taylor, Robert A. "Cow Cavalry: Munnerlyn's Battalion in Florida, 1864–1865." *Florida Historical Quarterly* 66 (1986): 196–214.

———. "Rebel Beef: Florida Cattle and the Confederate Army, 1862–1864." *Florida Historical Quarterly* 68 (1988): 196–214.

Thompson, Joseph Conan. "Toward a More Humane Oppression: Florida's Slave Codes, 1821–1861." *Florida Historical Quarterly* 71, no. 3 (January 1993): 324–38.

Towns, W. Stuart. "Honoring the Confederacy in Northwest Florida: The Confederate Monument Ritual," *Florida Historical Quarterly*, Vol. LVII, no. 2 (October 1978).

VanderVelde, Lea, and Sandhya Subramanian. "Mrs. Dred Scott." *Yale Law Journal* 106, no. 4 (January 1997): 1033–1122.

Waters, Zack C. "Florida's Confederate Guerrillas: John W. Pearson and the Oklawaha Rangers." *Florida Historical Quarterly* 70 (1991): 133–49.

———. "Tampa's Forgotten Defenders: The Confederate Commanders of Fort Brooke." *Sunland Tribune* 17 (1991): 3–12.

———. "'Tell Them I Died Like a Confederate Soldier': Finegan's Brigade at Cold Harbor." *Florida Historical Quarterly* 69 (October 1990): 156–77.

Weinert, Richard P. "Dickison: The Swamp Fox of Florida." *Civil War Times Illustrated* 5 (966): 4–11, 48–50.

Welke, Barbara Y. "When All the Women Were White, and All the Blacks Were Men: Gender, Class, Race, and the Road to Plessy, 1855–1914." *Law and History Review* 13, no. 2 (Autumn 1995): 261–316.

Willis, Lee L., III. "Secession Sanctified: Bishop Francis Huger Rutledge and the Coming of the Civil War in Florida." *Florida Historical Quarterly* 82, no. 4 (Spring 2004): 421–37.

Unpublished Thesis and Dissertations

Codieck, Barrett. "Keepers of History, Shapers of Memory: The Florida Division of the United Daughters of the Confederacy, 1895–1930," MA thesis, Florida State University, 2012.

Coles, David James. "Far from Fields of Glory: Military Operations in Florida during the Civil War, 1864–1865." PhD diss., Florida State University, 1996.

Dalton, Jack P. "A History of Georgia Baptists." PhD diss., University of Florida, 1952.

Graetz, Robert Bruce. "Triumph Amid Defeat: The Confederate at Natural Bridge." Bachelor's honors thesis, Florida State University, 1986.

Jackson, Jesse Jefferson. "The Negro and the Law in Florida, 1821–1921: Legal Patterns of Segregation and Control in Florida, 1821–1921." Unpublished MA thesis, Florida State University, 1960.

Kennington, Kelly Marie. "River of Injustice: St. Louis's Freedom Suits and the Changing Nature of Legal Slavery in Antebellum America." Unpublished diss., Duke University, 2009.

King, Jerry McDowell. "Shadow Warriors of the Confederacy" MA thesis, University of South Florida, 1990.

Lord, Mills M., Jr. "David Levy Yulee, Statesmen and Railroad Builder." MA thesis, University of Florida, 1940.

Nichols, Richard S. "Florida's Fighting Rebels: A Military History of Florida's Civil War Troops." MA thesis, Florida State University, 1967.

Parker, Amy Suzanne. "Love Is a Battlefield: The Marriages of Confederate Soldiers and Their Wives in Florida during the Civil War." Honors thesis, Florida State University, 2009.

Electronic Sources

www.battleofolustee.org

www.florida-scv.org

Cannon, Jeff, "The Brooksville-Bayport Raid and the Civil War in Hernando County," http://www.pascocemeteries.org/Brooksville_bayport_raid.html

"County Name Origins," www.flheritage.com/facts/reports/names/county.cfm

Cox, Dale. "Historic Apalachicola Arsenal—Chattahoochee, Florida," http://www.exploresouthernhistory.com/arsenall.html

Contributors

Chris Day is a history instructor at Maclay College Preparatory School in Tallahassee, Florida. His research focuses on the Long Civil Rights Movement in Florida, which he views through the lens of legal history. The scope of this endeavor can be found in his dissertation, "Civiliter Mortuus: The Florida Supreme Court and the Civil Rights Movement, 1845–1896." Chris's other research interests include antebellum Florida, Reconstruction in Florida, and race relations.

R. Boyd Murphree is the project manager for Florida Family and Community History at the University of Florida Smathers Libraries. His dissertation focused on the Civil War leadership of Governors John Milton of Florida and Joseph E. Brown of Georgia. He has published entries in the *Encyclopedia of the American Civil War*. He is currently coediting a book on the history of Florida's governors and writing a biography of Governor John Milton.

David Nelson is an associate professor of history at Bainbridge State College. A graduate of the University of North Florida (BA) and Florida State University (MA, PhD), Nelson's work focuses on Florida and Southern History, Public History, and Environmental History. He is also director of the Scotland Study Abroad Program for the University System of Georgia. He lives in Quincy, Florida, with his wife, Heather, and his son, Carter.

David B. Parker is a professor of history at Kennesaw State University. He is the author of works on Georgia writer Bill Arp, evangelist Sam Jones, the American carpet industry, *The Wonderful Wizard of Oz*, Confederate textbooks, "so help me God" in the presidential oath, and Georgia's bicentennial celebration, among other topics. He is most proud of having proven that "y'all," usually associated with lower-class native southern speakers, in fact began with seventeenth-century British poetry.

Tracy J. Revels is an award-winning professor at Wofford College. Revels received her PhD from Florida State University in 1990. She is the author of *Grander in Her Daughters: Florida's Women during the Civil War* (University of South Carolina Press), *Watery Eden: A History of Wakulla Springs* (Sentry Press), and *Florida's Civil War: Terrible Sacrifices* (Mercer University Press).

Jonathan C. Sheppard is a native Floridian who received his PhD at Florida State University in 2008. He was a lecturer at Florida State, where he earned a Distinguished Teaching Award. He is now the executive director at Mission San Luis: Florida's Apalachee-Spanish Living History Museum. He is the author of *By the Noble Daring of Her Sons: The Florida Brigade of the Army of Tennessee* (University of Alabama Press). He lives with his wife, Courtenay, in Tallahassee.

Robert A. Taylor is a professor of history and the associate dean/head of the School of Arts and Communication at the Florida Institute of Technology. He received a PhD from Florida State University. Taylor is the author, coauthor, editor, or coeditor of seven books, including *Rebel Storehouse: Florida in the Confederate Economy*. His articles and reviews have appeared in journals such as *Army History*, *Journal of Southern History*, and *Florida Historical Quarterly*.

Lauren K. Thompson is an assistant professor of history at McKendree University in Lebanon, Illinois. She received her PhD from Florida State University in 2015. Her research focuses on race and gender during the Civil War era. Her book *Friendly Enemies: Soldier Fraternization throughout the American Civil War* is forthcoming from the University of Nebraska Press.

Zack C. Waters is a retired attorney and teacher. He has authored numerous articles on America's Civil War and, with James C. Edmonds, the Florida Historical Society award-winning book *A Small but Spartan Band: The Florida Brigade in Lee's Army of Northern Virginia*. He is currently completing a book on Confederate guerrillas in East and South Florida. Born in Florida, he resides in Rome, Georgia, with his wife.

Seth A. Weitz is an associate professor of history at Dalton State College. His research focuses primarily on the New South history, African American history, and Florida history. A graduate of Tulane University (BA) and Florida State University (MA, PhD), Weitz has published in the *Historian*, *Tampa Bay Journal of History*, and *FCH Annals: Journal of the Florida Conference of Historians*, among others. He is currently working on a book project on Florida governor George Franklin Drew.

Index

African American Episcopal Church, 128–29

Alison, A. K., 54

American Freedmen's Inquiry Commission recommends creating the Freedmen's Bureau, 148

Babcock, William, 48

Baya, Francis, 189

Baya, Joseph, 188

Baya, William, 185, 190–91

Beauregard, P. G. T., 82, 103

Bell, John, 48

Benjamin, Judah P., 66, 101; guerilla warfare, refuses to authorize, 73; guerilla warfare, revises view on, 74

Bird, Daniel E., 76

Bowen, W. L. L., 80

Bragg, Braxton, 95

Bravo, Alonzo, 186

Beard, John, 31–34

Breckinridge, John C., 48

Brooksville, 83–84

Broome, James E., 19–20; elected governor of Florida (1852), 37

Brown, Joseph E., 108

Brown, Thomas, 24; "Southern Convention," refuses to endorse, 27–28; Unionism and compromise, support of, 25

Buchanan, James, 124

Buchman, Thomas, placement of torpedoes on St. John's River, 82

Bullock, Edward C., 53

Bureau of Florida Folklife, 207

Butler, Benjamin, decision not to return contraband to owner, 142–43

Cabell, Edward, 31–34; loses reelection, 37; unites with David Levy Yulee and Jackson Morton to endorse "Southern Convention," 27

Calhoun, John C.: author of "Southern Address," 25; suggests "Southern Convention," 26

Call, Richard Keith, 116; and belief that slavery was protected under the US Constitution, 48; 1852 gubernatorial campaign of, 33; as member of the "nucleus," 8; reaction to the Compromise of 1850, 30–31; second term as territorial governor, 9; and selection of Tallahassee as Florida's territorial capital, 6; supports Thomas Brown during Crisis of 1850, 26

Canova, Andreas, 186

Canova, Antonio, 191–92

Canova, Bartola, 189

Capers, Henry D., leads expedition against loyalists in Taylor County, 83

Carreas, Gaspar, 186

Castillo, David, 189

Catholic Church in Florida, 121–22; number of members in 1860, 117

Cavedo, Louis D., 188

Cedar Keys, 59, 84, 102

Clark, Frank J., 76

Collins, Leroy, creates Florida Civil War Centennial Commission, 209

Compromise of 1850, 20; aftermath of passage in Florida, 31–32; need for, 24; passed by Congress, 30; proposed by Henry Clay, 27
Confederate symbolism: debate over Confederate, 215–16; and reaction against, 214–15
Confederate memorials, construction of, 202–3
Constitutional Union Party (1860), 4

David S. Walker, Appeallant v. James H. Griffin, Appellee, 155–58
Davis, Jefferson, 2; and conscription, 104; and popularity in post-Civil War South, 199; refuses to authorize guerilla warfare, 73; and regulatory legislation pertaining to blockade running, 107–8
Davis, W. G. M., 97
Democratic Party of Florida, 8; reaction to Thomas Brown's stance on "Southern Convention," 20; reaction to passage of Compromise of 1850, 30
Dickinson, J. J., 84, 85; background of, 77; capture of the steamboat *Columbine*, 82; captures Welaka and Saunders, 83
Dilworth, William Scott, 184; on defenses of Amelia Island, 62; requests slave labor to assist with work on Amelia Island, 6
"Dixiecrats," 207
Donaldson v. The State, 149–50
Douglas, Stephen: and Compromise of 1850, 30; and election of 1860, 48–44
DuBose, John, 116
DuPont, Samuel, 66; and seizure of Amelia Island, 66–68, 74; and seizure of Port Royal Sound, 64
Duval, William Pope, 7

East Florida, 6, 11
East Gulf Blockading Squadron, 2, 80, 83
8th Florida Infantry Regiment, 184; Hispanics serving in, 186
Ellis, William J, preaches sermon in reaction to Abraham Lincoln's election, 123–24
Emmons, George F, returns contraband to their owner, 142
Episcopal Church in the United States, number of members in 1860, 117
Eppes, Susan Bradford, 14

Fernandez, Edward A., 187
Fernandina: economy of, 59; identified as strategic location, 60; occupation by Union forces, 68, 101
Finegan, Joseph, 14, 77, 190
Finley, Jesse J., 21–22
Florida: economy at the outbreak of the Civil War, 10–11; and importance of cattle during Civil War, 12; and observance of Confederate holidays, 213–14; occupation of Gulf Coast islands by Union troops, 78–79; production of salt in, 13l; secession convention of, 52–55; secession of, 42, 54–55; secession rhetoric in, 49–50, 51–52; supplies cattle to Confederate army, 81; Unionists in, 79–80
Florida Baptist Association, purchases Confederate bonds, 12

Florida Baptist Convention: approves resolution that endorses secession, 116; number of members in 1860, 117
Florida Civil War Centennial Commission, 210; controversies associated with, 211; and first reenactment of the Battle of Olustee, 211–12
Florida Executive Council, 100–10
Florida Library and History Commission, 207
Florida Methodist Conference, 117–18, 128; number of members in 1860, 117
Florida Park Service, 196–97, 207; and lack of decision on construction of Union monument, 218; and Olustee reenactment, 216
Florida State Archives, 207
Florida State Library, 207
Florida State Museum, 207; and Civil War exhibit, 213
Footman, William, 84
Fort Clinch, 62
Fort Myers, 84
Fort Pickens, 94
Fourteenth Amendment, 153
Freedmen's Bureau, establishment of, 148–49
Fremont, John C., issues emancipation decree in Missouri, 141–43
1st Florida Infantry Regiment, Hispanics serving in, 186
1st Florida Cavalry Regiment, 97
1st Florida Special Battalion, 82
4th Florida Infantry Battalion, 82
4th Florida Infantry Regiment, 65, 95–96
54th Massachusetts Infantry Regiment, 196, 216

Gainesville, 83
Gaskins, Thomas G, manumission case over will of, 150–52
Genovar, William, 188
Gist, William Henry, 141
Gonzalez, August, 188
Gonzalez, Celestine, 185–86
Grayson, John B., 63

Hart, Isaiah, 10
Hemming, J.C., 75
Hernandez, A. J., 188
Hernandez, Joseph, 188–89
Hernandez, Randolph, 186
Higginson, Thomas Wentworth, 145
Hilton, R. B., 108
Hopkins, Edward, 94, 96–97
Huston, George, brief, but violent career of, 76

Indian Removal Act (1830), 44

Jacksonville, fire of 1863 in, 123, 125–26

Kansas-Nebraska Act (1854), 47

Lang, David, 184
Lee, Robert Edward, 66; assignment to command Department of South Carolina, Georgia, and Florida, 64; defense of Amelia Island, 64–65; on importance of Florida to Confederate war effort, 12; orders withdrawal from Amelia Island, 67; suggests on the interior of Florida be defended, 75
Lincoln, Abraham: blockade proclaimed by, 60; and Election of 1860, 49; issues Emancipation

Proclamation, 144–45; Southern reaction to election of, 42–43
Long, Ellen Call, 14
Long, G. W., 76
Lopez, Alonzo, 186
Lopez, Emmanuel M., 188
Luke v. Florida, 137–39
Lutterloh, E. J., 84

McGehee, John C., 19; addresses Southern Rights Association of Madison County, 35–36; as president of Florida's Secession Convention, 37
McQueen, McIntosh, 124, 138
Middle Florida, 7, 11, 12, 19, 44; holds political and economic power of Florida, 22–23
Milton, John, 2–3; Amelia Island's capture, reaction to, 74; and call for improved defenses of Florida, 14; background of, 89–91; blockade running regulations, support of, 108; confronts problem of Unionism in Taylor County, 83; cavalry units, criticism of, 97; conscription, support of, 104–6; dispatches Florida soldiers to Virginia, 82; and deserters, 106–7; elected governor of Florida (1860), 94; Florida, defense of, 95–96, 98–99, 106; governorship, evaluation of, 110–11; political career, 92–93; and railroad construction, 101–3, 109; state press's criticism of, 100; suicide, 15, 81, 89, 110
Morton, Jackson, 21; elected as US senator by Florida legislature, 24; unites with Yulee and Cabell on "Southern Convention," 27
Moseley, William Dunn, 30; warning against abolitionists' designs on slavery, 21
Mosquito Inlet, skirmish at, 77
Munnerlyn, Charles J., organizes "Cow Cavalry," 81

Natural Bridge, Battle of, 14, 84, 109
99th United States Colored Troops, 14
"Nucleus, The" 7–8

Ocean Pond (Olustee): battle of, 1, 13–14, 106; in Civil War memory, 3–4; Confederate monument at, 204–6; origins of the campaign, 81–82; reenactment of, 216–18; Sons of Confederate Veterans protest construction of Union monument at battlefield of, 197; Sons of Union Veterans propose constructing a monument at battlefield of, 196; Union burials of battlefield of, 208; women's role in the aftermath of, 176
Oliveras, John B., 186
Oratogus, Predentes, 191

Palatka, 126
Papy, Mariano, 101; congressional bid by, 34
Partridge, Benjamin, 63, 66
Pasco, Samuel, 63
Pearson, John W., 75, 76
Pelot, John C., 115
Perry, Madison Starke, 20; blamed by John Milton for state of affairs in Florida, 96; elected governor of Florida (1856), 38; rhetoric on secession, 51–52

Ponce, Thomas, 188
Pope, Leroy Pope, 61, 95
Presbytery of Florida, 120–21; number of members in 1860, 117
Protestant Episcopal Church of the Confederate States of America, formed, 123

Randolph, William D., 95
Reid, Raymond, 8–9; death of, 10
Republican Party, 47
Ruffin, Edmund, 53; suicide of, 110
Rutledge, Francis Huger, 124–25

Salla, Gomocindo, 189
Sanchez, Francis, 188
Sanchez, Henry C., 187
Sanchez, John, 188
Sanchez, Manuel, 188
Sanchez, Roman, 188
Sanchez, S. J., 188
Saxon, Rufus, and 1863 expedition to occupy Jacksonville, 78
2nd Florida Infantry Battalion, 82
Second Seminole Indian War (1835–1842), 44–45; 50–51
Scott, John Jackson, 125
Seddon, James, 107
Sherman, Thomas W., 64, 66
Sherman, William T., 108
Simmons, William H., 6
6th Florida Infantry Battalion, 81–82, 66, 101
Slave population in Florida (1860), 45
Southern Baptist Convention, established, 119
South in popular culture, 213
Stanton, Edwin, 145; creates the American Freedmen's Inquiry Commission, 147
St. Augustine, 2
"St. Augustine Blues," composition of company, 184
Stephens, Winston, 75, 125–26
Stickney, Lyman, attempts to harvest timber around abandoned Fort Myers, 74
St. Joseph Convention (1838), 7
Strain, Matthew, 76
Strickland, William, and organization of Unionists in Taylor County, 83
Summerlin, Jacob, defends Fort Myers against Stickney's expedition, 74
Sumner, Charles, 147–48

Tampa, FL, 80
Taney, Roger, and Dred Scott decision, 137
3rd Florida Infantry Regiment, 62, 77, 95-96, 184; Hispanics serving in, 186
Thirteenth Amendment, 153
Trapier, James: criticism of, 68,100; suggests a withdrawal from Amelia Island, 67
Treaty of Moultrie Creek (1823), 44
Treaty of Payne's Landing (1832), 44
Truman, Harry, civil rights reforms of, 207

United Daughters of the Confederacy: activities in Florida of, 200–201; creation and goals of, 199; involvement in creation of the Florida Civil War Centennial Commission, 209
United States Blockade Board: formed, 60; strategy of, 60–61

Verot, Augustus, 121–23; 129

Ward, George T., 21–23, 62; death of, 54; delegate to Florida's Secession Convention, 53–54; defeated in gubernatorial campaign (1852), 37; Florida's coastal defenses, concern for, 61
Webb, William, 64
West Florida, 6, 11
Whig Party of Florida, 8–10; collapse of, 37–38; ensures a moderate delegation elected to represent Florida at "Southern Convention," 29; height of power, 20
Williamson, John Lee, 6; describes Middle Florida's agricultural promise, 7
Women: absent soldiers, interaction with, 170; bondage, 173–75; captured Unionists, react to harsh treatment of, 128; "a conquered people," 177; Florida's secession, reaction to, 165–66; and hardships caused by the war, 170–72; and Lost Cause ideology, 198–99; as refugees, 176–77; sendoffs for departing soldiers, 166; sewing organizations, 166–67; support for hospitals, 167–68; Unionists and Federal soldiers, encounters with, 169; war efforts, raise funds for, 167

Yulee, David Levy, 8; election of 1840, 9; Florida's statehood, advocate for, 10–11; plantation burned, 80; as protégé of John C. Calhoun, 25–26; selling of sugar to Savannah during Civil War, 190; "Southern Rights Party," suggests formation of, 26